WITH US OR AGAINST US

The CERI Series in International Relations and Political Economy

Series Editor, Christophe Jaffrelot

This series consists of works emanating from the foremost French research center in international studies, the Paris-based Centre d'Etudes et de Recherches Internationales (CERI), part of Sciences Po and associated with CNRS (Centre National de la Recherche Scientifique).

Founded in 1952, CERI has about sixty fellows drawn from different disciplines who conduct research on comparative political analysis, international relations, regionalism, transnational flows, political sociology, political economy and on individual states.

This series focuses on the transformations of the international arena, in a world where the state, though its sovereignty is questioned, reinvents itself. The series explores the effects on international relations and the world economy of regionalization, globalization (not only of trade and finance but also of culture), and transnational flows at large. This evolution in world affairs sustains a variety of networks from the ideological to the criminal or terrorist. Besides the geopolitical transformations of the globalized planet, the new political economy of the world has a decided impact on its destiny as well, and this series hopes to uncover what that is.

Published by Palgrave Macmillan:

Politics In China: Moving Frontiers
    edited by Françoise Mengin and Jean-Louis Rocca
Tropical Forests, International Jungle: The Underside of Global Ecopolitics
    by Marie-Claude Smouts, translated by Cynthia Schoch
The Political Economy of Emerging Markets: Actors, Institutions and Financial Crises in Latin America
    by Javier Santiso
Cyber China: Reshaping National Identities in the Age of Information
    edited by Françoise Mengin
With Us or Against Us: Studies in Global Anti-Americanism
    edited by Tony Judt and Denis Lacorne

WITH US OR AGAINST US

STUDIES IN GLOBAL ANTI-AMERICANISM

Edited by

Tony Judt

and

Denis Lacorne

First published in 2005 by
PALGRAVE MACMILLAN™
175 Fifth Avenue, New York, N.Y. 10010 and
Houndmills, Basingstoke, Hampshire, England RG21 6XS
Companies and representatives throughout the world.

PALGRAVE MACMILLAN is the global academic imprint of the Palgrave Macmillan division of St. Martin's Press, LLC and of Palgrave Macmillan Ltd. Macmillan® is a registered trademark in the United States, United Kingdom and other countries. Palgrave is a registered trademark in the European Union and other countries.

ISBN 1–4039–6951–5

Library of Congress Cataloging-in-Publication Data

With us or against us : studies in global anti-Americanism / edited by Denis Lacorne, Tony Judt.
    p. cm. — (CERI series in international relations and political economy)
    Papers derived from a conference jointly organized by the Remarque Institute and the Paris Center for the Study of International Relations (CERI) held in Paris in the fall of 2002.
    Includes bibliographical references and index.
    ISBN 1–4039–6951–5
    1. Anti-Americanism—Congresses. 2. United States—Relations—Foreign countries—Congresses. 3. September 11 Terrorist Attacks, 2001—Congresses. I. Lacorne, Denis. II. Judt, Tony. II. Series.

E840.W56 2005
327.73′009′0511—dc22   2005040025

A catalogue record for this book is available from the British Library.

Design by Newgen Imaging Systems (P) Ltd., Chennai, India.

First edition: June 2005

10 9 8 7 6 5 4 3 2 1

Printed in the United States of America.

CONTENTS

ACKNOWLEDGMENTS

Our primary purpose in publishing this volume—derived from a conference jointly organized by the Remarque Institute and the Paris Center for the Study of International Relations (CERI), held in Paris in the Fall of 2002—is to describe the complexity of anti-American sentiment in six distinct parts of the world: Western and Eastern Europe, Russia, the Middle-East, and Central and Southeast Asia. Publication of the conference proceedings was delayed in order to allow all the contributors to update their essays after the American invasion of Iraq. The case studies in this volume were selected to present a comprehensive understanding of Western and non-Western perceptions of the United States since the second World War.*

We would like to thank Yasmin Alibhai-Brown, Ali Buzurukov, Christophe Jaffrelot, Ivan Krastev, Zaki Laïdi, Philippe Roger, and Olivier Roy for acting as participants and discussants at the conference. Their insightful comments were particularly helpful to the authors in preparing the present volume.

This project would not have been possible without the generous help of the German Marshall Fund of the United States.

* Some contributors have chosen to cover a longer historical period, starting either with the very foundation of the United States or with the first U.S. settlements in Asia. See chapters 10 and 11. For practical reasons, we were not able to include Latin American countries, India, China, and Japan among our case studies.

NOTES ON CONTRIBUTORS

Detlev Claussen, professor for sociology and theory of culture and science at Hannover University (Germany), is the author of *Theodor W. Adorno. Ein letztes Genie* (Frankfurt/Main: S. Fischer Verlag, 2003) and *Grenzen der Aufklärung. Zur gesellschaftsgeschichtlichen Genese des Antisemitismus* (Frankfurt/Main: S. Fischer Verlag, 2005).

F. Gregory Gause, III, associate professor of political science at the University of Vermont (United States) and director of the Middle East Studies Program. He is the author of *Oil Monarchies* (New York: Council on Foreign Relations Press, 1994) and has published numerous articles on the politics of the Arabian Peninsula and the broader Middle East.

Gérard Grunberg, deputy director and vice-provost for research, Institut d'Etudes Politiques de Paris (Sciences Po), is the author of *Vers un socialisme européen?* (Paris: Hachette, 1997) and the coeditor of *La démocratie à l'épreuve, Une nouvelle approche de l'opinion des Français* (Paris: Presses de Sciences Po, 2002).

Tony Judt, Erich Maria Remarque professor of European studies and director of the Remarque Institute at New York University (United States), is the author of *Past Imperfect. French Intellectuals, 1944–1956* (Berkeley: University of California Press, 1992), *The Burden of Responsibility: Blum, Camus, Aron, and the French Twentieth Century* (Chicago: University of Chicago Press, 1998), and *Postwar: A History of Europe Since 1945* (Penguin, United States, 2005).

Denis Lacorne, research director at the CERI/Fondation Nationale des Sciences Politiques (Paris, France), and director of studies at the Graduate School of the Institut d'études politiques de Paris, is the author of *L'Invention de la république. Le modèle américain* (Paris: Hachette, 1991) and *La Crise de l'identité américaine Du melting pot au multiculturalisme* (Paris: Gallimard, 2005, 2nd edition). He is the coeditor, with Tony Judt, of *Language, Nation and State. Identity*

Politics in a Multilingual Age (New York: Palgrave, 2004) and is completing a book on religion and politics in the United States (Paris: Gallimard, 2006).

Camille Mansour, professor of international relations and Middle Eastern Studies at Paris I and Versailles Universities, is the author of *Beyond Alliance: Israel in U.S. Foreign Policy* (New York: Columbia University Press, 1994) and the editor of *Israel: A General Survey* (Beirut: Institute for Palestine Studies, 2004). He is the editor-in-chief of the *Palestine Yearbook of International Law*, published jointly by the Institute of Law at Birzeit University and Martinus Nijhoff Publishers (The Hague).

Farish A. Noor, a Malaysian political scientist and human rights activist, is a researcher at the Zentrum Moderner Orient (Berlin, Germany) and the author of *Islam Embedded: The Historical Development of the Pan-Malaysian Islamic Party PAS'* (Kuala Lumpur: MSRI, 2004) and *The Other Malaysia* (Kuala Lumpur: Silverfish, 2003). He has written extensively on religiopolitical movements and parties in Southeast Asia.

Jacques Rupnik, research director at the CERI/Fondation Nationale des Sciences Politiques (France), is the coauthor of *L'Europe des Vingt Cinq* (Paris: Autrement, 2004), the editor of *Les Européens face à l'élargissement. Perceptions, acteurs, enjeux* (Paris: Presses de Sciences Po, 2004), and the coeditor with Denis Lacorne and Marie-France Toinet of *The Rise and Fall of Anti-Americanism. A Century of French Perception* (London: Macmillan, 1990).

Morad Saghafi, is the editor-in-chief, *Goft-o-gu* (Tehran, Iran).

Mohammad Waseem, professor of political science and chair of the international relations department at the Quaid-i-Azam University (Islamabad, Pakistan), is the author of *Politics and the State in Pakistan* (1989) and of *The 1993 Elections in Pakistan* (1994). He held the Pakistan Chair at St Antony's College (Oxford), from 1995 to 1999 and is on the editorial board of three major academic journals: *Ethnicities* (Bristol), *Contemporary South Asia* (Bradford), and *International Studies* (New Delhi).

Nikolai V. Zlobin, former professor at Moscow State University is senior fellow and director of Russian and Asian Programs at the Center for Defense Information (Washington, D.C., United States) and the author of *International Communications* (Chicago: M.E.

Sharpe, 2004). A leading expert on international security, terrorism, and relations between the United States and Russia, he is the executive editor of *Demokratizatsiya*, the Journal of Post-Soviet Democratization and the president of *Washington ProFile*, an international news agency, which he founded in 2001. He also writes a regular column for the Russain daily, *Izvestia*.

INTRODUCTION

THE BANALITY OF ANTI-AMERICANISM

Denis Lacorne and Tony Judt

Anti-Americanism is above all about perceptions. Nothing is more difficult to preserve than the good image of a country, particularly when the country—like the United States—claims to set the tone for the rest of the world and insists on the highest possible standards of freedom and democracy. Unexpected events can deeply affect perceptions. The traumatic events of 9/11 certainly generated sympathy throughout the world. But the invasion of Iraq, the split between the United States and "Old Europe," the poor management of an unprecedented experiment in nation building, and the revelations about the tortures in the Abu Ghraib jail have seriously damaged the image of the United States and led numerous Americans to reassess their understanding of the proper response to the attack of 9/11.

The first, most obvious form of anti-Americanism is anti-Bushism—a widespread phenomenon, both in the United States and in the rest of the world. Consider, for instance, the opinion of a prominent British Tory, Michael Portillo, who had strongly supported the war in Iraq and initially saw no problem with "the younger Bush's robust foreign policy." Shocked at the Abu Ghraib prison atrocities, astonished that "such a formidable executive has made so many disastrous mistakes," he could only conclude that "For America to brush away its recent disgraces, the electorate will have to bin this administration. I never expected to say this to my American friends: vote Democrat."[1] Or again, consider the opinion of a leading American businessman, Eric Best, a managing director at Morgan Stanley, who declared at about the same time: "I can testify to the extraordinary destruction of 'American Brand Value' accomplished by this administration, from Europe to Hong Kong to Shangai to Tokyo, and beyond [. . .] If any

CEO of a global multinational had accomplished this for his enterprise as quickly and radically as George Bush Jr. has done for the U.S., he would be replaced by the board in no time."[2]

A poor image can be repaired and the Bush administration has spent considerable time and energy, in 2004, trying to improve perceptions through renewing a more consensual form of multilateral diplomacy, as demonstrated in a series of diplomatic events: the D-Day commemorations in Normandy, the G-8 gathering in Georgia, the reunion with EU leaders in Dublin, and the Istanbul NATO summit. June 2004 was "arguably . . . the most intense month of summitry in the history of the Atlantic alliance."[3] Bush has been frantically trying to achieve what John Kerry had announced he would do a genuine trans-Atlantic reconciliation. But, in the end, it is not a board of directors that decides who is responsible for the destruction of the "American Brand Value," but the American people themselves.

Of course, there are other forms of anti-Americanism than anti-Bushism. Anti-Americanism is as old as America itself. It can be defensive or reactive, rational or irrational, popular or elitist, political or cultural; it can center on economic or religious issues or on no particular issue at all.[4] In its mildest form, anti-Americanism is merely criticism of some American policies or social characteristics. At the other extreme, it expresses a real clash of civilizations, the complete rejection of anything and everything "American," to the point of denying that there even is such a thing as an American culture or an American democracy.

Thus, when French philosopher Jean Baudrillard formulates a radical death wish—the total destruction of America—simply because the United States has become too hegemonic for his taste, his *ressentiment* can in no way be compared to the refusal of President Chirac or Chancellor Schröder to support the American decision to invade Iraq. The French philosopher's Americanophobia is so extreme that it does not lend itself to rational interrogation. By contrast, Chirac's and Schröder's strategic opposition to invading Iraq, however displeasing to the Bush administration, belongs in the realm of reasonable and reasoned disagreement. It is important to distinguish between the two.

What is often disappointing about the existing literature on anti-Americanism is its repetitive nature: old stereotypes are endlessly reproduced, as if nothing had changed for years, if not centuries, between the United States and its critics, whether or not they used to be friends or allies. We take issue with such an approach in our own contributions to this book (chapters 1 and 2). Anti-American sentiments do change over time and pro-American feelings exist as well, but are often ignored because they weaken the arguments of those on both sides who see the world in black and white. There are indeed clashes of cultures, conflicts of ideas, and strong political rivalries between the United States and its critics. But expressions of friendship, support, and sympathy coexist with these, even though they are rarely reported. We have attempted to describe the full nature of Western and non-Western perceptions of America, while respecting the ambiguities, contradictions, and frequent reversals of these perceptions.

Anti-Americanism today, as Tony Judt argues in chapter 1, is the master narrative of the age. It is also, by its nature, immensely diverse. It finds its source in a variety of religious, cultural, political, and philosophical experiences, which vary from one continent to the next and sometimes divide entire blocks of nations within a single continent. Such, for example, was the nature of the debate that opposed the misleadingly labeled "Old" and "New" Europes at the time of the Iraq war, as Jacques Rupnik demonstrates in chapter 5.

Such *varieties* of anti-Americanism are well documented by the authors of this volume. Less obvious and perhaps more worrisome for American policymakers is another pervasive phenomenon that one might call, with due acknowledgment to Hannah Arendt, the *banality* of anti-Americanism. This is nicely illustrated by the following comments, made recently by some French high-school seniors to their English teacher in one very well-regarded French *lycée*:[5]

> America is an extreme country a new country, where the reality is often cruel and hard for more than half the population. It is the most powerful country [in the world], but it is also the most dangerous.
>
> America wants to look like God because they [the US government] want to decide who must die or not.
>
> George Bush wants to control the world. He is not a good president. . . . There is very much racism because the society is controlled by the WASPs . . . It's not a democratic country.
>
> I just hate the politics in the United States.
>
> The United States is great, without the Americans . . . I hate their president because he abuses his power, and makes war everywhere.
>
> I hate America, because it makes war in Iraq for its oil.

These quotes suggest a sustained level of anger, resentment, and even hatred—widely shared feelings among a new generation of European high-school students. But these sentiments are quite detached from anti-American rhetoric of even the relatively recent past: the Vietnam War and the old anti-imperialist struggles of the European Left evoke practically no memories or empathy among today's teenagers, who simply do not like "America" and dislike President Bush and his policies even more. The America they do like—and for them it is often the *real* America—is that of Michael Moore, the beloved hero of contemporary French, German, and Spanish moviegoers. There are, of course, discordant voices—intellectuals who truly "love" America—but they are few and isolated and their opinions carry almost no weight.[6]

The banal universality of anti-Americanism is well documented in the case studies presented in this volume. The emergence of anti-American sentiment cannot be attributed to a single cause. It results, rather, from widely different contexts, each with its own distinctive history. In Iran, for example, as Morad Saghafi demonstrates (chapter 10), Americanophilia was the norm until the early 1950s. Post–World War II America was seen as "liberating" the country from Soviet occupation. But the 1953 CIA-sponsored coup against Mossadegh seriously tarnished the reputation of the United States and transformed the American ally into a "disloyal and deceitful" friend.

Later in the century, when the American-backed monarchy became the enemy of the insurgent mullahs, anti-Americanism emerged as the key slogan of the age, unifying two radically different discourses—the traditional propaganda of the communist left and the religious discourse of the Islamists—and lending a very particular and enduring vigor to Iranian anti-Americanism. Today, the "Great Satan" is no longer such a threatening demon, and in the aftermath of 9/11, the Iranian middle class expressed a surprising level of sympathy for their American counterparts. The Iranian case thus perfectly illustrates the cyclical nature of pro- and anti-American perceptions. It also suggests that anti-Americanism is often a reactive phenomenon and is one that cannot be easily separated from the study of *pro*-American sentiment.

Palestinian perceptions of America, as argued by Camille Mansour (chapter 8), are in no way monolithic. What the population at large resents to the point of enduring hatred is U.S. foreign policy (and particularly George W. Bush's Middle East policy), which is perceived as one-sided and "blindly pro-Israel." But the opinions of the "Palestinian street" should not be confused with those of the political elites. American society and its culture are often greatly admired, particularly by the educated middle class, whether they are in Palestine or in exile. The anti-Americanism of many middle-class Palestinians allows for a certain pragmatism: the realization that the United States is the only superpower and therefore the only country that can have an influence on Israel. Palestinians, concludes Mansour, do not see themselves in some grand clash of civilizations, despite the efforts of local Islamists to "universalize their local anti-Israeli struggle."

Anti-Americanism in Southeast Asia is inextricably tied to the region's colonial past and America's involvement in the area, particularly in the Philippines. The strength of anti-American sentiment is related to the size of local Muslim minorities, their treatment by ruling elites, and the respective influence of radical and moderate Islamists. Opinions are not fixed, however, and they are directly related to the nature of domestic policies. One of the most unfortunate (and unanticipated) consequences of 9/11, as demonstrated well by Farish Noor (chapter 11), has been the increasingly repressive policies of Asian governments against Muslim minorities. This has had the predictable consequence of exacerbating the anti-Americanism of "many Islamists and pro-democracy activists," who can now readily demonstrate the link between U.S. interests and their own government's authoritarian rule. The effort to "export democracy" to Afghanistan and Iraq has, in fact, strengthened authoritarian Southeast Asian regimes, which have been only too pleased to clamp down on local democratic movements in the name of an ill-defined struggle against terrorism.

The key to understanding Pakistani–American relations, as argued by Mohammad Waseem (chapter 9), is foreign policy. America was never a colonial power in that part of the world and is not perceived as one. On the contrary, it cultivated friendly relations with Pakistan—the most anti-Communist country of the region—particularly following the Soviet invasion of Afghanistan. There was thus a "convergence" of outlooks between the United States and Pakistan. This convergence, and the pool of sympathy that it generated, disappeared for a while after the collapse of the U.S.S.R. With 9/11 and the subsequent U.S. invasion of Afghanistan, the two countries were free to "rediscover each other," at least at the elite level. Pakistan had become a necessary, if occasionally embarrassing, ally in the struggle against Al Qaeda.

But the divergence between elite and mass public perceptions of the United States in Pakistan has remained substantial. Public opinion is steadfastly and increasingly anti-American, particularly because it is all too well informed about the conflicts that oppose the Muslim and non-Muslim worlds. The Islamic media "explosion" of the 1990s, according to Waseem, has greatly tarnished the positive image of the United States, which is held directly responsible for the mistreatment of Muslim populations throughout the world. By globalizing local conflicts (and, indeed, giving local meaning to international developments), the modern Islamic media—television above all—fuels the anger and resentment of a public whom Waseem describes as "ignorant and gullible."

In Saudi Arabia, of course, anti-Americanism is endemic; this is in part because here, too, public opinion is increasingly well informed—albeit selectively—about the world, and is especially sensitive to the violence unleashed by the Israeli–Palestinian conflict. But even here, anti-Americanism, as Gregory Gause points out (chapter 7), is not monolithic. It is highly segmented, reflecting the diverging views of intellectual elites, governmental leaders, and *salafi* Islamist circles. The *salafis* are clearly the most likely to denounce the United States, for religious reasons, as an evil crusader that should be removed from the region.

But a number of prominent *salafis*, together with certain liberal intellectuals, have favored greater dialogue with the West in the name of pragmatism and realism. In fact, Gause argues, the true nature of the relationship between the United States and Saudi Arabia should be judged only at the elite level: "On neither side is there a strong *public* constituency for the relationship. It is a relationship between elites, based on very clear understandings of mutual interest. There is no sentiment in it. . . . It is on oil that the relationship began, and it will be on oil that the relationship will in the future evolve."

Does public opinion in Europe differ significantly from non-Western, Middle Eastern, or Asian sentiment? As Gérard Grunberg demonstrates in chapter 3, it certainly does not with regard to the American invasion of Iraq. Europeans as a whole were hostile to the war in Iraq, even when their leaders favored the American intervention. It is, in fact, striking that two-thirds of the Poles, 90 percent of the Spanish, and over 50 percent of the British declared their opposition to the war. Once the war started, to be sure, Tony Blair was able to benefit from a "rallying around the flag" effect, as nearly two-thirds of the British expressed support for the intervention. But that support faded very quickly, and in the absence of any evidence of Iraqi "weapons of mass destruction," it has now almost completely evaporated. In any case, and notwithstanding the British exception, Grunberg's conclusion should be seriously pondered: "The Europeans are no longer certain that they defend the same causes and strive for the same objectives as the Americans."

The new German anti-Americanism, as convincingly demonstrated by Detlev Claussen (chapter 4), does indeed mimic older anti-American narratives and revive older anti-American memories based on the struggles of the 1960s and 1970s. But "new anti-Americanism" is not merely a *reprise* of older political debates. It expresses a new phenomenon: the social psychology of the new German middle classes in a reunified Germany, eager, for the first time in six decades, to reaffirm their identity and willing to denounce America's use of military force as the manifestation of an unacceptable "arrogance of power."

German anti-Americanism is well established among both cultural elites and the public at large. It is reinforced and legitimized by what many Germans see as their country's distinctive approach to international affairs, with its emphasis on peaceful engagement and a high moral tone. This self-congratulatory and rather self-regarding outlook helps explain, in Claussen's view, why Europeans have not always grasped the underlying significance of the events of 9/11—reinforced by the Madrid train bombings of March 2004—that the attacks targeted not just the United States, but the entire Western world: "Only when the international community acknowledges that international terrorism is a shared threat will anti-Americanism recede in strength."

In examining the rather contrasting feelings expressed by East European leaders (but, again, not their publics), Jacques Rupnik in chapter 5 raises an uncomfortable question: was it just appreciation of and admiration for the U.S. "liberator" or were there other, less noble motivations? Genuine gratitude, Rupnik argues, was mixed with more opportunistic considerations, particularly on the part of the Polish and Rumanian leadership: ex-Communist leaders, eager to erase the memories of their own Communist past, eagerly seized the occasion to cultivate friendship with America. As America's most "trusted" allies, they openly expressed the hope that their backing would, in turn, generate tangible economic and military rewards. Above all, friendship with America was cultivated for its "equalizing effect" on Europe's dominant economic and political partners—France and Germany. "New Europe" plus America was supposed to counterbalance the excessive influence of "Old Europe."

Russian perceptions of America are truly distinct from Western and Eastern European perceptions, partly because of the persistence of old attitudes inherited from the Cold War, and partly because of Russia's "growing disenchantment" with the experience of market democracy during the years of the Yeltsin presidency, as explained by Nikolai Zlobin (chapter 6). In addition, Russia's global loss of influence—the fact that it can no longer claim to be a superpower—has had a traumatic impact on Russian political elites. As a result, the dramatic events of 9/11 did not significantly alter Russian perceptions of the United States. The revival of the Russian "national idea" and Russian "pride" under Vladimir Putin's rule, together with a certain nostalgia for the "cultural values of Soviet times," is well documented. Paradoxically, this makes Russian public opinion less vulnerable to the sort of resentful anti-Americanism of states and peoples who seek to escape from the shadow of American power. Russians don't object to the emergence of a "closer relationship" with America, as long as this relationship is understood to be a relationship of "equals."

*   *   *

The chapters in this volume, while covering considerable ground, are not intended to be a comprehensive, country-by-country survey of anti-American sentiment in the contemporary world. Certain important countries are not discussed in detail—the United Kingdom, to take one example—and, as noted above, we have not attempted to cover every part of the world. Thus, Latin America, whose various nations have complicated and differing relationships with both the idea of "America" and the policies of the United States, is not covered here. We have sought, rather, to engage with anti-American sentiment in certain regions that are key to America's own foreign policy dilemmas and interests, and in countries, such as France and Russia, where the sources and varieties of attitudes to America are not always well understood—not least by Americans themselves.

As volume editors, we have not sought to impose a single interpretation or perspective upon our contributors. On the contrary, we believe that one of the distinctive merits of this collection is that it not only reflects a range of scholarly opinion but also captures rather well the different approaches to the subject itself, as they emerge from very different national and cultural angles. It is also perhaps worth noting, in view of the highly contentious and sensitive nature of the subject itself, that we have not tried to align the views of our contributors. These cover quite an eclectic range, as readers will discover—and that is as it should be.

This book, then, is decidedly not a contribution to the anti-American "case," nor is it a defense of the United States in the face of its many critics. In both categories, there is a voluminous and growing literature that casts diminishing light upon the subject. If, as we have suggested, "anti-Americanism" is the banal but decidedly widespread discourse of our age—the rhetorical form through which much of the world organizes its understanding of the age we live in—then what is called for is sustained attention to the *sources* of this new master narrative, to its present variety and likely trajectory. The chapters in this book may thus serve as an analytical introduction: a prolegomenon to what we hope will be a growing body of scholarship on a subject destined to play a crucial role in twenty-first-century public affairs.

July 22, 2004

NOTES

1. Michael Portillo, "There's only one way forward for America—Vote Democrat," *The Sunday Times,* July 4, 2004.
2. As cited in Jackie Calmes, "Chinks appear in Bush's pro-business armor," *The Wall Street Journal* (Europe), June 29, 2004.
3. Philip Gordon and Jeremy Shapiro, "An alliance waiting for November," *International Herald Tribune,* June 29, 2004.
4. Most of the authors in this volume present one definition or other of anti-Americanism. We have not tried to impose a single definition to be used throughout: each author assumes his own choice and theoretical justification.
5. The name and exact location of the school have not been provided to preserve the anonymity of the students and their teachers.
6. See Yves Berger, *Dictionnaire amoureux des Etats-Unis* (Paris, Plon, 2003) for a rare example of such Americanophilia.

1

A New Master Narrative?
Reflections on Contemporary
Anti-Americanism

Tony Judt

"Anti-Americanism" is the master narrative of the age. Until quite recently, political argument—first in the West, latterly everywhere—rested firmly, and, for most people, quite comfortably, upon the twin pillars of "progress" and "reaction." The idea of progress encapsulated both the moral confidence of the Enlightenment and the various and ultimately conflicting political projects to which it gave rise: liberalism, democracy, socialism, and, in the twentieth century, communism. Each of these heirs to the Enlightenment project had a confident story to tell of its own origins, its desirability, its necessity, and ultimately its grounds for confidence in impending victory. Each, in short, was not merely a narrative of human progress but a *master* narrative, aspiring to contain within itself and, where necessary, explain away all other accounts of modernity.

Reaction—beginning, quite literally, with the reaction of certain early-nineteenth-century thinkers to the Revolution in France—was thus in this sense a *counter*-narrative: a denial, sometimes epistemological, often ethical, always political, of the projects and programs born of the optimistic eighteenth century. The political forms of reactionary politics were almost as protean and diverse as those of its nemesis: Catholic, paternalist, nostalgic, pastoral, pessimistic, authoritarian, and, ultimately, Fascist. But reactionary accounts of the human condition shared one common evaluative conclusion with progressivism: they tended, in every case, to the view that the modern world was, or would soon be, divided into two opposed and irreconcilable camps. The end of the Cold War appeared to close this centuries-long cycle of

Manichean political and intellectual apposition. Not only had capitalism and communism, the West and the East, democracy and authoritarianism, apparently become reconciled—largely through the unambiguous victory of the former in each case—but the very intellectual premises on which the distinctions rested, broadly associated with Marxism and its various heirs, seemed to have crumbled. If "capitalism" was no longer a passing and regrettable stage on the historical high road from backwardness to socialism (a core article of radical faith since the 1840s), but rather the default condition of well-regulated societies, as free-market liberals had long asserted and even social democrats now conceded, then even the distinction between "Left" and "Right" was unclear. "History," as some pundits unwisely announced, had come to an "End."

A mere 15 years after the fall of the Berlin Wall, it is clear that such pronouncements were a little premature. The wretched of the earth and their better-heeled sympathizers and spokesmen in the rich world have once again found common cause. Capitalism, to be sure, is no longer the avowed target of opprobrium, though it is worth noting that it is much less universally admired or desired than many fondly suppose—or than was the case two decades ago. And outside of unreconstructed Trotskyist *groupuscules*, the prospects for a radical transition from present discontents to future idylls—the dream of revolution and socialism—are not widely discussed. And yet, there is, once again, an international rhetoric of rejection that binds politics, economics, and ethics into a common story about how the world works and why it doesn't. And those who invoke this language, even if they have yet to find a common sense of purpose or even a common strategy, have chanced upon something much more important, at least in the medium term—a common target. That target is the United States of America.

It is tempting to dismiss out of hand the new politics of anti-Americanism. For what, after all, can this "America"—a huge and differentiated society, as ethnically and culturally diverse as any other and whose constituent peoples have diasporic ties to most of the rest of the world—stand for? Capitalism? Sweden, Spain, New Zealand, Nigeria, and Brazil, along with dozens of others, are all "capitalist" countries. Imperialism? The United States of America is without doubt the only empire of our times. But "anti-imperialism," albeit a well-established radical politics in its own right, is hardly a self-sufficient account of the world—a "master" narrative. It is beholden to other narratives—theories of race and anti-racism, socialist explanations for capitalism's voracious search for foreign markets, and so on.

If anti-Americanism were indeed just the latest anti-imperialism, appropriately adjusted to the latest empire itself—in the manner, say, of the 1960s—it would hardly be so interesting, or so appealing to so many. America today is the object of suspicion and fear—mixed as ever with an element of fascination and seduction—because its global reach goes well beyond political or economic power, though it rests on these. Stretched to a planetary scale, the American way of modernity—*globalization*, to acknowledge the shorthand account if it—threatens local interests and identities in ways that no past empire could ever have imagined.

A world apparently busy remaking itself in what Americans all too readily claim is their own image stands challenged in many intersecting spheres: the decline of indigenous language; the dilution of high culture; the internationalization of popular culture; the uncontained risks to environmental health; the virtual disappearance of economic autonomy; the etiolation of public policy, and the apparent diminution of national sovereignty. Local commentators can hardly hope any longer to explain or address such concerns within their own borders. They are obliged to look beyond; and what they see there has become material in many people's eyes for a new, all-embracing explanation of our current woes. If America is the *fons et origo malorum*, the source and origin of all miseries, then it is America—whatever that is—that is the problem. If you want to understand how America appears to the world today, consider the sport-utility vehicle (SUV). Oversized and overweight, the SUV disdains negotiated agreements to restrict atmospheric pollution. It consumes inordinate quantities of scarce resources to furnish its privileged inhabitants with supererogatory services. It exposes outsiders to a deadly risk in order to provide for the illusory security of its occupants. In a crowded world, the SUV appears as a dangerous anachronism. Like U.S. foreign policy, the SUV comes packaged in sonorous mission statements; but underneath, it is just an oversized pickup truck with too much power.

In short, America is everywhere. Americans—just 5 percent of the world's population—generate 30 percent of the World's Gross Product, consume nearly 30 percent of global oil production, and are responsible for almost as high a share of the world's output of greenhouse gases. Our world is divided in many ways: rich/poor, North/South, Western/non-Western. But more and more, the division that counts is the one separating America from everyone else.

The United States, by virtue of its unique standing, is exposed to the world's critical gaze in everything it does or fails to do. Some of the antipathy the United States arouses is a function of what it is: long before

America rose to global dominion, foreign visitors were criticizing its brash self-assurance, the narcissistic confidence of Americans in the superiority of American values and practices, and their rootless inattentiveness to history and tradition—their own and other people's. The charge sheet has grown since the United States took the world stage, but it has not changed much. This "cultural" anti-Americanism is shared by Europeans, Latin Americans, and Asians, secular and religious alike. It is not about antipathy to the West, or capitalism, or freedom, or the Enlightenment, or any other abstraction exemplified by the United States. It is about America.

To foreign critics, these contradictions in American behavior suggest hypocrisy—perhaps, the most familiar of the accusations leveled at the United States. They are all the more galling because, hypocritical or not, America is indispensable. Without American participation, most international agreements are dead letters. American leadership seems to be required even in cases—such as Bosnia between 1992 and 1995—where the British and their fellow Europeans had the means to resolve the crisis unaided. The United States is cruelly unsuited to play the world's policeman—Washington's attention span is famously short, even in chronically troubled regions like Kashmir, the Balkans, the Middle East, or Korea—but it seems to have no choice. Meanwhile, everyone else, but the Europeans especially, resent the United States when it fails to lead, but also when it leads too assertively.

The position of the European Union is, on the face of it, a paradox. Fifty-five percent of the world's development aid and two thirds of all grants-in-aid to the poor and vulnerable nations of the globe come from the European Union. As a share of GNP, U.S. foreign aid is barely one third the European average. If you combine European spending on defense, foreign aid, intelligence gathering, and policing—all of them vital to any sustained war against international crime—it easily matches the current American defense budget. "Europe" is not inherently weak.

But decades of American nuclear reassurance induced unprecedented military dystrophy. The Franco-German condominium of domination was sooner or later bound to provoke a backlash among Europe's smaller nations. The inability of the European Union to build a consensus on foreign policy, much less a force with which to implement it, has handed Washington a monopoly in the definition and resolution of international crises. No one should be surprised if America's present leaders have chosen to exercise it. What began some years ago as American frustration at the Europeans' failure to organize and spend in their own defense has now become a source of satisfaction for U.S. hawks. The Europeans don't agree with us? So what! We don't need them, and anyway what can they do? They're feeling hurt and resentful in Brussels, or Paris, or Berlin? Well, they've only themselves to blame. Remember Bosnia.

Moreover, in the shadow of the recent invasion of Iraq, the present and future member states of Europe fell to internecine squabbling, unable to agree on a common response to America's martial activism. Some, like Britain, Spain, and Italy, chose to line up with their long-standing American protector. Others, like France, Germany, and Belgium, asserted a "European" difference that certainly reflects public opinion across the continent, but may lead them into a strategic cul-de-sac. The East Europeans buckled under unprecedented American diplomatic pressure and bribery; for those in Brussels, Paris, and elsewhere who didn't want them in the Union anyway, that will not be forgotten soon. If this squabbling, uncoordinated "Union" is indeed the only geostrategic challenger America now faces, Washington ought to be able to rest easy. America, it would seem, is not just the sole surviving super power, but the only sure source of international initiative and well being.

And yet, in little more than two years since 9/11, President George W. Bush and his advisers managed to make America seem to the over-whelming majority of humankind as the greatest threat to global stability. By staking a monopoly claim on Western values and their defense, the United States has prompted other Westerners to reflect on what divides them from America. By enthusiastically asserting its right to reconfigure the Muslim world, Washington has reminded Europeans, in particular, of the growing Muslim presence in their own cultures and its political implications. In short, the United States has given a lot of people occasion to rethink their relationship with it.

Resented for what it is, America thus stokes further antipathy by what it does. Here, things have indeed changed for the worse. The United States is often a delinquent international citizen: it is reluctant to join international initiatives or agreements, whether on climate warming, biological warfare, criminal justice, or women's rights; it is one of only two states (the other being Somalia) that have failed to ratify the 1989 Convention on Children's Rights. The present U.S. administration has "unsigned" the Rome Treaty establishing an International Criminal Court and has declared itself no longer bound by the Vienna Convention on Law of Treaties, which sets out the obligations of states to abide by treaties they have yet to ratify. The American attitude toward the United Nations and its agencies is cool, to say the least.

Washington's stance toward the International Criminal Court, in particular, is especially embarrassing. It makes a mockery of the U.S. insistence on international pursuit and prosecution of terrorists and other political criminals; and it provides a cover for these countries and politicians who have real cause to fear the new Court. All of Washington's friends and allies on the UN Security Council voted against the United States when this matter was discussed in 2002; meanwhile, Washington's opposition to the International Criminal Court is shared by an unholy alliance of Iran, Iraq, Pakistan, Indonesia, Israel, and Egypt.

Indeed, the United States has more than once found itself in questionable company. When the Bush Administration vetoed a protocol designed to put teeth into the 30-year-old Biological Weapons Convention and effectively destroyed a generation of efforts to halt the spread of these deadly arms, only a handful of the 145 signatories to the Convention took Washington's side: among these were China, Russia, India, Pakistan, Cuba, and Iran. All too often, Washington's position now pits it against the Western Europeans, Canadians, Australians, and a majority of Latin American states, while American "unilateralism" is supported (for their own reasons) by an unseemly rogues' gallery of dictatorships and regional troublemakers. The impact of this on America's overseas image and influence is incalculable. Even the mere appearance of taking the world seriously would enhance American influence immeasurably—from European intellectuals to Islamic fundamentalists, anti-Americanism feeds voraciously off the claim that the United States is callously indifferent to the views and needs of others.

America's apparent "indifference" has distinctive roots. Just as modern American leaders typically believe that in domestic public life, citizens are best left to their own devices, with limited government intervention, so they project this view onto international affairs as well. Seen from Washington, the world is a series of discrete challenges or threats, calibrated according to their implications for America. Since the United States is a global power, almost anything that happens in the world is of concern to it; but the American instinct is to address and resolve any given problem in isolation. Of course, this reflects, in part, a refreshingly American confidence that problems may indeed *be* resolved—at which point, the United States can return home. This emphasis upon an "exit strategy," upon being in the world but not quite of it, always at liberty to retire from the fray, has its domestic analogue in modern American life. Like many of its citizens, especially since 9/11, the United States feels most comfortable when retreating to its "gated community."

This long-standing American sense of being both engaged in the world and somehow apart from it has been further complicated by the confrontational rhetoric of the newest generation of advisers and rulers in Washington. The foreign strategy of the United States, in the words of two influential neo-conservative writers, must be "unapologetic, idealistic, assertive and well funded. America must not only be the world's policeman or its sheriff, it must be its beacon and guide."[1] By confidently equating the United States' own interests with those of every right-thinking person on the planet, such a strategy is doomed to arouse the very antagonism and enmity that provoke American overseas intervention in the first place. In American governing circles today, it is widely held that America can do as it wishes without listening to others, *and* that in so doing, it will unerringly echo the true interests and unspoken desires of friends and foes alike.

*   *   *

The anti-Americanism now preoccupying commentators should thus come as no surprise. But, in America especially, it is much misunderstood. Thus, in the prelude to the Iraq war, it was widely asserted in Washington that "pro-American" Europeans could be conveniently distinguished from their "anti-American" neighbors. But this is not the case. In a poll by the Pew Research Center, Europeans were asked whether they thought "the world would be more dangerous if another country matched America militarily." The "Old European" French and Germans—like the British—tended to agree. The "New European" Czechs and Poles were less worried at the prospect. The same poll asked respondents whether they thought that "when differences occur with America, it is because of [my country's] different values" (a key indicator of cultural anti-Americanism): only 33 percent of French respondents and 37 percent of Germans answered "yes." But the figures for Britain were 41 percent, for Italy 44 percent, and for the Czech Republic 62 percent (almost as high as the 66 percent of Indonesians who feel the same way).[2]

In Britain, the *Daily Mirror*, a mass-market tabloid daily that had hitherto supported Tony Blair's New Labour Party, ran a full-page front cover on January 6, 2003, mocking Blair's position; in case you haven't noticed, it informed him, Bush's drive to war with Iraq is about oil for America. Half the British electorate opposed war with Saddam Hussein under any circumstances. In the Czech Republic, just 13 percent of the population endorsed an American attack on Iraq without a UN mandate; the figure in Spain was identical.

In traditionally pro-American Poland, there was even less enthusiasm: just 4 percent of Poles would back a unilateralist war.

In Spain, voters from José Maria Aznar's own Popular Party overwhelmingly rejected his support for President Bush; his allies in Catalonia joined Spain's opposition parties in condemning "an unprovoked unilateral attack" by the United States on Iraq; and most Spaniards remained adamantly opposed to a war with Iraq even with a second UN resolution.[3] If America is to depend on what Secretary of Defense Donald Rumsfeld called its "New European friends," then, it had better lower its expectations. Among the pro-U.S. signatories singled out for praise by Mr. Rumsfeld, Denmark spends just 1.6 percent of its GNP on defense, Italy 1.5 percent, Spain a mere 1.4 percent—less than half the defense commitment of Old European France.

As for East Europeans: yes, they like America and will do its bidding if they can. The United States will always be able to bully a vulnerable country like Romania into backing it against the International Criminal Court. But in the words of one Central European foreign minister opposed to U.S. intervention at the time of the 1999 Kosovo action: "We didn't join NATO to fight wars." In a recent survey, 69 percent of Poles (and 63 percent of Italians) oppose any increased expenditure on defense to enhance Europe's standing as a world power. It is one thing to like America, quite another to make sacrifices on her behalf.[4]

And what of Germany? American commentators were so offended at Germany's willingness to "appease" Saddam, so infuriated by Chancellor Schröder's lack of bellicose fervor and his "ingratitude" toward America that few have stopped to ask why so many Germans share Günter Grass's view that "the President of the United States embodies the danger that faces us all." The sources of German ambivalence toward American policy are distinctive. Germany today is different. It has a distinctively pacifist culture (quite unlike, say, France). If there is to be war, many Germans feel, let it be *ohne mich* (without me). If America stands for "war," however justified, many Germans will be anti-American on that ground alone.

However, the German stance is not representative. Pace Robert Kagan, the world is not divided into a pacifistic, post-Kantian Europe and a courageous, martial America.[5] It was only very recently that European infantrymen were dying on peacekeeping missions in Asia, Africa, and Europe while American generals foreswore foreign ground wars lest U.S. soldiers get killed. If Americans are from Mars, as Kagan puts it, they rediscovered the martial virtues only recently. Indeed, when asked in 2002 whether they approved of the use of military power to protect their interests, British, French, Italian, and Polish respondents all showed more support for military action than did American respondents. Only the Germans were less enthusiastic. Europeans may not like wars—in which respect they are indeed at odds with the current U.S. administration, though in tune with many Americans—but they are not pacifists, either.[6]

*   *   *

Contemporary suspicion of America—its leaders, its motives, its way of life—is part of an old story everywhere. America has been an object of foreign suspicion for even longer than it has been a beacon and haven for the world's poor and downtrodden. Eighteenth-century commentators—on the basis of very little direct observation—believed America's flora and fauna to be stunted, and of limited interest or use. The country could never be civilized, they insisted, and much the same was true of its unsophisticated new citizens. From the perspective of a cosmopolitan European conservative like Joseph de Maistre, writing in the early years of the nineteenth century, the United States was a regrettable aberration—and too crude to endure for long. Charles Dickens, like Alexis de Tocqueville, was struck by the conformism of American public life. Stendhal commented upon the country's "egoism"; Baudelaire sniffily compared it to Belgium (!) in its bourgeois mediocrity; everyone remarked upon the jejune patriotic pomp of the United States back in the nineteenth century, just as they do today. But in the course of the twentieth century, European commentary shifted perceptibly from the dismissive to the resentful. By the 1930s, the United States' economic power was giving a threatening twist to its crude immaturity. For a new generation of antidemocratic critics, the destabilizing symptoms of modern life—mass production, mass society, and mass politics—could all be traced to America.

Like anti-Semitism, to which it was often linked, anti-Americanism was a convenient shorthand for expressing cultural insecurity. In the words of the Frenchman Robert Aron, writing in 1935, Henry Ford, F.W. Taylor (the prophet of work rhythms and manufacturing efficiency), and Adolf Hitler were, like it or not, the "guides of our age." America was "industrialism." It threatened the survival of individuality, quality, and national specificity. "America is multiplying its territory, where the values of the West risk finding their grave," wrote Emmanuel Berl in 1929. Europeans owed it to their heritage to resist their own Americanization at every turn, urged Georges Duhamel in

1930: "We Westerners must each firmly denounce whatever is American in his house, his clothes, his soul."[7]

World War II did not alleviate this irritation. Left-wing anti-Americanism in the early–Cold War years echoed to the letter the sentiments of right-wing anti-Americanism 20 years earlier. When Simone de Beauvoir charged that America was "becoming Fascist," Jean-Paul Sartre claimed that McCarthyite America "had gone mad," and *Le Monde* declared that "Coca-Cola is the Danzig of European Culture," they were denouncing the same American "enemy" that had so alarmed their political opponents a generation before. American behavior at home and abroad fed this prejudice but did not create it. In their anger at the United States, European intellectuals had, for many decades, been expressing their anxieties about changes closer to home.[8]

The examples I have quoted are from France, but English ambivalence toward America is also an old story. The present author grew up in post-war Britain where the United States was envied by many, dismissed by some (often the same people)—and *terra incognita* to almost everyone. The German generation of the 1960s blamed America above all for the crass consumerism and political amnesia of their parents' post-war Federal Republic; and even in Donald Rumsfeld's new Europe—the Czech republic, for example, or Hungary—the United States, representing "Western" technology and progress, is increasingly held responsible on all sides of the political spectrum for the ethical vacuum and cultural impoverishment that global capitalism brings in its train.[9] Nevertheless, anti-Americanism in Europe, at least, has always had a distinctively French tinge. As some recent publications suggest, it is in Paris that European ambivalence about America takes a most acute polemical form.

* * *

In his recent history of French anti-Americanism, a learned and witty "genealogy" of the "semiotic bloc" of French anti-American writings, Philippe Roger demonstrates not only that the core of French anti-Americanism is very old indeed, but also that it was always fanciful, and loosely, if at all, attached to American reality. Anti-Americanism is a *récit*, a tale (or fable), with certain recurring themes, fears, and hopes. Starting out as an aesthetic distaste for the New World, French anti-Americanism has since moved through the cultural to the political; but the sedimentary evidence of earlier versions is never quite lost to sight.[10]

Roger's book is strongest on the eighteenth and nineteenth centuries. His coverage of the twentieth century stops with the generation of Sartre—the moment, as he reminds us, when it became conventional for French anti-American texts to begin by denying that they were. That seems reasonable—there are a number of satisfactory accounts of the anti-Americanism of our own times and Roger is interested in tracing origins, not outcomes.[11] And by ending short of the present, he can permit himself a sardonic, upbeat conclusion: "What if anti-Americanism today were no more than a mental slavery that the French impose on themselves, a masochist lethargy, a humdrum resentment, a passionless Pavlovian reaction? That would offer grounds for hope. There are few vices, even intellectual ones, that can long withstand the boredom they elicit." Unfortunately, there is a fresh twist in the story. Anti-Americanism today is fueled by a new consideration. Most Europeans and other foreigners today are untroubled by American products, many of which are, in any case, manufactured and marketed overseas. Most of them don't despise America, and they certainly don't hate Americans. What upsets them, as noted above, is the U.S. foreign policy; and they don't trust America's current president. This is new. Even during the Cold War, many of America's political foes actually quite liked and trusted its leaders. Today, even America's friends don't like President Bush: in part for the policy he pursues, in part for the manner in which he pursues it.

This is the background to a recent burst of anti-American publications; in Germany, in England, but above all in Paris. The most bizarre of these was a book by one Thierry Meyssan, purporting to show that the 9/11 attack on the Pentagon never happened. No airliner ever crashed into the building, he writes: the whole thing is a hoax perpetrated by the American defense establishment to advance its own interests. Meyssan's approach echoes that of Holocaust deniers. He begins by assuming the nonexistence of a well-accredited event, and then reminds us that no amount of evidence—*especially* from firsthand witnesses—can prove the contrary. The method is well summarized in his dismissal of the substantial body of eyewitness testimony running counter to his claim: "Far from warranting their evidence, the quality of these witnesses just shows how far the US Army will go to distort the truth" (*Loin de créditer leurs dépositions, la qualité de ces témoins ne fait que souligner l'importance des moyens déployés par l'armée des États-Unis pour travestir la vérité*).[12]

The most depressing thing about Meyssan's book is that it was a best seller. There is an audience in France for the farther reaches of paranoid suspicion of America, and 9/11 seems to have aroused it.

More typical, though, is the shopping list of complaints in books with titles like *Pourquoi le monde déteste-t-il l'Amérique?*, *Le Livre noir des États-Unis*, and *Dangereuse Amérique*. The first two are by British and Canadian authors, respectively, though they have sold best in their French editions; the third is coauthored by a prominent French Green politician and former presidential candidate.[13]

Characteristically presented with real or feigned regret ("We are not anti-American, but . . ."), these works are an inventory of commonly cited American shortcomings. The United States is a selfish, individualistic society devoted to commerce, profit, and the despoliation of the planet. It is as uncaring of its own poor and sick as it is indifferent to the rest of humankind. The United States rides roughshod over international laws and treaties and threatens the moral, environmental, and physical future of humanity. It is inconsistent and hypocritical in its foreign dealings and wields unparalleled military clout. It is, in short, a bull in the global china shop, wreaking havoc. Much of this is recycled from earlier criticisms of America. Peter Scowen's complaints (his chapter headings include "Les atrocités de Hiroshima et de Nagasaki" and "Une culture vide"), like those of Sardar and Davies ("American Hamburgers and Other Viruses") or Mamère and Farbiaz ("L'américanisation du monde," "Une croisade qui sent le pétrole" [A crusade smelling of oil]), blend traditional themes with new accusations. They are a mixture of conservative cultural distaste (America is ugly, rootless, and crass); anti-globalization rhetoric (America is polluting the world); and neo-Marxist reductionism (America is run by and for the oil companies). Some of the criticisms of American policy and practice are well founded; others are drivel. In their catalogue of claims against America, Sardar and Davies blame the United States for the Cold War imposed on a reluctant Western Europe: "Both France and Italy had major Communist Parties—and still do [*sic*]—but with their own very specific histories that owed little to Russia." "International Communism," in other words, was an American invention. This revisionist myth died many years ago. Its posthumous revival suggests that an older, political anti-Americanism is gaining new traction from the Bush administration's foreign ambitions. Once a rogue state, always a rogue state.[14]

According to Emmanuel Todd, however, there is no need to worry. In his recent book, *Après l'empire* (also a best seller), he argues that the sun is setting on imperial America. We are entering a post-American age. America will continue to jeopardize international stability. But Europeans (and Asians) can take some comfort from the knowledge that the future is theirs. American military power is real, but redundant; meanwhile, its tottering economy is vulnerably dependent upon the rest of the world, and its social model holds no appeal. Between 1950 and 1990, the United States was a benevolent and necessary presence in the world, but not anymore. The challenge today is to manage America's growing irrelevance.[15]

Todd is not at all a conventional "anti-American" and some of what he has to say is of interest—though English-readers seeking to understand the case for American decline would do better to read Charles Kupchan.[16] Todd is right to say that asymmetric globalization—in which the United States consumes what others produce, and economic inequalities grow apace—is bringing about a world unsympathetic to American ambition. Post-communist Russia, post-Saddam Iraq, and other modernizing societies may adopt capitalism ("the only reasonable economic organization") and even become democratic, but they won't mimic American "hyper-individualism" and they will share European preferences on many things. The United States, in Todd's view, will cling desperately to the vestiges of its ambition and power; to maintain its waning influence, it will seek to sustain "a certain level of international tension, a condition of limited but endemic war." This process has already begun, and 9/11 was its trigger.

The problem with Emmanuel Todd, and it will be immediately familiar to anyone who has read any of his previous books, is less his conclusions than his reasoning. There is something of the Ancient Mariner about this writer. He is an anthropological demographer by training, has a demographic tale to tell, and he recounts it in book after book, gripping the reader relentlessly as though to say "Don't you get it? It's all about fertility!" In 1976, he published *La Chute finale: Essai sur la décomposition de la sphère soviétique*, in which he prophesied the end of the USSR: "A slight increase in Russian infant mortality between 1970 and 1974 made me understand the rotting away of the Soviet Union back in 1976 and allowed me to predict the system's collapse." According to his account, the decline in the Soviet birthrate revealed to him "the likely emergence of normal Russians, perfectly capable of overthrowing communism."

Emmanuel Todd was not the only person back in the 1970s predicting an unhealthy future for communism. Nevertheless, the link he claims to have uncovered between fertility and regime collapse has gone to his head. In his new book, world history is reduced to a series of unidirectional, mono-causal correlations linking birthrates, literacy rates, timeless family structures, and global politics. The Yugoslav wars were the result of "fertility gaps" between Slavs and Muslims. The American Civil War can be traced to the low birthrates of the Anglo-Saxon settler class. And if "individualistic" America faces grim prospects today, this is because the "family structures" of the rest of the world favor very different political systems.

In Emmanuel Todd's parallel universe, politics—like economic behavior—is inscribed in a society's "genetic code." The egalitarian family systems of Central Asia reveal an "anthropology of community" that made communism more acceptable there (elsewhere he has attributed regional variations in French, Italian, and Finnish voting patterns to similar differences in family life[17]). Today, the "universalist Russian temperament" based on the extended Russian family offers a nonindividualistic socioeconomic model that may be the democracy of the future. "A priori, there is no reason not to imagine a liberal and democratic Russia protecting the planet against American efforts to shore up their global imperial posture."

Todd goes further. He absurdly exaggerates America's current woes, real as they are. Extrapolating from the collapse of Enron (but what of Parmalat?), he concludes that all American economic data are as unreliable as that of the Soviets: the truly parlous state of the U.S. economy has been kept hidden; and he offers his own variant on the "clash of civilizations." The coming conflict between Islam and the United States brings into opposition the "effectively feminist," women-based civilization of America and the masculinized ethic of Central Asian and Arab warrior societies. Here, too, America will be isolated, for Europeans will feel just as threatened by the United States as their Arab neighbors do. Once again, it all comes down to family life, with a distinctive modern twist: "The status of the American woman, threatening and castrating [*castratrice et menaçante*], [is] as disturbing for European men as the all-powerful Arab male is for European women." The Atlantic gap begins in the bedroom . . .

To leave Emmanuel Todd for Jean-François Revel is to abandon the mad scientist for the self-confident patrician. Revel is an august immortal of the Académie Française. He is the author of many books (31 to date), as the reader of his latest essay is firmly reminded.[18] Revel's style suggests a man unfamiliar with self-doubt and unused to contradiction. He tends toward sweeping, unsupported generalizations—by his account, most of Europe's political and cultural elite "never understood anything about communism"—and his version of French anti-Americanism, at times, approaches caricature. This is a pity, because some of what he writes makes good sense.

Thus, Revel is right to draw attention to the contradiction at the heart of much French criticism of America. If the United States is such a social disaster, a cultural pygmy, a political innocent, and an economic meltdown waiting to happen, why worry? Why devote so much resentful attention to it? Alternatively, if it is as powerful and successful as many fear, might it not be doing something right? As a Frenchman, Revel is well placed to remind his fellow citizens that France, too, has social problems—the much-vaunted French education system neither assimilates cultural and religious minorities nor does it support and nourish cultural difference. France, too, has slums, violence, and delinquency.

And Jean-Marie Le Pen's score in the presidential elections of 2002 is a standing rebuke to all of France's political class for its failure to address the problems of immigration and race. Revel makes legitimate fun of France's cultural administrators, who can vandalize their own national heritage at least as recklessly as the barbaric Americans. No American booster could ever match Culture Minister Jack Lang's 1984 "Projet Culturel Extérieur de la France," in which France's cultural ambitions are described by Lang himself as "probably unequaled in any other country." And what does it say about the sophistication of the French press and television who devoted so much credulous space to the elucubrations of M. Meyssan?

One could go on. Mocking the French for their pretensions (and their memory holes) is almost as easy as picking apart the hypocrisies of the U.S. foreign policy. And I agree with Revel that today's antiglobalization activists came as a "divine surprise" for the European left, a heaven-sent cause at a post-ideological moment when Europe's radicals were adrift. But Revel's astute observations of what is wrong in France are devalued by his inability to find *anything* wrong with America. His entire book is a paean of blinkered praise for a country that, regrettably, does not exist. Like the anti-Americans he disdains, he has conjured up his American subject out of thin air.

In Revel's America, the melting pot works "*fort bien*" and there is no mention of ghettos. According to him, Europeans misread and exaggerate U.S. crime statistics, whereas, in reality, crime in America is not a problem. Health coverage in America works well: most Americans are insured at work, the rest benefit from publicly funded Medicare and Medicaid. Anyway, the system's shortcomings are no worse than those of France's own provisions for health care. The American poor have the same *per capita* income as the *average* citizen of Portugal; so, they can't be called poor (Revel has apparently never heard of cost-of-living indices). There is no "underclass." Meanwhile, the United States has had social democracy longer than Europe, and American television and news coverage is much better than you think.

As for American foreign policy: in Revel-land, the United States has stayed fully engaged in the Israel–Palestine conflict, is resolutely non-partisan, and its policy has been a success. The American missile defense program worries M. Revel a lot less than it does some American generals. Unlike 50 percent of the U.S. electorate, Académicien Revel saw nothing amiss in the conduct of the 2000 presidential election. As for evidence of growing American anti-French sentiment, stuff and nonsense: *pour ma part, je ne l'ai jamais constaté* ("as for me, I've never seen it"). In short, whatever French critics and others say about the United States, Jean-François Revel maintains the opposite. Voltaire could not have done a better job satirizing traditional French prejudices. M. Revel is Pangloss in Wonderland.

*   *   *

Somewhere between Emmanuel Todd and Jean-François Revel, there is emerging an interesting European perspective on George Bush's America; for anti-Americanism, in Europe at least, draws on a genuine Atlantic gap. The two sides of the ocean really are different today, in many ways. To begin with, there is religion. America is a credulous and religious society: since the mid-1950s, Europeans have abandoned their churches in droves; but in the United States, there has been virtually no decline in churchgoing and synagogue attendance.

In 1998, a Harris poll found that 66 percent even of non-Christian Americans believed in miracles and 47 percent of them accredited the Virgin Birth; the figures for all Americans are 86 and 83 percent, respectively. Some 45 percent of Americans believe there is a Devil. In a recent *Newsweek* poll, 79 percent of American respondents accepted that biblical miracles really happened. According to a 1999 *Newsweek* poll, 40 percent of all Americans (71 percent of Evangelical Protestants) believe that the world will end in a battle at Armageddon between Jesus and the Antichrist. An American president who conducts Bible study in the White House and begins cabinet sessions with a prayer may seem a curious anachronism to his European allies, but he is in tune with his constituents.[19]

Second, the inequalities and insecurities of American life are still unthinkable across the Atlantic. Europeans remain wary of excessive disparities of income, and their institutions and political choices reflect this sentiment. Moreover, it is prudence, rather than the residue of "socialism," that explains European hesitation over unregulated markets and the dismantling of the public sector and local resistance to the American "model." This makes sense for most people in Europe—as elsewhere in the world—unrestricted competition is at least as much a threat as an opportunity. Europeans want a more interventionist state at home than Americans do, and they expect to pay for it. Even in post-Thatcher Britain, 62 percent of adults polled in December 2002 would favor higher taxes in return for improved public services. The figure for the United States was under 1 percent. This is less surprising when one considers that in America (where the disparities between rich and poor are greater than anywhere else in the developed world), fully 19 percent of the adult population claims to be in the richest 1 percent of the nation—and a further 20 percent believe they will enter that 1 percent in their lifetime![20]

What Europeans find perturbing about America, then, is precisely what most Americans believe to be their nation's strongest suit: its unique mix of moralistic religiosity, minimal provision for public welfare, and maximal market freedom—the "American way of life"—coupled with a missionary foreign policy ostensibly directed at exporting that same cluster of values and practices. Here, the United States is ill-served by globalization, which highlights for the world's poorer countries the costs of exposure to economic competition and reminds West Europeans, after the long sleep of the Cold War, of the true fault lines bisecting the hitherto undifferentiated "West." Indeed, a truth that is clearer now than even just a few years ago is that in many crucial respects, Europe and the United States are actually less alike than they were 50 years ago. This observation flies in the face of claims about "globalization" and "Americanization" advanced not just by enthusiastic proponents of the process, but also by its angry critics. Yet there is less to the promise of a new American century than meets the eye. In the first place, we have been there before. It is a cardinal tenet of the prophets of globalization that the logic of economic efficiency must sweep all before it (a characteristically nineteenth-century fallacy they share with Marxists). But that was also how it seemed at the peak of the last great era of globalization, on the eve of World War I, when many observers, likewise, foresaw the decline of the nation-state and a future age of international economic integration.

What happened, of course, was something rather different, and 1913 levels of international trade, communication, and mobility would not be reached again until the mid-1970s. The contingencies of domestic politics trumped the "laws" of international economic behavior, and they may do so again. Capitalism is indeed global in its reach, but its local forms have always been richly variable and they still are. This is because economic practices shape national institutions and legal norms and are shaped by them in their turn; they are deeply embedded in very different national and moral cultures.

Partly for this reason, the American model is not obviously more appealing to people elsewhere and its triumph is far from assured. Europeans and Americans live quite different sorts of lives. More than one American in five is poor, whereas the figures for continental Western Europe hover around one in twelve. In their first year of life, 60 percent more babies die in the United States than in France or Germany. The disparity between rich and poor is vastly greater in the United States than anywhere in continental Europe (or than it was in the United States 20 years ago); but whereas fewer than one American in three supports significant redistribution of wealth, 63 percent of Britons favor it and the figures are higher still on the European continent.

Even before modern European welfare states were established, most employed Europeans had compulsory health insurance (since 1883 in the German case), and all Western Europeans now take for granted the interlocking mesh of guarantees, protections, and supports whose reduction or abolition they have consistently opposed at the polls. The social and occupational insecurity familiar to tens of millions of Americans has long been politically intolerable anywhere in the European Union. If fascism and communism were the European reactions to the last great wave of laissez-faire globalization, then "welfare capitalism" is Europe's insurance against a rerun. On prudential grounds, if for no other reason, the rest of the West is not about to take the American path.

But what of the claim that Europeans, like everyone else in the world, will have little choice? Much is said about the coming ineluctable triumph of American economic practice at the expense of the lumbering, unproductive, inflexible European variant. Yet handicapped as they are by all the supposed impedimenta of their statist past, the economies of Belgium, France, and the Netherlands last year were actually *more* productive for each hour worked than that of the United States, while the Irish, the Austrians, the Danes, and the Germans were very close behind.[21]

Between 1991 and 1998, productivity on average actually *grew faster* in Europe than in the United States. The United States, nonetheless, outpaces Europe in gross terms. This is because more Americans work; the state takes less from their wages (and provides less in return); they work longer hours—28 percent more than Germans and

43 percent more than the French; and they take shorter vacations or none at all.

Whether Europe (or anywhere else) would look more like America if the American economic model were adopted there is a moot point. The modern American economy is not replicable elsewhere. The "war on terror" is not the only matter in which the United States is critically dependent upon foreigners. The American economic "miracle" of the past decade has been fueled by the $1.2 billion per day in foreign capital inflow that is needed to cover the country's foreign trade deficit, currently running at $450 billion per year. It is these huge inward investment flows that have kept share prices up, inflation and interest rates down, and domestic consumption booming. If a European, Asian, or Latin American country ran comparable trade deficits, it would long since be in the hands of the International Monetary Fund. The United States is uniquely placed to indulge such crippling dependence on foreign investors because the dollar has been the world's reserve currency since World War II. How long the American economy can operate thus before it is brought painfully to earth by a loss of overseas confidence is a much-debated topic; as is the related claim that it was these rivers of foreign cash, rather than the unprecedented productivity of the new high-tech sectors, that drove the prosperity of the 1990s.[22] What is clear is that for all its recent allure, the American model is unique and not for export.

Far from universalizing its appeal, globalization has, if anything, diminished foreign enthusiasm for the American model: the reduction in public ownership of goods and services in Europe over the past 20 years has not been accompanied by any reduction in the state's social obligations—except in Britain where, tellingly, governments have had to backtrack in the face of public opposition. And it is because they inhabit such very different societies that Europeans and Americans see the world so differently, and value sharply contrasting international processes and outcomes.

But Europe, especially "old Europe," is much more in tune than the United States with the thinking of the rest of the world on everything from environmental threats to international law, and its social legislation and economic practices are more congenial to foreigners and more readily exportable than the American variants. U.S. domestic policy and politics are poorly adapted to the complexity of today's world. And it is the United States, not Europe that is increasingly dependent on foreign investment to feed its deficit-laden economy and sustain its vulnerable currency.

Thus when American leaders throw fits of pique at European dissent, and provoke and encourage internal European divisions, these might reasonably be interpreted as signs of incipient weakness, not strength. Real power is influence and example, backed up by understated reminders of military force. When a great power has to buy its allies, bribe its friends, and blackmail its critics, something is amiss. The energetic American response to 9/11 may thus be misleading. The bedrock reality is a world from which the United States will either retreat in frustration or with which it will have to engage on cooperative terms. Either way, the "American era" is passing.

*   *   *

And yet America is still esteemed and even revered overseas, not because of globalization but in spite of it. America is not epitomized by MTV and McDonald's, or by Enron or WorldCom. America is not even particularly admired abroad for its awesome military establishment, any more than it is respected for its unparalleled wealth. If American power and influence are actually very fragile, it is because they rest upon an idea, a unique and irreplaceable myth: that the United States really does stand for a better world and is still the best hope of all who seek it. Radical anti-Americans acknowledge the force of this myth, even as they disparage it.

What gives America its formidable international influence is not its unequaled capacity for war but the trust of others in its good intentions. That is why Washington's opposition to the International Criminal Court does so much damage. It suggests that the United States does not trust the rest of the world to treat Americans fairly. But if America displays a lack of trust in others, the time may come when they will return the compliment. The greatest threat to America is that in the face of American neglect and indifference, the American image will fade and "large proportions of key societies [will] turn against the United States and the global values of free trade and free society."[23]

This process is already well under way. "Anti-globalizers," environmentalists, advocates of a European (or French) "alternative model," all share a common anti-Americanism that takes its cue from U.S. behavior and serves as a broad church within which the discontented of the world can now congregate. Whether this coalition of sentiments and interests will ever move beyond rhetorical unison is unclear and perhaps unlikely. Europeans may see themselves as increasingly at odds with the United States, but from the point of view of much of the rest of humanity, the wealthy West still looks like a single bloc with fundamentally similar interests.

But it may be that today's transatlantic schisms and distinctions will come to matter more, not less, in years to come. Long-standing social and cultural contrasts are being highlighted and reinforced by irresolvable policy disagreements. Already the schism over the U.S. war on Iraq has revealed something new. In the early years of the Cold War, anti-American demonstrations in Europe took their cue from Soviet-financed "peace movements," but the political and economic elites were firmly in the American camp. But today's mass anti-war protests require no manipulation, and the widespread anger toward the United States is a new development.

This is not good news for America's European allies—as Aznar, Blair, and their collaborators wrote in their controversial open letter of January 30, 2003, "Today more than ever, the transatlantic bond is a guarantee of our freedom." But it augurs ill for America, too. If the world needs the United States, the converse is no less true. If anti-Americanism becomes the shared default sentiment of much of humanity, then America will be compelled increasingly to resort to force, or the threat of force, to achieve its own ends, having lost the means to persuade or convince friends and foes alike. The outcome would be further suspicion and dislike, very possibly triggering a new American retreat from international responsibility. It is an unappealing prospect.

NOTES

1. Lawrence F. Kaplan and William Kristol, *The War over Iraq. Saddam's Tyranny and America's Mission* (Washington: Diane Pub. Co., 2003), pp. 120–121.
2. See *The Economist*, January 4, 2003.
3. For Czech and Polish attitudes to war with Iraq, see *The Economist*, February 1, 2003. For Spanish opposition to Aznar, see *El País*, February 3, 2003.
4. See the survey of transatlantic attitudes in a poll conducted by the Chicago Council on Foreign Relations and the German Marshall Fund of the U.S. at www.worldviews.org. For NATO member-state defense expenditures, see *La Republica*, February 11, 2003. The critical views of a Central European diplomat were expressed in a private communication. Like many other politicians from former Communist Europe, he was reluctant to air his criticisms of American policy in public.
5. See Robert Kagan, *Of Paradise and Power: America and Europe in the New World Order* (Knopf: New York, 2003), and my review in *The New York Review of Books*, vol. 50, no. 6, April 10, 2003.

6. See Craig Kennedy and Marshall M. Bouton, "The real transatlantic gap," *Foreign Policy*, November–December 2002, based on a recent survey by the Chicago Council on Foreign Relations and the German Marshall Fund. For American views, see www.gallup.com/poll/releases/pr030228.asp. In late February 2003, 59% of Americans opposed a war on Iraq without UN support.

7. Emmanuel Berl, *Mort de la pensée bourgeoise* (Paris: Bernard Grasset, 1929; reprinted, 1970), pp. 76–77; André Siegfried, *Les États-Unis d'aujourd'hui* (Paris: Colin, 1927), quoted in Michel Winock, *Nationalisme, antisémitisme et fascisme en France* (Paris: Seuil, 1982), p. 56. See also Georges Duhamel, *Scènes de la Vie future* (Paris: Mercure de France, 1930); Robert Aron and Arnaud Dandieu, *Le Cancer américain* (Paris: Rieder, 1931); and my own "America has gone mad: anti-Americanism in historical perspective," in *Past Imperfect: French Intellectuals, 1944–1956* (Berkeley: University of California Press, 1992), pp. 187–204.

8. For Simone de Beauvoir, see her *L'Amérique au jour le jour* (Paris: Morihien, 1948), pp. 99–100. Sartre was commenting on the trial and execution of the Rosenbergs. For *Le Monde*, see the editorial "Mourir pour le Coca-Cola," *Le Monde*, March 29, 1950.

9. For German representations of the price of Americanization, see Rainer Werner Fassbinder's *Marriage of Maria Braun* (1979); or Edgar Reitz's *Heimat: Eine deutsche Chronik* (1984), where the American impact on "deep Germany" is depicted as far more corrosive of values than the passage through Nazism. And it was Václav Havel, no less, who reminded his fellow dissidents back in 1984 that rationalism, scientism, our fascination with technology and change, were all the "ambiguous exports" of the West, the perverse fruits of the dream of modernity. See Václav Havel, "Svedomí a politika," *Svedectví*, vol. 18, no. 72 (1984), pp. 621–635 (quote from page 627).

10. Philippe Roger, *L'Ennemi américain: Généalogie de l'antiaméricanisme français* (Paris: Seuil, 2002).

11. See Philippe Mathy, *Extrême Occident: French Intellectuals and America* (Chicago: University of Chicago Press, 1993), and *L'Amérique dans les têtes: Un siècle de fascinations et d'aversions*, edited by Denis Lacorne, Jacques Rupnik, and Marie-France Toinet (Paris: Hachette, 1986).

12. Thierry Meyssan, *11 septembre 2001: L'Effroyable Imposture* (Chatou: Carnot, 2002), p. 23. In the same key, see Andreas von Bülow, *Die CIA und der 11. September* (Munich, 2003). A representative selection of British views, none of which descends to the paranoid absurdities of Meyssan or von Bülow, can be found in "What we think of America," *Granta*, vol. 77 (spring 2002).

13. Ziauddin Sardar and Merryl Wyn Davies, *Pourquoi le monde déteste-t-il l'Amérique?* (Paris: Fayard, 2002), Peter Scowen, *Le Livre noir des États-Unis* (Paris: Editions Mango, 2003); Noël Mamère Patrick Farbiaz, *Dangereuse Amérique: Chronique d'une guerre annoncée* (Paris: Ramsay, 2002).

14. We are back in May 1944, when Hubert Beuve-Méry, future founder and editor of *Le Monde*, could write that "the Americans constitute a real threat to France. . . . [They] can prevent us accomplishing the necessary revolution, and their materialism lacks even the tragic grandeur of the materialism of the totalitarians." Quoted by Jean-François Revel in *L'Obsession anti-américaine* (Paris: Plon, 2002), p. 98.

15. Emmanuel Todd, *Après l'empire: Essai sur la décomposition du système américain* (Paris: Gallimard, 2002).

16. Charles Kupchan, *The End of the American Era* (New York: Knopf, 2002). See my discussion of Kupchan in *The New York Review*, April 10, 2003.

17. Emmanuel Todd, *La troisième planète: Structures familiales et systèmes idéologiques* (Paris: Seuil, 1983). "Communism's success is principally explained by the existence . . . of egalitarian and authoritarian family structures predisposing people to see Communist ideology as natural and good": See *Après l'empire*, p. 178.

18. Revel, *L'Obsession anti-américaine, op. cit.*

19. See www.pollingreport.com/religion.htm, and www.pollingreport.com/religion2.htm

20. "A tale of two Legacies," *The Economist*, December 21, 2002; *Financial Times*, January 25–26, 2003.

21. See *Financial Times*, February 20, 2002.

22. For a relentlessly negative account of the deficiencies of the American model, see Will Hutton, *The World We're In* (Boston: Little Brown, 2002), to which I am indebted for some of the figures cited above.

23. Michael J. Mazarr, "Saved from ourselves?" in *What Does the World Want from America?* edited by Alexander T.J. Lennon (from MIT Press, Boston, November 2002), p. 167; first published in *The Washington Quarterly*, vol. 25, no. 2 (spring 2002).

2

Anti-Americanism and Americanophobia: A French Perspective

Denis Lacorne

French anti-Americanism has never been as much the focus of debate as it is today. This is true both in France, where a crop of books has appeared on the subject, and in the United States, for reasons linked to the French refusal to support the American invasion of Iraq. Some authors have underlined the unchanging nature of the phenomenon, defining anti-Americanism as a historical "constant" since the eighteenth century, or again as an endlessly repetitive "semantic block" to use Philippe Roger's expression. Others, like Jean-François Revel, have tried to show what lies hidden behind such a fashionable ideology: a deep-rooted critique of economic liberalism and American democracy. Yet others, while rejecting the anti-American label, like Emmanuel Todd, have attempted to lift the veil and lay bare the weaknesses of American democracy and the extreme economic fragility of an American empire "in decline," despite appearances.[1]

Contradictions and Swings in Public Opinion

What I propose to do here—rather than pick out historical constants, defend the virtues of the liberal model, or pontificate upon the inevitable decline of great empires—is to take a closer look at the contradictions of what I view as a changing and ambiguous phenomenon, a subject of frequent swings in public opinion. In *The Rise and Fall of Anti-Americanism*, Jacques Rupnik and I pointed out that:

> France is a heterogeneous country made up of countless different groups, every one of which has its "own" image of America, which frequently changes in the light of circumstances or political events. However, it sometimes happens that this multitude of contradictory perceptions coalesces into a major trend of opinion and for a while the attitudes of the country as a whole are either exaggeratedly favourable or excessively unfavourable to American realities.[2]

Such contrasting swings of opinion have indeed occurred over the past three years, first due to France's reaction to the tragic events of 9/11, and later to France's opposition to the second Gulf War.

To properly bring out the complexity of French opinion, its ambiguities and frequent contradictions, I propose going back to the year 2000, before the upheavals of the 2001–2003 period. This was a peaceful time in Franco-American relations. According to a 2000 SOFRES poll, sympathy for the United States (41 percent of French respondents) was stronger than animosity (10 percent), and at first sight, French respondents seemed to be more Americanophile than anything else. However, the very proportion of those who refused to commit themselves one way or another (48 percent) was disquieting—suggesting a kind of discomfort before the American big brother.[3] To get a clearer picture, SOFRES, in the same poll, included an open-ended question, leaving a wide margin to respondents: "When you think of the United States, what words and images come to your mind?"

As table 2.1 clearly shows, most spontaneous images of America (56 percent) turned out to be negative. When the French thought of the United States, the first thing that came to mind was violence (mentioned by 21 percent of the respondents) in every form (physical violence, drugs, the death penalty, uncontrolled gun sales), or again the weird or excessive aspects of the American character (14 percent), including the "obesity of Americans" and the "junk" they eat (3 percent). The complaints so common in the 1960s and 1970s against "American imperialism" or "capitalism" were now barely mentioned (3 and 2 percent of responses, respectively). As for spontaneously mentioned positive aspects, what is striking is that none of them had anything to do with American democracy. When the French hold a positive opinion of the United States, they cite, in order of importance, American grandeur or gigantism (14 percent), American power (12 percent), or superior technology . . . It is clear that for the French, America is not a political model. An insignificant number of the respondents specifically

Table 2.1 French responses to the question: "When you think of the United States, what words and images come to your mind?" (all values in %)

Positive Aspects	**43***	*The economy*	7
(% respondents who mention)		"American imperialism"	3
Grandeur/gigantism	14	Economic hegemony	2
Power of the United States	12	Capitalism/profit-seeking	2
Wealth	4	*Food*	3
Freedom	4	Poor food	2
Superior technology	4	The obesity of Americans	1
Modernism	3	*Other negative aspects*	2
"I like this country"	1	**Neutral Aspects**	**43***
Dynamism	1	Money	4
The economy	6	Economic liberalism	3
Economic strength/	4	A multiracial society	3
a strong economy		Weapons	3
A strong currency/	1	Capitalism	2
a strong dollar		A federation of states	2
Politics	4	The dollar	2
"Gives military support		The "American Dream"	1
to other countries"	3	*Geography*	8
Other positive aspects	3	The Statue of Liberty	2
Negative Aspects	**56***	Wide open spaces	2
"I don't like the United States"	2	Hollywood	2
Violence	21	Skyscrapers	2
Violence (unspecified)	14	Other geographical features	2
Crime, delinquency, drugs	7	*Food*	6
The death penalty, executions	2	McDonald's	3
Free sale of arms	2	Fast food restaurants	3
Negative psychological traits	14	Coca-Cola	2
"They're excessive in everything"	3	*American personalities*	6
Vanity, arrogance	2	Among them, Bill Clinton	4
Individualism	2	*Politics*	5
Extremism	1	Power	3
Puritanism	1	A world power	2
Craziness/"a crazy people"	1	A military power	1
Selfishness	1	*Other neutral aspects*	2
Intolerance	1	Brings nothing to mind	2
Criticism of American influence	11	*No answer*	5
They control other countries	9		
"They think they're the			
world's policemen"	2		
"They want to impose their			
way of life"	2		

* Multiple responses account for totals greater than 100.

Source: "France-Etats-Unis: regards croisés," SOFRES/French American Foundation poll, May 2000.

referred to key elements of economic or political liberalism, such as "individualism" (2 percent), "freedom" (4 percent), "liberalism," or capitalism, without elaborating (3 percent). One even comes away with the impression—and this goes to prove the ignorance of the average Frenchman about America—that recent immigrants are more easily assimilated in France than in the United States.[4]

These few data suggest that the French didn't turn anti-American all of a sudden in 2003, at the time of the American invasion of Iraq. They were so before the Gulf War; or rather, they were already of two minds, their empathy mingled with indifference, their admiration with doubt and distrust of the abnormalities of the American society.

Who shapes opinion? The SOFRES study does not give a clear answer. But we could suggest a few explanations, particularly for the frequent criticism in France against the violence and racism of American society. The media may be partly to blame: films, news, and current affairs programs, and all the French debates about the injustice and barbarity of the death penalty in the United States. There seem to be good reasons for the United States to become unpopular with the French, even if, as I hope to show, some of our *belles âmes* have overdone it to the extent of losing all credibility.[5]

Let us now consider the three quick swings of public opinion that have occurred since September 2001.

First Phase. Extreme sympathy. Most of the French shared in the suffering of Americans, in the aftermath of the 9/11 attacks. One of the most well-known newspaper editors marked the occasion with a slogan somewhat unusual in the post-war daily press: "We are all Americans!"[6] French compassion expressed itself in a hundred different ways: from the ecumenical service performed at the American Church of Paris to the three mandatory minutes of silence imposed by the government on every school and public agency, the hundreds of drawings elementary school students in Normandy sent to the U.S. embassy in Paris, and other more modest but symbolically significant gestures like the planting of a tree of liberty next to Bartholdi's small bronze replica of the Statue of Liberty in the Luxemburg gardens in Paris. During the Bastille Day festivities of July 14, 2002, the new compassionate love for America reached its climax with a red New York Fire Department truck leading the parade. It was followed by an entire class of West Point cadets that came to Paris to celebrate the bicentennial of their school—founded in the same year as the French military academy— their Saint Cyr comrades marching alongside.

Second Phase. Emergence of differences of opinion between France and the United States with the UN resolutions on Iraq. What came as a surprise in France, was the near-unanimous public support for Chirac's critical stance, a situation where the political left, right, and far right seemed to have joined the same chorus. Stranger still, French opinion coincided perfectly with widespread European popular opposition to the war, making it possible to say that there is such a thing as a common, unified European public opinion.[7] On March 28, when the war began, French public opinion confirmed its massive support for Chirac's foreign policy: 78 percent of a polled sample opposed the American intervention. More surprisingly, a quarter of the French (and nearly two-thirds of French Muslims) felt themselves "on the Iraqi side" and, according to the same survey, "deep down," 33 percent of the respondents "did not wish the United States to win" (among them, 72 percent of French Muslims).[8] In a most unprecedented declaration, the Prime Minister felt obliged to say, in Clermont-Ferrand on March 31, 2003: "Be careful not to pick the wrong enemy. . . . Opposing the war doesn't mean that we're hoping for dictatorship to win over democracy."[9]

A note of discord did emerge within the French elite. Influential intellectuals such as Pierre Hassner (otherwise extremely critical of the methods used by the Bush administration) spoke out in support of good sense and realism, against French diplomatic activism and the ephemeral alliance it forged with Russia, Germany, and China, a combination intended to counterbalance the power of the United States: "Even if we refuse to take orders from Bush, we can't have the butcher of Chechnya or Tibet commanding us instead."[10]

Third Phase. Appeasement and reconciliation. Preparations for the G8 summit at Evian (June 2003) became an opportunity to resume friendly French-U.S. relations. Indeed, Bush concluded his *Le Figaro* interview with an unexpected "Vive la France!," preceded by the admission that "between allies, we might have our differences, but what brings the United States closer to France, to Europe, is far more important."[11] At the same time, an officer of the American forces posted at Kabul stressed the eminently positive role of the French forces helping the Americans rebuild an Afghan army. "Out here," he pointed out to a visiting American senator, "we've still got French fries."[12] French Defense Minister Alliot-Marie's visit to the Pentagon, on January 22, 2004, was a major step in the restoration of frayed ties between France and the United States. It was designed to prepare a visit to Normandy by President Bush in June 2004 to participate in the commemoration of the sixtieth anniversary of D-Day—the planned highlight of a genuine Franco-American reconciliation.[13]

Still, whatever the ups and downs of the transatlantic relationship, we would be well advised not to ignore the vigor and tenacity of anti-American feelings in France. This is proven by the sales figures of a whole new literary genre of books about the "murky side of America." These publications indiscriminately denounce the more monstrous aspects of American civilization. For example: Noël Mamère and Patrick Farbiaz, *Dangereuse Amérique [Dangerous America]* (Ramsay, 2002); Peter Scowen, *Le Livre noir des États-Unis [The Black Book of the United States]* (Mango, 2002); Ziauddin Sardar and Merryl Davies, *Pourquoi le monde déteste-t-il l'Amérique? [Why Does the World Hate America?]* (Fayard, 2002); Thierry Meyssan, *L'Effroyable imposture [The Appalling Imposture]* (Carnot, 2002); Gilbert Achcar, *Le choc des barbaries [The Clash of Barbarians]* (Complexe, 2002); Eric Laurent, *La guerre des Bush: les secrets inavouables [Bush's War: The Unspeakable Secrets]* (Plon, 2003).

All these books tell a similar tale of misdeeds, horrors, and threats—the American colonization of the world compounded with an even more real colonization of minds, a foreign policy that is nothing but a series of terrible conspiracies (of oil barons, genetically modified food barons, the CIA and the Pentagon), brutal domineering behavior, complete indifference to poverty and mass killings in the world—an indictment of American abuse of power and dominant position, U.S. disrespect for international law, in a word the neocolonial violence of a new Roman Empire. The portrayal of Bush in the media fulfilled all expectations. It seemed tailor-made—at last a president that America-haters always dreamt of—a splendid blend of the brutal sheriff and the fanatic missionary. These studies, as we might suspect, lacked scientific rigor. Guesses and impressions passed for truths and every manner of sophistry was deployed to prove the barbarity of America. George W. Bush, for instance, when he was still the governor of Texas, was first portrayed as a bloodthirsty leader, with a finger firmly pressed on the switch of an electric chair. Elected president, commander in chief of the U.S. Armed Forces, Bush suddenly appeared in the role of a Christian crusader king, out to shake up the world, flying the standard of a puritan fundamentalist horde gone out of control. News headlines spoke of "George Bush's Holy Crusade" (*Libération*), "War or Jehad?" (*Le Courrier International*), "Holy Wars" (*Le Point*), "Holy War against Jehad" (*Le Nouvel Observateur*), "The Clash of the Fundamentalists" (*Le Monde*), for over three weeks.[14]

JOSÉ BOVÉ AND JEAN-MARIE MESSIER:
TWO GRAND CAUSES, TWO FALLEN
HEROES OF FRENCH MODERNITY

We see that the protean anti-Americanism of the past few years has been nourished by contemporary world events, and fed also by fears and fantasies inherited from the nineteenth or early twentieth centuries. The antiglobalization rhetoric of José Bové, the "shepherd of Larzac," is, in fact, little but a remake of the 1920s attacks on "Americanism," pointing to the subservience of modest independent artisans to American corporate power, brutal assembly-line discipline, and the "dehumanized settings" of an industrial society excessively rationalized by the rules of Fordianism or Taylorism—in short, a world devoid of pride in personal initiative and accomplishment.[15]

Single-handedly taking on the American Goliath and its Taylorized food outlet—the McDonald's fast-food chain—José Bové proved that society had not totally silenced individual voices and that a lone David could check the inexorable advance of the juggernaut of food standardization. Wholesome food was contrasted to American "junk" (*la malbouffe*), the rich taste of a slice of Roquefort was compared with a tasteless, greasy, grilled mass of ground beef. A modern incarnation of the *personnaliste* philosophy of the 1930s, José Bové symbolized a typically French form of resistance to American trade imperialism. His spectacular political protests launched with the support of the French Farmers' Confederation—the destruction of a McDonald's restaurant at Millau in the Aveyron[16] (euphemistically termed a "dismantling" operation), or his active participation in antiglobalization protests at the WTO's Seattle Summit were happenings which established his omnipresence in the French media (he was, of course, barely mentioned in the U.S. media).

Acclaimed by leaders of the right and the left, united in their opposition to the uncontrolled globalization process, José Bové became a self-made myth: he embodied the virtues of great comic book heroes. He was at once Tintin in America, going after the evil producers of genetically modified foods, and Astérix at war against the legions of a new imperial Rome.

Oddly enough, the rejection of "American" globalization, symbolized by José Bové, coincided with the emergence of a new type of French corporate globalization, embodied by a truly Americanized French CEO, Jean-Marie Messier. A classic product of the elite "Grandes écoles" (Polytechnique and the National School of Administration), a high-ranking, respected civil servant in the Balladur government,

Messier demonstrated that it was possible to live the American dream in France—first by changing careers, then by taking control of an old-style corporation, the Compagnie Générale des Eaux, and turning it into one of the biggest media and communications companies in the world, with its name appropriately changed to Vivendi Universal, after a series of spectacular mega-mergers. Like the frog in the fable that blew itself up to the size of an ox, this ordinary French company became one of the leading American multinationals, highly rated on Wall Street, gaining control of one of Hollywood's major studios (Universal Studios), and adopting English as its working language to satisfy the wish of the majority of its board of directors. Messier, the exemplary Parisian bureaucrat, even chose to transfer his private residence to Park Avenue, in Manhattan, to better establish his American credentials.[17]

However, these two emblematic figures of French modernity ended up as fallen heroes. José Bové landed in prison, sentenced by a French court for attacks on private property, and Messier, in the end, was forced to quit the chairmanship of a company he had driven to the verge of bankruptcy. Both kinds of zeal led to failure. José Bové and Jean-Marie Messier, men who symbolized the difficult French transition to modernity and globalization, only revealed the paradox of French public opinion—generally "suspicious" of globalization (72 percent of polled opinions), but acknowledging at the same time that globalization was a "good thing for France" (53 percent), and "especially good for French industry" (63 percent).[18]

This inconsistency of the French surely reflects another paradox, observed in a recent study by Philip Gordon and Sophie Meunier: "While the French (often stridently) resist globalization, they also adapt to it (discreetly and usually better than many would suspect)."[19] Anti-American rhetoric should, therefore, never be taken literally: it is often accompanied by blatantly Americanophile rhetoric, an aspect too often overlooked by the media, and by authors who have made a career out of anti-Americanism.[20]

Still, French anti-Americanism has a bright future. It feeds on a century-old tradition, and enjoys continuing support from leading political figures of all stripes, as well as from new lobbies, such as the Farmers' Confederation founded by José Bové in 1987, and ATTAC, an antiglobalization public interest lobby launched in 1998 at the initiative of the editors of *Le Monde Diplomatique*. Echoing José Bové's radical slogan, "I have one enemy, it's the market!," Ignacio Ramonet, the editor-in-chief of *Le Monde Diplomatique*, declared in the same vein at about the same time: "Let us disarm and defeat the market at all cost!"[21] Bové was popular because the left-wing media readily supported his cause without questioning his motivations.[22]

The remarkable success of the French antiglobalization movement would not have been possible without the quasi-unanimous support of major French political parties. Among them are Jean-Marie Le Pen's National Front, belligerently opposed to the globalization of trade during the European elections of 1999, as well as Charles Pasqua and Philippe de Villiers' ultranationalist party, the Rassemblement pour la France, which lamented the sacrifice of the "grandeur of France upon the altar of globalization" (Pasqua termed it the "new totalitarianism of our times"). The Communist Party and its general secretary, Robert Hue, who denounced the horrors of "unbridled neo-liberal globalization" at WTO's Seattle Summit, to say nothing of the curious alliance of a Gaullist Chirac and a Socialist Jospin, both of whom have suggested ways to "tame" or "humanize" globalization as if it were some kind of wild beast that had to be reined in at all costs if the destruction of European cultures and economic systems were to be averted.

Worried about the increasingly important role of American pension funds in the workings of the French stock exchange, Chirac publicly attacked the selfish interests of "California and Florida pensioners" while Jospin denounced the "dictatorship of shareholders," imposed from across the Atlantic. Only the MEDEF (the leading organization of French business firms) and the centrists of Liberal Democracy, led by Alain Madelin, could see any good at all coming out of the globalization of liberal economies.[23]

The Illusion of Transparency

America is indeed an open society. News and information circulate freely, American media organizations dot the globe, European journalists encounter no special obstacles when they work in the United States, and the number of Europeans traveling to America rises from year to year. However, behind this apparent transparency, the real workings of American society are far from obvious. We believe we know a great deal about America, but, in fact, we know very little . . . There are numerous reasons for such ignorance: negligence, lack of in-depth research, excessive reliance on hearsay and reductionist stereotypes, old-fashioned prejudices, and no doubt, a certain arrogance, based on a feeling of European cultural and moral superiority. It is so much easier to speak without trying to understand, to look without really seeing, to condemn before checking the facts. Two controversial topics can illustrate the actual ignorance that characterizes French views of America: multiculturalism and the death penalty.

American multiculturalism has been, since the 1990s, the *bête noire* of the partisans of a secular, republican, and assimilationist French society, who decry the importing of a "politically correct" ideology, radically foreign to our own French ways.[24] Transplanted to France, American multiculturalism is perceived as a mortal challenge to the core of our centralist, republican tradition. The introduction of new forms of ethnic "identity politics," the critics argue, would balkanize French society into rival "ethnic ghettos" or territorial "communities." This, in turn, would prevent the assimilation of new immigrant groups and, in the end, precipitate the dissolution of the "One and Indivisible" French Republic. Worse, the acceptance of American-style multiculturalism could perpetuate regressive cultural practices like polygamy, female excision, or forced marriage.[25]

Criticism of the excesses of American multiculturalism is not entirely unjustified. The critics, however, seem to miss the forest for the trees. In fact, there hardly exists such a thing as "American multiculturalism." There are different types of multiculturalism, and most radical and separatist forms are rare even in the United States.[26] Multiculturalism, however divisive, did not prevent America's spontaneous surge of patriotism in the aftermath of the tragic events of 9/11. Beneath the apparent confusion of a multicolored mosaic, there did survive a *Unum*, a common political culture, a patriotic fervor shared by all Americans, whether they happened to be recent immigrants—Europeans, Latinos, or Asians. Multiculturalism is not, as we seem to believe in France, a source of irreconcilable differences. The "disuniting" of America is no more real than the "balkanization" of France. Opposition to multiculturalism, a French variant of anti-Americanism, is closely related to an ancestral, obsessive fear of the fragmentation of the "One and Indivisible French Republic"—a fear that can be traced back to the French Revolution and more specifically to the Jacobins' denunciation of their political enemies, the Girondins, unfairly accused of wanting to transform the new revolutionary regime into the chaos of a fragmented federal State, modeled on the American federal system.[27]

The French debate on the death penalty in the United States is an equally striking example of the ignorance of French commentators. The life stories of American death-row inmates, such as Karla Faye Tucker, Betty Lou Beets, Gary Graham, Odell Barnes, or Mumia Abu-Jamal are thoroughly familiar to readers of French newspapers and some of the most famous French intellectuals, like Jacques Derrida, have been mobilized to denounce the injustice of the death penalty.

Jack Lang, a former education minister, visited Texas to spend a few minutes with Odell Barnes in the hope of influencing the state's Board of Pardons. Robert Badinter, the former chief justice of the Constitutional Council, launched a press campaign against the U.S. death penalty, collecting close to a million signatures for a petition addressed to the newly elected American president, George W. Bush. Badinter found it deplorable that the "oldest democracy in the world and the greatest power on earth . . . has now joined the head pack of homicidal states, together with China, Iran, the Democratic Republic of the Congo and Saudi Arabia. . . . American society seems to be in the grip of a killing madness. And yet it has failed to rid itself of crime. All it has done is respond to killing with more killing."[28] Serge Tornay, a professor at the National Museum of Natural History, believed he had finally discovered the reason: it could all be explained by the "theocratic" nature of American democracy. "It just might be the case," he wrote, "that human sacrifice, the notorious historical privilege of theocratic and totalitarian states, still constitutes a last resort. Faced with the threat of annihilation of their social order, Americans today, like the Aztecs long ago, are terrified by the prospect that the current cosmic cycle is coming to an end. Only the deaths of countless human beings, could generate enough energy to ward off the danger."[29]

The maintenance of the death penalty in America and its abolition in all European nations greatly facilitated the critics' inference: Europeans were civilized, in contrast to their American cousins, the barbarians.[30] But the explanation was incomplete. Paradoxically, it is not due to a lack, but rather an excess of democracy, that America maintains such a cruel practice Indeed, contrary to what most French critics seem to assume, Congress in fact has no authority to abolish the death penalty across the United States. Criminal law (with the exception of federal crimes) falls within the province of the states and it is up to their legislatures to decide to abolish or to retain the death penalty. In France, a simple majority vote in the National Assembly was all it took, in 1981, to abolish the death penalty, at a time when 62 percent of the French still favored the practice. In the United States, federalism and local democracy tilt the balance in favor of a practice that many jurists recognize as cruel and unjust, especially vis-à-vis ethnic minorities. The death penalty lives on simply because it is the will of the people! Also, contrary to what has often been said in France, when George W. Bush was governor of Texas, he was not personally responsible for his state's high rate of executions: final authority was not his, it resides exclusively with an independent Board of Pardons.

Our ignorance can be explained by the tenacity of our centralist, Jacobin tradition. The concentration of power in the One and Indivisible French Republic has not prepared us French, to understand the workings of a federal government. Why in the world haven't they, Americans, abolished the death penalty like we have? Could this be because they are less democratic, and therefore less civilized? The answer, as I have tried to show, is not quite as simple as it seems.

There is indeed a "knowledge gap" between France and the United States. It concerns issues as different as the role of religion in American politics, the ravages—more imaginary than real—of "political correctness" and other such typically French exaggerations about the "horrors" of American feminism, or the seething anger of the American ghetto, verging on open warfare. The greater our ignorance, the more fanciful the stereotypes that serve to decipher American reality.

THOSE NOT WITH US ARE AGAINST US

Francophobia, no doubt encouraged by the Bush administration, is an old phenomenon, which can be traced back to Protestant England and was instrumental in building modern British nationalism, as well demonstrated by Linda Colley.[31] It was unleashed in the United States for a simple reason: the Bush administration could not tolerate any criticism from Western allies, particularly those who should have been eternally grateful for the U.S. intervention in two world wars. In the field of international relations, eternal praise is not a common political value, even from friends and allies, and yet it was expected from the Bush administration. "Those not with us are against us" was the motto of the age. There was therefore no hesitation on the part of the American press, eager to please the White House, to describe French foreign policy as that of a "perfidious" if not "treacherous" nation, the sole aim of which was the failure of the U.S. military strategy (despite the thin evidence presented to the UN by Colin Powell of the existence of Iraqi weapons of mass destruction).[32] We know today that this evidence was more fictitious than real and that the French criticism of an untimely war against Iraq was based on a healthy dose of critical thinking, perfectly justified under the circumstances. The French manner was, perhaps, inelegant: the threat to use the French veto at the UN "whatever the circumstances" was clumsy, to say the least, and the inability of the French to envisage an end to repeated rounds of inspections aroused doubt about the good faith of French diplomats.[33] But to go so far as to accuse the French of treason was a line that only the most vicious Francophobes could cross. That line was indeed crossed by several established (and not so established) members of the American press. It was a good time for bashing the French, those disgusting "cheese eating surrender monkeys" (The Simpsons)—a phrase that was endlessly repeated in signed and unsigned editorials. Murdoch's press pictured President Chirac as a "weasel" running away from responsibility (*The New York Post*), or a wriggling worm (*The Sun*, in England), and stranger still, *The Wall Street Journal* portrayed Chirac as a "transvestite, balding, pygmy Joan of Arc."[34] French leaders became a band of cowards who slunk away the moment things got hot, forgetting how America had saved France twice from disaster. As for our intellectuals, suffering, in the words of Jonah Goldberg, the editor of the *National Review On Line*, from "mental fecal impaction," they naively believed that Old Europe still meant something, that it still carried weight in the world arena. This is why, our visionary explained, "Hollywood morons and French Intellectuals alike find the taste of Fidel Castro's posterior so palatable."[35] At the U.S. Congress cafeteria, French fries had become "liberty fries" to play up to the most xenophobic of American congressmen. One of the most merciless cartoons of President Chirac portrayed him as a transvestite, in a "compromising position" with a particularly virile Saddam Hussein, in simulated advertisements for condoms, with the legend: " 'Republican Guard': the only proven protection for your weapon of mass destruction."[36]

THE HISTORICAL ORIGINS OF FRENCH AMERICANOPHOBIA

Just as American Francophobia must be distinguished, for the sake of clarity, from American critiques of French politics and society, Americanophobia must be distinguished from mere anti-Americanism. By anti-Americanism, I mean the critical and reasoned expression of a disagreement with what Americans say or do. By Americanophobia, I mean the total visceral rejection of anything that has to do with American culture, democracy, or economy, in short, with American civilization. Anti-Americanism expresses itself through critical acts or words; it may not be reasonable, but it is openly debated in the public sphere and is related to the concrete events that mark the ups and downs of Franco-American relations. Philippe Roger and Jean-François Revel's recent books abound in examples of this nature (see chapter 1).

The story of French Americanophobia is an old one, going back to the beginnings of the transatlantic relationship. It was best expressed in Cornelius de Pauw's virulent thesis of American degeneracy. In his

Recherches Philosophiques sur les Américains, published in 1768, the primary concern of this Dutch priest who wrote in French and worked at the court of Frederick the Great, was to serve the interests of his master. Realizing that the prince wished to discourage German emigration to North America, and inspired by Buffon and some French explorers, de Pauw argued that, in America, all natural forms, whether vegetal, animal, or human, had degenerated to the point of having a shrunken appearance. His essay was clearly aimed at terrifying the future North European settlers. Hence his dramatic description of the pernicious effects of the American climate on four-legged animals "more than six times smaller than their European counterparts," on moronic human creatures, contaminated in every part of their organism[37] and rendered feeble by the horrors of famine and hunger. De Pauw did not hesitate to affirm that:

> American tigers and lions were entirely mongrelized, undersized, cowardly and a thousand times less dangerous than those of Asia and Africa . . . wolves, wolverines and bears also occurred as miniatures in this land, and were less audacious than their counterparts on the old continent. . . . Finally, a generalized mutation and bastardization had affected all four-legged creatures in this part of the world, deep down to the very principles of life and its regeneration.[38]

Animals brought from Europe survived with difficulty in the New World, to the point of "dogs losing their voice, and ceasing to bark in most of the countries of the new continent." On the contrary, the most repugnant animals escaped this phenomenon and were of sufficiently impressive sizes to discourage potential emigrants:

> Here the earth's rotting surface was overrun with lizards, eels, snakes, reptiles and monstrous and highly poisonous insects . . . Most caterpillars, butterflies, centipedes, beetles, spiders, frogs and toads, were giant-sized, and multiplying in number beyond imagination.[39]

The new colonizers, still according to de Pauw, encountered terrible reproductive difficulties, since the "climate of the New World concealed a hidden vice, which to this day is inconducive to the multiplication of the human race." Worse, the rare children who were born in this new land had a low life expectancy: "the suffocating malignancy of the atmosphere affected them right from the cradle, and strange illnesses cut them down at a young age."[40]

Such exaggerations explain, in turn, why Founding Fathers like Franklin, Jefferson, and Madison devoted so much energy, and much of their correspondence, to refuting the arguments put forth by de Pauw—the first example of a European truly committed to the systematic denigration of America.[41]

Two centuries later, it was no longer possible to characterize the United States as a country that could not be civilized. On the contrary, it was now the excess of American civilization, American hyper-modernity, that nourished anti-American sentiment. Some Americanophobes, like the communist writer Roger Vailland, mixed humor and irony in their perfectly reactionary denunciation of the French enthusiasm for what was, then, a recent American invention, the refrigerator:

> I have never really understood what use a Frigidaire could ever be in a country like France, where, apart from two moderate months in a year, and then again not every year, the climate is uniformly so cold that a window pantry is quite enough to keep till Monday, Tuesday or Wednesday the leftovers from Sunday's lamb roast. Those of my friends who own one use it mainly to produce little cubes of ice, which are meant to be added to a glass of wisky [sic], and which alter its taste. Wisky, besides, has grown so dear that their Frigidaire no longer serves anything but a symbolic purpose.[42]

In its most extreme form, Americanophobia today expresses itself in a morbid desire for the military defeat of America, or even for the destruction of America. To sweeten his deadly pill, Dr. Baudrillard thus claimed, a few days after the trauma of 9/11, that each of us, French, secretly wished the death of America. This was our *schadenfreude*, our secret joy at the suffering of others—a suffering that is necessary and justified because Americans well deserved it! Our jubilation, according to Baudrillard, was proportional to our "terrorist imagination," supposedly shared by all well-meaning men and women. The "sacrificial" nature of the attack was beyond description. It displayed violence at its best—a strange mixture of "the white magic of cinema, and the black magic of terrorism." The destruction of the twin towers ultimately fulfilled the dream of the West: "our aversion to any final or permanent world order." Hence this stubborn "fact," more real than all others, despite Baudrillard's well-known aversion for the very possibility of a reality principle:

> We desired this event, each one of us wished it to happen, for it is impossible not to wish the annihilation of such an hegemonic superpower. Even though this is quite contrary to Western moral values, *it is a fact*, and this fact precisely reveals the pathetic violence of all efforts to deny it.[43]

And yet, such an extreme example of Americanophobia is not a recent phenomenon in France. It was well entrenched in the France of the 1930s, with classics on the subject of French decadence like Georges Duhamel's *Scènes de la vie future (Scenes from the Future,* 1930), Robert Aron's and Arnaud Dandieu's *La decadence de la nation française (The Decadence of the French Nation,* 1931) or their *Cancer américain (American Cancer)* published in the same year, or again Daniel Rops's *Le Monde sans âme (A World Without a Soul,* 1932), to which should be added the works of partisans of a French spiritual renaissance like Jacques Maritain, Alexandre Marc, and Emmanuel Mounier.[44] But the latter did not secretly wish the death of America; their only dream was to check the evil of the age: the proliferation of American materialistic values.

For Robert Aron and Arnaud Dandieu, the editors of *Ordre Nouveau,* the degradation of the French spirit, or French "republican decadence," was due to "the full rationalization of modern society, which under the auspices of Ford, Taylor and Young, has dehumanized all our frames of reference."[45] The adoption by the French elites of a new "industrial dogma," amounted to a two-fold betrayal: betrayal of the old patriotic, emotional enthusiasm derived from the French revolutionary tradition, and betrayal of the French capitalistic tradition. From a purely "material and quantitative" perspective, according to Aron and Dandieu, France had "already lost the battle, and sacrificed itself upon the altar of social structures utterly hostile and foreign to her." In this perspective, the French had become the "parasites" of the American empire, "conquered minds" comparable to the *Graeculi* of the old Roman Empire, poor teachers oblivious of the meaning of what they "copied or taught."[46] In a grand *élan* heralding the anticapitalist utopias of the 1930s, Aron and Dandieu attacked the "cosmopolitan plutocracy," which in submitting France to the supranational order of the Young plan, had destroyed "all manifestations of love for the land and the nation." The war debt settlement did produce the terrible feeling, accepted as a matter of fact by all the *grands bourgeois,* "that France was done for." Anticipating the *personnalistes* theses of Emmanuel Mounier, the future editor-in-chief of the quarterly *Esprit,* Robert Aron and Arnaud Dandieu offered a new solution to the utter degeneration of France: a "return to a real, sentimental and anti-rational individualism." The aim was vague but grandiose. Whatever the cost, it was an urgent task to recover the revolutionary patriotic *élan,* a taste for self-affirmation, a renewed acceptance of the "risks of victory, which demand energy and aggressiveness."[47] The Americanophobia of the 1930s effectively expressed, to use

François Furet's words, a certain "pseudo-Nietzcheism"[48] that gave central importance to the exaltation of the will against the cold rationalizations of an *Homo œconomicus*, supposedly exemplified by American bankers and captains of industry.

In *Le Cancer Américain*, Robert Aron and Arnaud Dandieu took stock of the gravity of the American disease, a subtly insidious, surreptitious cancer, which penetrated all human communities, beginning with our cities, our universities, indeed our minds, since, they pointed out, "America is a method, a technique, a sickness of the mind."[49] The link with Georges Duhamel is undeniable; it is akin also to the concerns of Emmanuel Mounier who, in his written review of Duhamel's *Scènes de la vie future*, warmly applauded the author for his denunciation of "Americanism," that "barbarism which threatens the entire human edifice" in the name of a progressive civilization destined to control the fate of the human species. An ultimate consequence would be nothing less than the "extermination of all individual life forms." Faced with the terrifying emergence of "idolatrous mechanism," the civilized individual, according to Mounier, had no choice but to "wake up to the alarm" in order "to save the future of mankind, whatever it might hold."[50]

The founding manifesto of the quarterly *Esprit* took up the same themes in 1932, implicitly targeting the grand American tyranny, whose drastic effects called for a healthy revolt. The consequences, if the authors of the manifesto were to be believed, were quite clear: "Societies governed like businesses; savings dilapidated to adapt man to machine and to extract only material profit from human effort; a private life torn apart by appetites and desires, totally disordered and pushed to all forms of homicide and suicide (. . .)." The solution, again, was to save man "by making him conscious of his true identity," while accepting the "permanent fate of the Spirit, without any attachment to its temporal manifestations," without enslaving it to the search for profit. The final call for freedom was: "It is time to free heroic action from bitterness and joy from mediocrity."[51]

Strictly speaking, the exalted rhetoric of the editors of *l'Ordre Nouveau* and *Esprit*, was not just French in inspiration. Behind the specter of a decadent France was that of a decadent Europe, and the defense of a French spiritual renewal echoed the thoughts and writings of an influential German philosopher, Martin Heidegger.[52] Heidegger shared with his French literary counterparts a similar Americanophobia. His enemy was the twin facets of modern capitalism: American and Bolshevik materialism and mechanism, the true causes of Europe's fatal sickness, and the manifestations of an unspeakable "emasculation (*Entmachtung*) of the Spirit."

Europe, according to Heidegger, "lies in a [pair of] pincers between Russia and America, which are metaphysically the same"[53] because they promote a single value: equality, that is, conformity and the destruction of all social ranks. This, in turn, according to Heidegger, produces in both countries a "boundless etcetera of indifference and always-the-sameness," which can only lead to the destruction of "every world-creating impulse of the Spirit." Hence this "onslaught" of what Heidegger defined as "the demonic, in the sense of destructive evil." What was the solution proposed by the great German philosopher? A Nietzschean solution, not without similarity to the Nazis' fascist ideology: the only way to recover the "true essence of the Spirit" consisted in recovering the "true power and beauty of the body, all sureness and boldness in combat, all authenticity and inventiveness of the understanding." The "awakening of the Spirit," concluded Heidegger, demanded that the German nation "take on its historical mission" in combating the Americano-Bolshevik axis of evil.[54]

TWO TOTALITARIANISMS, SOVIET AND AMERICAN

Post–World War II Americanophobia was remarkably similar to pre–World War II Americanophobia. Consider this statement written in 1981 by Alain de Benoist, one of the intellectual leaders of the French New Right: "The truth is that there exist two distinct forms of totalitarianism, with very different effects, but each as redoubtable as the other. The first, in the East, imprisons, persecutes, tortures the body; it however leaves room for hope. The other one in the West leads to the creation of happy robots. It air-conditions hell and kills the soul."[55] The same argument was untiringly repeated by authors as politically apart as Michel Jobert, Jacques Thibau, Jean-Marie Benoist, or Anicet Le Pors, in books with revealing titles: *Pavanes pour une Europe défunte* (1976), *La France Colonisée* (1980), *Marianne à l'encan* (1980), and so on.

It should be clear at this point that a significant part of Old Europe's intelligentsia was not just being critical of America. It rejected *all* U.S. social and political values as barbaric, to prevent, in Heidegger's cruel words, a horrible "emasculation of the Spirit."

"OLD AMERICA": A MODEL FOR EUROPE?

Are French intellectuals today as Americanophobic as they were in the 1930s or at the end of the Cold War? I do not believe so. Baudrillard's wild imagination is probably the exception that proves the rule. The critical stance taken by France and Germany during the Iraqi crisis was not a sign of a total rejection of American values, quite the contrary. Economic liberalism, economic globalization, and American democracy were not described as "cancers" or instruments of the "Spirit's emasculation." The stated goal of the Bush Administration—the elimination of weapons of mass destruction—was not being questioned. What was contested was the means chosen to attain these objectives and especially the timetable of military intervention adopted by the Pentagon. With his ironical comment about a powerless "Old Europe," Donald Rumsfeld forgot that Old Europe—the Europe of the Brussels Convention (to draft a future European constitution)—was also a remarkably creative political enterprise. The delegates of the European Convention had chosen the oldest political model available to them, that of "Old America," that is, the America of the Philadelphia Convention, of the Founding Fathers, of the rule of law, and of sophisticated constitutional compromises . . . A more vibrant homage could never be paid to America, at the very time when transatlantic misunderstandings were degenerating into mutual abuse.

How many in the Bush administration still cared for the glorious model of Old America? Certainly not the President or his praetorian guard. A little more attention paid to the creation of a new constitutional Europe, a little more respect for the reasonable (but no doubt debatable) criticism expressed by the leaders of Old Europe would probably have averted numerous misunderstandings. Indeed, in the end, nothing illustrates the proximity of the two models, European and American, better than the motto chosen by the two federated continents: "*E Pluribus Unum*," say the Americans; "*Unity in Diversity*," states the Preamble of the future European constitution, drafted by the Brussels delegates in the year 2003.[56] By choice, and without realizing it, we've all become Americans, in spite of it all!

NOTES

1. Philippe Roger, *L'ennemi américain. Généalogie de l'antiaméricanisme français* (Paris: Seuil, 2002); Jean-François Revel, *l'obsession anti-américaine* (Paris: Plon, 2002); Emmanuel Todd, *Après l'empire. Essai sur la décomposition du système américain* (Paris: Gallimard 2002). For a discussion of these works, see chapter 1 by Tony Judt in this volume.
2. Denis Lacorne and Jacques Rupnik, "France bewitched by America," in *The Rise and Fall of Anti-Americanism. A Century of French Perception*, edited by D. Lacorne, Jacques Rupnik, and Marie-France Toinet (Basingstoke: Macmillan, 1990), p. 2 (trans. from the original French by

Gerald Turner, *L'Amérique dans les têtes. Un siècle de fascinations et d'aversions* [Paris: Hachette, 1986]).

3. French American Foundation-SOFRES poll, May 2000. Responses to the question: "Would you rather say your feelings for the United States were a) positive; b) negative; or c) neither positive nor negative?"

4. In answering a closed question about the social integration of immigrants, 50% of the respondents believed that, in the United States, "things weren't better than in France" as opposed to 18% who thought the opposite. When asked to choose a word that best describes the United States (from a preestablished list), French respondents listed first "violence" (67%), and then, "power" (66%), inequality (49%), racism (43%). "Liberty" ranked eighth and was only mentioned by 16% of the respondents.

5. See, in this book, chapter 3, by Gérard Grunberg, for a detailed and nuanced analysis of French and European opinion.

6. Title of an editorial by Jean-Marie Colombani, chief editor of *Le Monde* (September 12, 2001). A year later, observing the rise in transatlantic tensions, Colombani wondered whether the French hadn't "all become anti-American." Id. "L'impasse américaine," *Le Monde*, September 11, 2002.

7. See Olivier Duhamel, "Une opinion publique européenne," *Journal du Dimanche*, February 9, 2003. In Europe, never did more than 10% of any polled sample express an opinion favoring unilateral intervention in Iraq. In Britain, a relative majority of the polled population was opposed to any war (41%); the antiwar majority was significant in Germany (50%), substantial in France (60%), and massive in Spain (74%). EOS-Gallup Europe Poll, January 29, 2003, quoted by Duhamel.

8. Polls, *Le Monde*-TF1, March 28–29, 2003 and IPSOS-*Le Figaro*, April 1–3, 2003, *Le Figaro*, April 5, 2003 (based on a national sample of French Muslims).

9. Quoted in *Le Monde*, April 3, 2003.

10. Pierre Hassner, "Europe/Etats-Unis: la tentation du divorce," *Politique Internationale*, no. 100 (summer 2003), p. 173. Equally strong criticism was expressed by French business leaders and supporters of the "*droit d'ingérence*," among them André Glucksmann, Bernard-Henry Lévy, Bernard Kouchner, Bruno Latour, and Pascal Bruckner. See Laure Belot and Sophie Fay, "Les milieux d'affaires redoutent un divorce franco-américain," *Le Monde*, April 4, 2003; André Glucksmann, "L'étrange renversement," *Le Monde*, April 5, 2003, and Bruno Latour, "Pourquoi cet abîme?," ibid.; "America, je t'aime toujours," Bernard-Henri Lévy (interview with Matthew Campbell), *Sunday Times*, November 2, 2003.

11. Bush, "Je suis décidé à travailler avec la France" (interview), *Le Figaro*, May 30, 2003. Curiously, *The Times* in London interpreted the same event in a quite different way, under the title: "Bush diplomacy begins with attack on France," *Times*, May 31, 2003, p. 23.

12. Andrew Higgins, "For U.S., waging peace still requires support from contrarian allies," *Wall Street Journal* (Europe), June 17, 2003.
13. Keith Richeburg, "French defense minister visits U.S. in fence-mending mission," *Washington Post/Wall Street Journal Europe*, January 16, 2004.
14. See D. Lacorne, "Mais non, cette guerre ne fut pas une croisade!," *Le Monde*, April 17, 2003.
15. Robert Aron and Arnaud Dandieu, *Décadence de la nation française* (Paris: Editions Rieder, 1931), pp. 107–108.
16. Paradoxically, at the time when José Bové was attacking McDonald's, sales of the 932 French McDonald's went up by about 3% (between 2000 and 2001), while they fell by 1% in the United States. See Shirley Leung, "McHaute Cuisine," *Wall Street Journal*, August 30, 2002.
17. See José Bové and François Dufour, *The World is not for Sale. Farmers against Junk Food* (London: Verso, 2001) and Jean-Marie Messier, *J6M.com. Faut-il avoir peur de la nouvelle économie?* (Paris: Hachette, 2000).
18. According to an IPSOS poll for *Figaro Magazine* of May 26, 2000, well analyzed in Philip Gordon and Sophie Meunier, *Le Nouveau défi français. La France face à la mondialisation* (Paris: Odile Jacob, 2002), pp. 143, 154 (trans. from id., *The French Challenge. Adapting to Globalization* [Washington D.C.: Brookings Institution Press, 2001]). According to the same poll, 35% of the French believe that "globalization is not a good thing for France" and 46% consider that it is not beneficial to workers (against 36% contrary opinions). Furthermore, 51% of the French questioned by the CSA on June 30, 2000 declared themselves favorable to José Bové's views on globalization (p. 143).
19. *Le Nouveau défi*, ibid., p. 19.
20. For numerous expressions of Americanophilia, see Lacorne, Rupnik, and Toinet, *The Rise and Fall of Anti-Americanism. op. cit.*
21. Cited in Gordon and Meunier, *Le Nouveau défi français, op. cit.*, pp. 148–159.
22. Ibid., pp. 17–19, 147, 150–155. ATTAC is said to have over 34,000 active members and to enjoy the support of 130 French parliamentarians.
23. Ibid., pp. 17–19, 150–155.
24. For widely differing analyses of the "multiculturalist danger," see the writings of Jean-Claude Barreau, Paul Yonnet, Alain Peyrefitte, etc., all analyzed in depth in D. Lacorne, *La crise de l'identité américaine. Du melting-pot au multiculturalisme [The American Identity Crisis. From Melting Pot to Multiculturalism]*, 2nd revised edition (Paris: Gallimard, coll. Tel, 2003), pp. 31–36.
25. Christian Jelen, "La régression multiculturaliste," *Le Débat*, no. 97, November 1997, pp. 137–143, and more generally, id., *Les casseurs de la Republique* (Paris: Plon, 1997). Six years later, Education Minister Luc Ferry denounced the "American logic" of the right to difference, a perfect "calamity," which according to him, would aggravate the "communal excesses" that have proved so harmful for our schools. See Luc Bronner

and Xavier Ternisien, "Le mauvais débat du communautarisme," *Le Monde*, April 12, 2003.

26. For a critical analysis of three competing visions of American multiculturalism, see *La crise de l'identité américaine, op. cit.*, pp. 341–343.

27. The Girondins, according to Laurence Cornu (who quotes Buzot) were unjustly accused of "naturalizing in France the government of America." Laurence Cornu, "Fédéralistes! et pourquoi?" in *La Gironde et les Girondins*, edited by François Furet and Mona Ozouf (Paris: Payot, 1991), note 24, p. 284.

28. Robert Badinter, "L'Amérique et la mort," *Nouvel Observateur*, March 17, 1999.

29. Serge Tornay, "De la théocratie en Amérique," *Le Monde*, February 2, 1998.

30. See D. Lacorne, "The barbaric Americans," *Wilson Quarterly* (spring 2000), pp. 51–60 and Emmanuelle Le Texier, "L'Amérique au miroir de la presse française (1998–2000)," *Revue Tocqueville*, no. 1 (2001), pp. 139–161. On the recent period, see the thorough and well-informed account by Justin Vaïsse, "The future of transatlantic relations: a view from Europe," Committee on International Relations. U.S. House of Representatives, June 17, 2003.

31. Linda Colley, *Britons. Forging the Nation, 1707–1837* (New Haven: Yale University Press, 1992). See also Denis Lacorne, "Les dessous de la francophobie," *Le Nouvel Observateur*, February 27, 2003 (interview).

32. Geoffrey Nunberg, "A lexicon of Francophobia, from Emerson to Fox TV," *New York Times*, February 9, 2003. Charles Krauthammer, a *Washington Post* columnist, denounced the "sabotage" France had resorted to one month before the invasion of Iraq: "Yet the lengths to which France has gone to oppose the United States show that the stakes are much higher. France has gone far beyond mere objection, far beyond mere obstruction. It is engaged in sabotage . . . ," *Washington Post*, February 21, 2003.

33. Pierre Hassner, "Guerre: qui fait le jeu de qui?," *Le Monde*, February 25, 2003; id., "Etats-Unis-Irak-Europe: le troisième round," *Le Monde*, April 26, 2003.

34. As cited in "Francophobia.com," www.tf1.fr, February 12, 2003.

35. *The American Enterprise Magazine Online*, December 2002, *www.taemag.com/taedec02d.htm*

36. Image posted on the website www.StrangeCosmcs.com. See Julie Loudner, "La nouvelle francophobie" dissertation for the Cycle supérieur d'études américaines of the Ecole doctorale at the IEP, Paris, June 2003; Justin Vaïsse, "Etats-Unis, le regain francophobe," *Politique Internationale*, no. 97 (fall 2002); D. Lacorne, "Les dessous de la francophobie," *Le Nouvel Observateur*, February 27, 2003 (interview); "Fuck la France. Comment les Américains nous jugent aujourd'hui," special issue of *L'Echo des Savanes*, May 2003.

37. Cornelius de Pauw, *Recherches philosophiques sur les Américains*, in *Œuvres Philosophiques de Pauw* (original edition: 1768) (Paris: Jean François Bastien, an III de la République. 1792), vol. 1, p. 2.

38. Ibid., p. 8.

39. Ibid., p. 6.

40. Ibid., p. 34.

41. See James W. Ceaser, *Reconstructing America* (New Haven: Yale University Press, 1997), pp. 19–65 and D. Lacorne, "L'écartèlement de 'l'homme atlantique'," in *L'Amérique des Français*, edited by Christine Fauré and Tom Bishop (Paris: François Bourin, 1992), pp. 169–175.

42. Roger Vailland, *La Tribune des Nations*, March 14, 1956, quoted in *L'Amérique dans les têtes, op. cit.*, p. 29.

43. Jean Baudrillard, "L'esprit du terrorisme," my italics, *Le Monde*, November 2, 2001. For François Guery, there is an obvious and direct connection between Duhamel and Baudrillard. When young students read the *Scènes de la vie future*, writes Guery, they think "it's Baudrillard talking about America. They haven't heard of Duhamel. But Duhamel is nothing but Baudrillard." F. Guery, "L'Amérique impensable?," *Philosophie Politique*, no. 7 (December 1995), pp. 14–15.

44. Philippe Roger writes, "The intellectual Americanophobia of the Twenties and the Thirties still remains the unsurpassed horizon of French anti-Americanism," *L'ennemi américain, op. cit.*, p 358. On this period, Jean-Louis Loubet del Bayle, *Les non-conformistes des années trente* (Paris: Seuil, 1969) is essential reading.

45. Robert Aron and Arnaud Dandieu, *Décadence de la nation française* (Paris: Rieder, 1931), pp. 107–108.

46. Ibid., pp. 115–116. Continuing this tradition, Régis Debray describes the attitude of a true *graeculus* of modern times in his pamphlet, *L'édit de Caracalla ou plaidoyer pour les Etats-Unis d'Occident par Xavier de C**** (Paris: Fayard, 2002).

47. A. Dandieu and R. Aron, ibid., p. 243 and 57.

48. The expression is borrowed from François Furet, *Le passé d'une illusion* (Paris: Livre de Poche, 1998), p. 504.

49. *Le cancer américain*, p. 80, quoted in Loubet del Bayle, *op. cit.*, p. 259.

50. Mounier, *Revue de culture générale*. October 1930, pp. 14–21, quoted in Jean-Louis Loubet del Bayle, *Les non-conformistes des années trente* (Paris: Seuil, 1969), p. 258. On Mounier and America, see especially Seth Armus, "The eternal enemy: Emmanuel Mounier's *Esprit* and French anti-Americanism," *French Historical Studies*, no. 2 (spring 2001), pp. 271–303.

51. Folder announcing the founding of *Esprit*, February 1932, reproduced in J-L Loubet del Bayle, *op. cit.*, pp. 448–449.

52. The influence of Heidegger on the editors of *Ordre nouveau* is well documented by J-L Loubet del Bayle, ibid., p. 90. Another probable source of inspiration is the essay by Gina Lombroso, *La rançon du machinisme* (Fr. trans.) (Paris: Payot, 1931).

53. Martin Heidegger, *An Introduction to Metaphysics* [1935] (New Haven: Yale University Press, 1974), p. 45. (Based on a lecture delivered in 1935 at the University of Freiburg. "I have made no change in the content," explained Heidegger in his Preface to the 1953 German edition.)

54. Ibid., pp. 46, 47, 50, respectively.

55. Alain de Benoist, quoted in D. Lacorne et al., *L'Amérique dans les têtes, op. cit.*, p. 33. Curiously, the same argument was defended by more moderate politicians, strongly inspired by the Gaullist political tradition, such as Michel Jobert, Jacques Thibau, or Jean-Marie Benoist. Other major intellectuals like Maurice Merleau Ponty, Jean-Paul Sartre, or Etienne Gilson defended comparable viewpoints at the end of the 1940s. See Tony Judt, *Past Imperfect: French Intellectuals, 1944–1956* (Berkeley: University of California Press, 1994).

56. See D. Lacorne, "E Pluribus Unum, a motto for Europe?" *Le Débat*, January 2003, pp. 88–97 and a special issue of *Critique Internationale* on U.S. and European constitution-making (*Critique Internationale*, October 2003, pp. 118–187).

3

ANTI-AMERICANISM IN FRENCH AND EUROPEAN PUBLIC OPINION

Gérard Grunberg

The British–American intervention in Iraq served to reveal the depth of European anti-Americanism. The intervention did not create anti-Americanism, but it increased it and gave it form. The frequent opinion surveys conducted recently can be used to analyze present-day anti-Americanism and to explore its varying contours. American intervention in Iraq was, for the most part, seen through the prism of a previous, already largely negative image of America, which provided a framework for interpretation. In a sense, the war in Iraq served to confirm in the eyes of many Europeans the manifold reasons they had to distrust the United States. This chapter, largely devoted to the French case but which will include other European countries as well, sets out to analyze the varying contours of anti-Americanism and to measure its significance.

HOSTILITY TO THE WAR IN IRAQ

On the eve of military intervention in Iraq, at a time when war appeared practically certain, hostility to intervention was widespread in European public opinion. Roughly, four-fifths of the French were against it and remained so to the end of the war, even when coalition victory appeared imminent. Four-fifths of the Germans condemned the intervention and considered it unjustified. Ninety percent of the Spanish—despite the fact that their government had unequivocally sided with the United States—declared that they were opposed to the war, and this percentage remained high throughout the conflict. Three-quarters of Italians considered recourse to war unjustified even though in this country, as in Spain, the government backed the

United States. In Poland, where once again the government favored intervention, two-thirds of those polled were against their country taking part in the war. The same held true for 90 percent of the Swiss and 80 percent of the Danish. Ninety percent of the Russians considered that the Americans were wrong to intervene without a UN mandate. In Great Britain, on the eve of hostilities, 62 percent as against 22 percent disapproved of the way in which Prime Minister Tony Blair was "handling the situation in Iraq"; in February, 29 percent as against 52 percent were in favor of military intervention. Great Britain is the sole European country in which, once the intervention was launched, a sense of patriotism and the concern to support the troops in the field brought about a shift in public opinion toward increasing support for government policy. Tony Blair's approval rating, which was down to 31 percent in February, rose to 47 percent in April. In mid-April, 63 percent of the British as against 23 percent said they approved of the military intervention. Everywhere else, public opinion remained hostile to the Iraq war up to the end.

This opposition to the war in Iraq was marked by a serious deterioration of the image of the United States in European public opinion. Thus, between 2002 and 2003, according to a survey conducted by the Pew Research Center for the People and the Press, the percentage of people who had a positive image collapsed in all European countries: a drop of 36 percentage points in Germany, Italy, and Spain, 33 in Russia, 32 in France, 29 in Poland, and 27 in Great Britain. Beyond doubt, the Iraq war produced a strong upsurge of anti-Americanism in Europe. But, as can be seen from table 3.1, even if it was in the years 2002 and 2003 that the image of the United States

Table 3.1 Global attitudes toward the United States (% favorable)

	1999–2000	2002	2003
Britain	83	75	48
France	62	63	31
Germany	78	61	25
Italy	76	70	34
Spain	50	—	14
Poland	86	79	50
Russia	37	61	28
Turkey	52	30	12

Source: March 10/17, 2003, Pew Research Center for the People and the Press.

deteriorated significantly, the decline had already set in before the Iraq issue emerged. Despite 9/11, which produced a real, if short-lived, sense of compassion and solidarity for the United States, the changed international context and the new orientation of American policy after the terrorist attacks in the United States worked against the image of America in European eyes. With the exception of Germany and Russia, the deterioration of America's image is the general rule in Europe during this period, even if this deterioration was to accelerate during the period that followed (table 3.1).We must then try to understand what has modified the image of the United States in the course of the last few years so as to understand why American policy with regard to Iraq has been considered in such negative terms by European public opinion.

THE CONTOURS OF ANTI-AMERICANISM

The Sole Superpower

The period between the collapse of the Soviet Union and 9/11 was a time of gestation in international affairs when the old world was on the way out while the new world had not yet taken shape. But during this period, the image of the United States underwent a gradual change. The United States appeared undeniably as the sole superpower. In the words of Madeleine Albright, the Pew Center chairperson and secretary of state under Clinton, when commenting on the results of a survey conducted between July and October 2002, anti-American attitudes, "simply go with the territory of being the world's only superpower, with unmatched economic and cultural influence. In many ways, we are viewed as the rich guy living on the hill. . . . We have seen this coming since the end of the Cold War."

The extensive survey conducted by the German Marshall Fund of the United States and the Chicago Council on Foreign Relations in June/July 2002 revealed that the Europeans were not content for the United States to remain the sole superpower (see table 3.2). The survey report stated, "Europeans appear ready to take on a stronger world role. When asked if the United States should remain the only superpower or the EU should become a military and economic superpower like the United States, 65 percent of European respondents opt for the latter. The French (91%) and Italians (76%) are the most supportive of this notion, with the Germans (48%) the most cautious. Of those desiring the European Union to become a superpower, 9 out of 10 indicate they support this as a way for Europe to better cooperate with

Table 3.2   The United States as superpower
Roles of the U.S. and Europe as superpowers (all responses in %)

	GB	FR	GER	NL	IT	PL	EUROPE	U.S.
U.S. should remain the only superpower	20	3	22	11	7	12	14	52
E.U. should become a superpower like the U.S.	56	91	48	59	76	63	65	33

Source: The German Marshall Fund of the U.S. and The Chicago Council on Foreign Relations.

the United States, not compete with it. A majority of these would support increased defense spending if necessary to attain this status." During the period of the first Gulf War, 65 percent of the French considered that it was a good thing for the United States to play a dominant role; in January 2003, only 17 percent thought so.

The Use of Force

Mistrust of America as a superpower feeds largely on U.S. readiness to use force in international relations, on the increasing preference for Hard Power rather than Soft Power, and the open espousal of this new approach. The issue of the systematic use of force by the United States is increasingly the key element in determining European public opinion concerning American policy. More than the specifics of American policy, it is the overall tendency to have recourse to force that prompts European distrust, not to say hostility. In this regard, the first Gulf War appears an isolated exception. From the late 1990s on, a majority of the French (57 percent) were against the bombing of Iraq by the United States (February 1998). This majority reached 63 percent in December of the same year. In March 1999, 46 percent of the French condemned NATO bombing of Serbia as against 40 percent who approved, even though France was an active partner in the campaign.

With few exceptions, the Europeans do not apprehend with as great an intensity as the Americans the dangers that threaten their society, nor do they give them the same degree of importance, and they are less inclined to consider that force is the best solution. According to the German Marshall Fund survey, 91 percent of Americans but only 65 percent of the French considered that international terrorism was a danger that threatened the vital interests of their country. Almost as many Europeans consider that global warming is as great a threat as Iraq's development of weapons of mass destruction (50 and 58 percent), while on the American side the figures are 46 and 86 percent, respectively.

In combatting international terrorism, more Europeans than Americans think that "helping poor countries develop their economies" is the best course (91 percent as against 78 percent); on the other hand, more Americans than Europeans favor "air strikes against terrorist training camps and other facilities" (87 percent as against 68 percent).

The use of troops is considered as legitimate or effective by Europeans above all when it is a question of helping people suffering from famine or of imposing international law—for the Americans, when the issue is the destruction of terrorist training camps. Nevertheless, these differences in public opinion were not strongly marked until the question of armed intervention in Iraq became a pressing issue. Thus, in June/July 2002, a majority of both Europeans and Americans were in favor of the invasion of Iraq if the campaign was approved by the UN and backed by the allies. When it became evident that America would act unilaterally, U.S. and European public opinions increasingly diverged.

The Legitimacy of American Policy

European opposition to American foreign policy grew as doubts as to the legitimacy of the policy intensified. American foreign policy was considered as too egotistic, exclusively concerned with the interests of the United States. Even though the 9/11 attacks clearly marked the United States as target and victim, a majority of Europeans considered that American foreign policy had been a contributing factor (GMF survey). Sixty-three percent of the French were of this opinion, but 57 percent of the British as well. In June of 2003, only 59 percent of Europeans thought that "in its conduct since the 9/11 attacks, the U.S. aims to protect itself from future terrorist attacks rather than enforce its will around the globe." As the Pew Center presentation of the March 2002 survey put it: "More generally, criticisms of U.S. foreign policy are almost universal. Overwhelming majorities disapprove of President Bush's foreign policy and the small boost he received in the wake of Sept. 11 has disappeared. As a consequence, publics in seven of the eight nations surveyed believe that American policies have a negative effect on their country. Only the British are divided on the impact of American foreign policy on their country." As for the survey conducted by the same organization in June/October 2002, the accompanying commentary gives a clear picture of the findings: "A majority of people in three of those friendly countries—France, Russia and Germany—believe the United States is pushing for war to win control of Iraqi oil. Majorities totalling 75 percent in France, 76 percent in Russia, and 54 percent in Germany say that is why Washington wants war. Many people around the world believe the U.S. does not take into account the interests of their country when making international policies. Majorities in most countries also see U.S. policies as contributing to the growing gap between rich and poor nations and believe the United States does not spend the right amount to solve global problems."

This perception of America as egotistic explains, in part why European reactions to military intervention.in Iraq are seen as unjustified and illegitimate. Figures taken from surveys conducted in France demonstrate this clearly. Even if 83 percent of young people interviewed by the SOFRES in April agreed that Saddam Hussein was a dictator, the party responsible for the conflict was, in their eyes, the one that started it, namely the United States. According to IPSOS (March 2003), it is the United States (65 percent) and not Iraq (12 percent) which is responsible for the outbreak of the conflict. Seventy-one percent of the French consider that the U.S. role in the Iraq crisis was not justified; 56 percent of them expressed their lack of comprehension of America's role, 49 percent a sense of exasperation, 44 percent expressed hostility, with only 14 percent indicating a degree of understanding, 9 percent respect, and 9 percent solidarity. The United States was resented above all as a power seeking to dominate the world. Given the choice between liberating a country's people by overthrowing their tyrant and protecting "puny" little Iraq against the powerful and rich Americans, it would seem that the majority of the French opted for the latter alternative. When asked to which nation, the United States or Iraq, they felt closest to, 34 percent replied the United States, 25 percent Iraq, and 31 percent neither. And if 53 percent came in the end to prefer an American/British victory, there were still 33 percent in favor of Iraq winning.

The battles waged by France in the UN was massively approved by the French who fully supported the line adopted by President Chirac and his minister for foreign affairs. Thus, 64 percent of the French (IPSOS, March 2003) were against any form of involvement in the conflict if the United States were to intervene without a second resolution of the UN Security Council. The issue of the veto became the primary means to counter the United States: if the United States were to succeed in having a majority of the Security Council vote in favor of intervention, 69 percent of the French were in favor of France using its right to veto, which confirms the fact that stopping American intervention by all possible means was indeed a first imperative. This accounts for the French population's unqualified support for their president. Three-quarters of the French considered that Chirac had not gone overboard in his opposition to the United States (IPSOS, March 2003), and, according to all the opinion polls, Chirac's popular support rose dramatically during this period.

Even though the major reason given by French political leaders, and by the president of the Republic himself, for opposing the American position was the question of whether or not the UN was to authorize intervention, a significant minority of the French appear to have adopted a decidedly pacifist stance; that is to say, opposition to the war whatever the UN chose to do. Thus, 52 percent of those opposed to military intervention (78 percent of the total) declared that they would not change their minds even if weapons of mass destruction were to be discovered in Iraq. In January, 60 percent of the French, according to Gallup, were against intervention even if supported by the UN. According to IPSOS (March 2003), even were the UN to approve, only 13 percent wanted France to take part in the conflict, whereas 44 percent thought France should indicate support but not take part, and 41 percent thought France should stay completely out of it. This tendency can also be found in other European countries. Two thirds of the Spanish, three-quarters of the Swiss, and more than half of the Danish were against intervention even with the approval of the UN Security Council. Close to three-quarters of the Italians opposed intervention even if weapons of mass destruction were to be found.

The issue of the use of force and the aggressive nature of American foreign policy can be seen as elements that crystallized European opinion except in the case of the British. These are the factors that pushed the Europeans into the "peace camp." These are the issues that, for a major segment of public opinion, turned Jacques Chirac into the leader of the camp. Thus, in February 2003, two thirds of the Spanish wanted their government to adopt the Franco-German position and three-quarters of the Germans were in favor of closer cooperation between Chirac and Schröder.

The Europeans and the American Model

Returning once again to the conclusion of the July/October Pew Center report, opposition to the the American intervention "reflects a broader discomfort with the imposing U.S. presence around the world. Even those who are attracted to many aspects of American society, including its democratic ideas and free-market traditions, object to the export of American ideas and customs. People in every European country except Bulgaria are resentful of American cultural intrusion in their country."

Anti-Americanism, without doubt, spreads as well—and perhaps even primarily—as a reaction to a global model of society. In February 2003 (13–15 February), BVA asked respondents to say whether the French should take America as an example in terms of its economic system, its culture, foreign policy, and social structure. The reply was an emphatic "no" in all areas: 64 percent "no" for the economic system, 77 percent for cultural matters, 84 percent for the way of life, 80 percent for foreign policy, and 84 percent for the social structure. It is more than evident that the French see the Americans as very different from themselves and have no desire to see their society resemble the United States. Furthermore, a majority of the French think that France and the United States are increasingly taking opposite sides in the funda- mental economic and social debates of the day. The overriding impres- sion is that the two countries are growing steadily apart.

Anti-Americanism and "Anti-Bushism"

Present-day anti-Americanism is tinged, particularly in France, with a pronounced hostility directed at George W. Bush. From the IPSOS survey of March 2003, 82 percent have a negative image of the presi- dent of the United States (of which 46 percent are very negative). For BVA (February), 54 percent of those interviewed had a favorable opinion of the American people as against 35 percent unfavorable, whereas only 15 percent had a favorable opinion of George Bush as against 76 percent unfavorable. George Bush is held personally responsible for the war. Thus, for IPSOS in March, 76 percent considered that the American position was closely tied to the personality of George Bush; only 17 percent thought the United States would have acted similarly under another president. And the French blame the United States for the deterioration of relations between the two countries.

A survey conducted in France on the occasion of the spring elec- tions of 2002 (CEVIPOF/CIDSP conducted by the SOFRES) revealed the particular characteristics of the anti-Bush factor in the negative opinions of American policy. Anti-Bushism does not stem from the same sources as traditional anti-Americanism. Traditional anti- Americanism is primarily anticapitalism (table 3.3). The United States

Table 3.3 Anti-Americanism and anticapitalism

Attitudes	Negative image of the U.S. (%)
The word "profit" evokes:	
Something very positive	32
Something fairly positive	38
Something fairly negative	56
Something very negative	66
The term "globalization" evokes:	
Something very positive	23
Something fairly positive	34
Something fairly negative	56
Something very negative	70
Making money is:	
Not very important	62
Fairly important	51
Very important	41
Extremely important	35

Source: CEVIPOF/CIDSP/SOFRES.

stands at the heart of the capitalist system, as the prime agent of globalization and its foremost beneficiary. It appears as a society that values money above all else.

On these issues, there is no significant difference between anti-Americanism and anti-Bushism. This decidedly does not hold true when it comes to universal values (such as cultural liberalism, antiracism). The differences here emerge when the replies to a question concerning the United States are compared to those concerning Bush. The question on the United States was framed in these terms: "Does the word United States bring to mind something positive or something negative?" The question on Bush consisted of score of likableness (on a scale of 0 to 10). Half of the people interviewed had a negative opinion of the United States and likewise little liking (under a score of 5) for George Bush.

Close analysis of the survey results shows that the image of the United States and that of George Bush do not entirely correspond. In fact, in comparison with traditional anti-Americanism, anti-Bushism retains its distinct characteristics. Table 3.4 lists the issues for which the differences between anti-Americanism and anti-Bushism were the most marked. Table 3.4 reveals, according to certain attitude and social class variables, the specific attributes of Bush's image as opposed to that of the United States. These attributes concern

Table 3.4 Anti-Americanism and anti-Bushism

	Negative image of the U.S. (%)	Dislike of Bush (%)
France has too many immigrants		
Yes, absolutely	42	28
No, not at all	65	76
The death penalty should be reinstated		
Yes, absolutely	44	32
No, not at all	60	67
Islam evokes something		
Entirely negative	51	38
Entirely positive	46	74
Liberty is		
Extremely important	54	57
Not very important	54	30
National defence is		
Extremely important	45	37
Not very important	65	78
Ariel Sharon		
Extremely favorable opinion	37	17
Extremely unfavorable opinion	66	71
Voted Le Pen in the first ballot of the presidential elections of 2002	40	27
Class self-identification		
Middle class	38	53
Working class	53	45
Educational level		
Elementary school	47	41
College	41	61

problems of immigration, Islam, national defense, individual liberty, and the image of Ariel Sharon. Dislike of Bush is strongest for those who are most opposed to the use of military force, who have a positive view of Islam and of immigrants, and who favor cultural liberalism and the defence of individual liberty. Bush stands clearly, for better or worse, for an aggressive interventionist America, authoritarian, repressive and racist, and supportive of Sharon's government. Conversely, pro-Bushism is stronger than pro-Americanism in the case of those who are the most xenophobic, those who attach greater importance to the military capacity of their country, who are in favor of the death penalty, and who support Israeli policy. Jean-Marie Le Pen's electorate is far less anti-Bush than anti-American.

Table 3.5 Anti-Americanism in relation to economic liberalism and xenophobia

	Negative image of the U.S. (%)	Dislike of Bush (%)
High economic liberalism		
Very xenophobic	37	34
Not very xenophobic	44	56
Low economic liberalism		
Very xenophobic	54	38
Not very xenophobic	65	76

It is thus evident that Bush's personality and policies constitute a factor apart within the larger context of anti-Americanism in general. It is a form of anti-Americanism based less on opposition to economic liberalism and more on hostility to cultural liberalism. Moreover, a number of studies have shown that a strong correlation exists between educational level and belief in cultural liberalism. Table 3.4 indicates, in effect, that French people on the lower end of the social scale were more anti-American than those of the higher classes, whereas their dislike of the president of the United States was not as great as that of the latter. Table 3.5 indicates that for non-xenophobic economic liberals, anti-Bush sentiment runs higher than anti-Americanism, whereas for those who are not economic liberals but are xenophobes, anti-Americanism is higher than anti-Bushism. However, the distinction between anti-Bushism and anti-Americanism should not be overdrawn. Those who are against both cultural and economic liberalism are both anti-American and anti-Bush.

Relations between Europe and the United States

Has the Iraq crisis brought about a change in relations between Europe and the United States? Are Europeans seeking to distance themselves from the United States? According to the report of the Pew Research Center survey of March 2003: "While critics of America's foreign policies mostly blame the president, rather than America more generally, the poll finds strong support for the idea that Western Europe should take a more independent approach to security and diplomatic affairs. Majorities in four of five Western European countries surveyed hold this opinion and a 48% plurality in Great Britain agrees. In the U.S., by contrast, 62% believe diplomatic and security ties with Western Europe should remain as close as they have been."

Data gathered on the French side suggests the existence of a genuine crisis in Franco-American relations as seen by the French, but above and beyond the crisis, there exists a sizeable built-in minority who no longer sides with the United States. France and the United States appear to be drawing apart and this has serious implications for the traditional alliance between the two countries: whereas 57 percent of the French, according to a BVA poll in February 2003, considered the alliance with the United States to be a positive factor, 39 percent did not. To be sure, 57 percent is a relatively high figure and it should warn us against concluding that today's anti-Americanism reflects a refusal of the alliance. But the size of the minority opinion should be borne in mind. In the eyes of the French, what America has gained in power, it has lost in terms of legitimacy; as a result, the idea of what the ties between the two countries should be has of necessity undergone a change. The serious differences of opinion between the various European governments, that the handling of the Iraq crisis revealed, have led the French to reformulate their images of the heads of other European governments. They disapprove of leaders or governments that have taken a stand in favor of the war. According to the IFOP survey of March, the percentage of favorable opinions of government leaders was Aznar 24 percent, Blair 22 percent, Berlusconi 20 percent, and Bush 14 percent. On the other hand, percentages for those opposed to the war were: Chirac 85 percent, Schröder 71 percent, and Poutine 47 percent. The issue is not simply one of transatlantic relations but of political divisions within Europe as well. One of the questions raised indirectly by the Iraq crisis is whether or not the governments of countries that supported the American intervention will suffer from it in the next general elections.

As of now, the British exception goes to show that there is no common European public opinion. The British, after having disapproved of their government, ended up by adopting the official line. Tony Blair remains the favorite for the next British elections. Above all, the Iraq crisis has brought Britain closer to the United States. In 2002, when the British were asked what country was the most important to Britain—Europe, the Commonwealth, or the United States—50 percent replied Europe, 19 percent the Commonwealth, and 29 percent the United States. In 2003, when the Iraq war was winding down, the proportions were 42, 16, and 34 percent, respectively. And when asked which country was the most reliable ally and which country the least reliable, the answer was America as the most reliable for 73 percent and France the least reliable for 55 percent. It is clear that even if the British were at first opposed to the war, they remain faithful to their special relationship with the United States. As for Spain, the regional and local elections of May 25, 2003 did not turn into a defeat for Aznar's party, contrary to what opinion polls had predicted. But Aznar lost the legislative election after the March 11, 2004 Madrid terrorist attack.

In a wider perspective, the new survey of the Pew Global Project Attitudes released in June 2003 revealed that one month after the end of the war in Iraq, the level of anti-Americanism had dropped in Europe (table 3.6). But the size of the decline varied from country to country. It was least pronounced in the case of Russia and of France. Anti-Americanism appeared relatively weak in Great Britain and Italy, fairly strong in other countries.

Public opinion in all European countries favored, to varying degrees, the evolution of diplomatic and security ties between Europe and the United States, and the development of a greater sense of independence (table 3.7). The British and the Germans were more concerned

Table 3.6   Favorable view of the United States (in %)

	March 2003	May 2003	Difference
Great Britain	48	70	+22
Italy	34	60	+26
Germany	25	45	+20
France	31	43	+12
Spain	14	38	+24
Russia	26	38	+8

Source: Pew Global Project Attitudes

Table 3.7   United States–European diplomatic and security ties (in %)

March 2003	Should remain close	Should be more independent	Don't know
U.S.	62	29	9
Britain	40	48	12
France	30	67	4
Germany	46	52	3
Italy	30	63	7
Spain	24	60	16

Source: Pew Research Center, March 2003.

with maintaining close relations than were the Spanish, the French, and the Italians. There emerges a distinction between northern Europe and southern Europe—a distinction that does not correlate with the positions taken by the governments concerned. In addition to the differences between countries, there are differences within each country according to the political orientations of the respondents (table 3.8). This is particularly true of France where, anti-Americanism becomes more pronounced as political orientation moves further to the left. In addition, whereas the French electorate close to the left "sided" with the Iraqis as frequently as with the Americans, the electorate close to the right clearly "sided" with the United States (44 percent as against 18 percent). Only 47 percent of the left electorate favored a coalition victory; on the other hand, the percentage rose to 69 for those on the right. These differences are reflected in the level of support for the alliance with the United States as revealed by the

Table 3.8 The image of the United States according to political orientation

Political orientation on a left/right scale	Negative image of the US (%)
Left	65
Center-left	51
Center	48
Center-right	42
Right	38

Table 3.9 The French American alliance
How strongly do you yourself support the alliance between France and the United States?

Support the alliance	Total (%)	Political orientation	
		Left (%)	Right (%)
Very strongly	17	15	23
Fairly strongly	40	38	45
Subtotal (support)	*57*	*53*	*68*
Not really strongly	28	34	22
Not at all	11	11	7
Subtotal (nonsupport)	*39*	*45*	*29*
No answer	4	2	3
Total	100	100	100

BVA survey of February 2003: those on the right were more supportive of the alliance than those on the left In France, the left is deeply split on the issue of the alliance with the United States. For some people on the left, the United States is not an ally but an adversary (table 3.9). It is here that radical anti-Americanism emerges most clearly.

The data that have been presented indicate that even if the Iraq crisis constituted a unique event that of itself precipitated a steep rise in anti-Americanism—the crisis served essentially to bring to the surface and reinforce an underlying level of anti-American sentiment. The foundations of the transatlantic alliance would appear, except in the case of Great Britain, to be fragile as far as European public opinion is concerned. The American superpower is a source of anxiety and U.S. policies are suspect. Europeans sense the gap to be widening between their societies and the United States. And the new foreign and military policies adopted by America run into strong objections because of its excessive reliance on military force and unilateralism. The Europeans are no longer certain that they defend the same causes and strive for the same objectives as the Americans. They fear that the American model of society will be forced upon them. In short, they feel that they are different.

4

IS THERE A NEW ANTI-AMERICANISM? REFLECTIONS ON GERMANY IN TIMES OF GLOBAL SIMULTANEITY

Detlev Claussen

With the Iraqi campaign of 2003, America has once again become the focus of world debate. Since 9/11, there has been a heated debate in Germany over its relationship with the leading power in the West—the United States. Though much has already been said against U.S. policies, the question now is whether there is a *new* anti-Americanism, one that has intensified since 1989 in the aftermath of the collapse of the Cold War's bipolar world order. Is this even anti-Americanism at all? This question cannot be answered if the situation in Germany is viewed in isolation. Like the devil and holy water, most participants in this discussion shy away from a more precise definition of anti-Americanism, the reason being that a closer examination would force the public parlor game of mutual accusation to give way to a serious analysis of the current global situation. Even those who argue in favor of the anti-American side do not want to be considered anti-American, at least not in the West anyway. While the manifest anti-Americanism preached by the group that surrounds bin Laden cannot be denied, it must be remembered that it is only since the 1980s—when Afghanistan's war with the Soviet Union ended—that this group's ideology turned against America. During the Cold War, bin Laden, like a magician's apprentice to the field of politics, fought with American support against the unbelievers of the Soviet Union. To him and his cohorts, the Soviet Union appeared to be the main secular enemy of the Arab world—the world from which they came and which shaped their motives. It was only after the Gulf War, in which one of the last representatives of Arab political nationalism, Saddam Hussein, styled himself in vain as the political leader of the Arab world, that the anti-American aspect of their worldview emerged. Manifest anti-Americanism in the Arab world has been well suited for its ongoing role of identifying guilty parties for the disaster of decolonization. As a cipher and symbol for the Arab world's failed liberation from colonial dependence, the state of Israel also continues to fulfill this function. Rather than recognizing that Israel's powerful position in the middle of the Arab world is related to the Arab world's own inability to create a peaceful, future-oriented social order, Israel's status has been attributed solely to the allegedly one-sided support by the United States. Since the 1920s, Arab nationalism in the form of Nasserism and Baathism has competed with the "corrupt regimes" that were held responsible for the failed modernization of the Arab world. Increasing in strength after the defeat of Nasser in the Six-Day War of 1967, political Islam, by contrast, declared both paths into the modern world equally corrupt. From nationalism, these Islamists inherited manifest anti-Americanism as a weapon in the Arab power struggle. After the victory of the Ayatollah Khomeini, with whom they had been competing, and after the *fatwah* against Salman Rushdie in 1989, the Islamists then integrated this weapon into their own worldview. The attacks of 9/11 constitute the previously unimaginable pinnacle of these activities. Though the attacks were meant to embarrass Arab regimes of all colors—modern and traditional alike—this struggle is no longer justified politically. Instead, it is justified in religious and cultural terms. It is in this respect that bin Laden's terrorism can be understood as a *new anti-Americanism*, even when it is put in the service of many old resentments.

Not the acts themselves, but aspects of their justification could count on a surprisingly worldwide sympathy. In the initial aftermath of 9/11, this sympathy was heard only in conversations at parties, then in public spaces, at universities, and on television and radio outlets. Then increasingly, these sympathies started to appear in print, first in feuilletons, and until finally they reached the editorial pages. The public was beginning to interpret the attacks of 9/11 and the central argument that emerged was that the world order was unjust. The current icon of this slant in the media is Arundhati Roy, who has taken on the role of spokesperson for a Third World that no longer exists. This post-colonial performance, which is intended for academic and mass media markets, has already been presented by the firebrand Edward Said. As both a spokesman for the Palestinian diaspora and a successful scholar within the American university system, Said was able to articulate himself in universal terms. In this way, he succeeded in establishing himself as a symbolic representative for people who identify with the Third World as well as for urban oriented intellectuals. The 1989 collapse of the bipolar world reflected a global simultaneity, which is bewildering. The social contradictions between the modern and the traditional coexist in every corner of the world; realities throughout the entire globe are characterized by bizarre mixtures of progress and backwardness. In the midst of this chaos, America serves as a point of orientation. It seems to have remained the same while the world has changed almost beyond recognition. Even the expression, "the only remaining superpower," strikes many people as a provocation, at the same time when it has become a social fact. The phrase, "new world order," already existed in 1990, even before the Gulf War, which came to symbolize this new world order. The halfhearted way in which this particular notion was staged can be criticized. The coalition may have succeeded in the war but the situation in the Middle East was left unresolved. Criticism of U.S. foreign policy in the Middle East is completely justifiable. However, this criticism veers toward anti-Americanism when it represents the U.S. government as the only responsible power that should still be concerned about the region's disarray. Anti-American emotions were running high when the embarrassingly excessive, "No Blood For Oil," was coined. In the early 1990s, Western societies did not settle this conflict either in the public arena or in terms of domestic policy. Saddam Hussein's disarmament hardly elicited any argument in 1991. Yet, the United States has dominated the last decade and in the eyes of most of its accusers, this makes it responsible for everything that has happened since then. The strongest power is always regarded as all-powerful. As a result, an anti-American worldview has become firmly established, a position that is always at hand and ready to be put to use.

Shock over 9/11 shaped the new reality of world politics. This shock only lasted a few days, however, before old reflexes, unresolved intellectual and political issues from the recent past, returned. The new anti-Americanism filled the void left by the lack of a theoretical conception of global society that would adequately reflect the way the world has changed since 1989. By employing such empty concepts as "globalization" social scientists have preferred to label, rather than to understand, the post-1989 period. What is underestimated is the extent to which the imperative to modernize as quickly as possible is more than ever colliding against lingering traditions. The long, post–World War II boom was accompanied by an international revolution in education, which created a new, globally competitive world middle class. Those who do not identify with America as the most advanced society in the world, or who cannot study it without emotion or bias, feel neglected or cheated—a well-known phenomenon in twentieth-century German social psychology. Since the last third of the twentieth century, the return to the past as a resource has been an integral part of this process. In the most advanced society in the world, this process has led to the public acceptance, far beyond the academic arena, of such categories as "ethnicity" and "identity." The recently formed middle classes, which had replaced the traditionally educated middle class in their cultural strongholds of schools and universities, founded a new, ethnic, religious, and, later, gender-based model of historical interpretation. This was appropriate for the United States, as it is a society characterized by immigration. Outside the United States, these very modernization processes, which had already found expression in the globally concurrent events of 1968, led to renationalized self-perceptions among the new middle classes. The "children of Karl Marx and Coca-Cola," as Jean-Luc Godard called them, became adults who invented their own ethno-cultural identity. In distancing themselves from America, their past could once again be national.

In other European countries, this renationalization of the past can happen with less restraint than in West Germany, which in contrast to France or Italy cannot define itself in unambiguously national terms, without playing down the National Socialist past. For this reason, heated debates over the German past constantly reoccur. Moreover, German relations with America are always connected with the fact that the United States liberated Germany from National Socialism through war and reeducation. This is hardly the case in the former East Germany. There, the discussions over the National Socialist past serve to validate or invalidate the winners and losers of reunification. Common German ground is only reached in discussions over the Allied bombing and the expulsions of Germans from the occupied territories after the war. Anyone who was not in Germany in the summer of 2003 would have trouble believing that, after the intervention in Iraq, the most-debated public issue in Germany concerned the correct interpretation of events that took place six decades ago. Only from a distance does Germany's cultural debate appear enviable. On closer inspection, these public disputes turn out to be a way of shifting contemporary social problems unto distant countries and the distant past. Uncertainty is the *chiaroscuro* that distorts reality. What is feared are the "American conditions," in which class predominates. Xenophobic fears are intertwined with anxiety over the end of the welfare state. Considered an old-European invention, it was not recognized that, beyond its specific forms, the welfare state was a common social development of the "short century." Without the welfare state, the concept of the West as the "abundant society," as Kenneth Galbraith put it, would never have looked attractive. Today, as in the past, the absolute oppositions that are presented between America and Europe are actually distortions of social differences. This gives the propagandist ideologues the opportunity to exploit the ambivalence of the public toward social change. As a result, America's present offers Europe a picture of its own future. In the population's anxieties about the future, old fears are reproduced in the new anti-Americanism.

The social basis of the new anti-Americanism is to be found in the middle classes that succeed through education and training. Their German spokespersons see themselves in agreement with the American anti-Bush opposition, which has grown since the end of the direct military confrontation in Iraq. On American campuses, resistance to the war on terrorism has been expressed in terms of the so-called new social movements of the 1970s and 1980s. In Europe, as well as in Latin America, the same social and political pink–purple–green categories are intertwined with national ones. During the protests in Germany against the war in Kosovo, Serb and Greek flags could be seen alongside new and old pacifist symbols. Now with the anti-Iraq war protests of 2003, a new transnational symbol has been found—the word "Pace" written over a rainbow flag—a poorly secularized version of ultra-Catholicism, a geopolitical St. Peter's Square. The forces of yesterday criticize those of today and that is fine with each new sheep that enters the flock, whether the sheep wanders in from the youth-oriented, antiglobalization movement or from the reawakened veterans of the 1970s and 1980s who have been incorrectly characterized as former "1968ers." This results in a harsh view of an America that appears omnipotent. In a world where America defines the rules to which the rest of the world orients itself, it is, nonetheless, fitting that it always occupies the number one spot. The academic left in Germany feels reassured by the reactions of its American colleagues, who for a long time appeared powerless against the unilateral course of the Bush administration but who have started to attack the Bush administration's foreign policy. As a result, the German academic left does not see itself as anti-American at all. Some of the American opposition's public statements against the policies of the Bush administration after 9/11 were rather muddled. On the level of domestic policies, however, George W. Bush's opponents, who already felt slapped in the face by the presidential election, have sought a better way to hinder his reelection. The behavior of the Democrats in the days leading up to the Iraqi invasion was purely tactical in motivation, leading the academic opposition to orient itself on the old "Vietnam Setting," as Charles Kupchan had accurately termed it in September 2001. It is for this reason that the peace demonstrations of 2003 had a nostalgic touch that spanned generations. In Europe, however, the demonstrations in London, Rome, Paris, and Berlin were celebrated as the birth of a new Europe. This would have been completely unthinkable during the anti-Vietnam demonstrations in 1968. The new anti-American propaganda has a bit of the illusion of a European society, an illusion that is necessary for the acceptance of a pan-national entity—just as Ernest Renan pointed out that historical lies were necessary in order to make the abstraction of the nation acceptable.

September 11 produced strange new battle lines. While the ruling coalition in Germany committed itself to "unconditional solidarity" with the United States, the activists of the once old, now revived, social movements rose up against this solidarity. In the mass media, the aversions integral to the convictions of the old left met with the new confidence of the recently emerged middle classes. The former consider war vulgar, whereas the latter accept "going along with it." The so-called German pacifism of today likes to see itself as the result of historical learning processes. Yet, at least since the 1970s, German pacifism has been used more as a means of flattering the self-confidence of the post-Nazi generation. This generation sees itself as, above all, superior to a nation of sycophants, which is how they define most of the older generations. Class distinctiveness intertwines with national distinctiveness. Professional politicians are singled out by the new middle classes as objects for contempt, despite the fact that professional politicians generally come from among their ranks—this is a phenomenon that Jimmy Carter already encountered in the previous generation. Such class-specific biases are now united against George W. Bush, Gerhard Schröder, and Joschka Fischer. The antipolitical protest stance of the academic American left denies that, in contrast to Vietnam, it is possible that, even if a different administration came to power in 2004, it would have to remain in Iraq. In German academic and mainstream media circles, this protest stance quickly becomes tinged with anti-American sentiment. From this perspective, politicians look like cynical opportunists and the majority of the population, which is not at all spontaneously anti-American, like easily manipulated fools, who are simply uninformed. In the same way that the arrogance of class distinctiveness feeds on ambivalence toward power, so does the new anti-Americanism. This is reflected in the common reproach, the "arrogance of power." Power is always envied and this jealousy leads to an exaggerated sense of power as omnipotence, thus making it possible to spread blame to everyone. At the same time, the powers that be, though hardly populist, look to the middle classes in educational institutions and in the media as their opinion leaders. The brand of anti-Americanism to which intellectuals subscribe, spans generation and stirs up resentment against any exercise of power. When contempt for politics becomes a social norm, society's ability to criticize power weakens.

The attacks of 9/11 underlined the necessity of an international peacekeeping organization. The U.S. government reacted to the terrorist attacks, however, with a "war on terrorism." If one takes the threat of terrorist attack scenarios seriously, then the logic of this war, which seeks to apprehend not only terrorists but also terrorist supporters, speaks for itself. Destroying Al Qaeda's training camps, which the Taliban concealed, seems only logical. The attention of the international community has put pressure on the U.S. government to adhere to rules that promote civilized warfare, but those who do not acknowledge the threat of terrorism, no longer have the right to debate the appropriateness of ends versus means. Supported by American Nobel laureates in an attempt to avoid accusations of anti-Americanism, German intellectuals damned the campaign in Afghanistan with a preachy tone that arose from the loss of this relationship between ends and means. Their demands to simply endure barbaric terrorist attacks merely mimic pacifism and hinder any recognition of the terrorist danger in their own country. Not even limited cooperation with America was possible under these conditions. As long as the attention of the world community is focused on U.S. foreign policy, this new form of anti-Americanism will have a great future. One of the main functions of this new anti-Americanism involves interpreting new developments with familiar tropes. In this way, new aspects of international terrorism need not be recognized and acknowledged as new developments. Terrorists, acting without regard to national borders, are then not seen as independent actors who only reach their goal by instilling fear and anxiety within the society. The threat of terrorism emerges from modern society itself, however. The openness of modern societies is precisely what makes them attractive targets for terrorists. The terrorists behave according to bin Laden's image as a son of the desert but, in reality, terrorists, such as the ones who carried out the 9/11 attacks, are children of multicultural societies and like fish in water, they circulate freely in these societies. By no means should they be seen as guerillas. What distinguishes them from free-dom fighters is their destructiveness. After all, terrorists and freedom fighters are not labeled arbitrarily. September 11 left the world com-pletely speechless because its violence was completely destructive. The relationship between ends and means burst apart. Even the demand to withdraw American troops from Saudi Arabia was only a pretext. In reality, 9/11 was intended to compensate the Islamic world for its imagined humiliation at being a third-rate world power. It is for this reason that the attacks of 9/11 are so lacking in perspective. Not faith, but willingness to deploy violence in a completely destructive manner is what binds the suicide bombers of America and Israel.

Only when the West recognizes 9/11 as a problem not just for America but also for the West as a whole will the new anti-Americanism lose the ground beneath its feet. If the modernization of society con-tinues to be equated with unwanted Americanization, anti-Americanism will maintain its social basis. The middle classes that the new education system produced started to look toward the past in reaction to the dis-appointments of 1968, when hopes for substantive changes in society collapsed in the face of reality. In urban areas, very small groups of people then turned to terrorism, which promised to undermine the prosaic "reality principle" of parliamentary democracy. The reality of this armed conflict left little to be romanticized, however. The conflict in Indochina, which had been used to justify violence, came to an end, robbing terror of any illusion to legitimacy. Since terrorists could no longer look to the present to justify their goals, they would have to find some justifications in the past. Once again, developments in Europe followed closely on the heels of those that took place in America. The similarity of these social processes was hardly noted as this change of society was considered, for the most part, to result from outside forces. The loss of a socially transforming vision of the future allowed the past to appear as a source of self-understanding. Corresponding to the need of the new middle classes for self-assurance was the discovery of identity as a formula that would explain social behavior. According to this formulation, the collapse of the bipolar world order and the subsequent disappearance of the Third World amounted to a gigantic, global leveling out that has made one's home-land less important. Indeed, the way that discourse is conducted has become globalized. Cultural criticism in New York, as well as in Cairo or Shanghai, is only a mouse click away. September 11 showed that educational institutions are threatening to turn from progressive nursery schools into conservative institutions. The turn to the Vietnam protests of the past might be a symptom. Outside of the United States, this symptom is augmented by the revival of anti-American memories. Memory is deceptive, however, as it is difficult to discern the difference between fact and fiction. In Vietnam, the intervention of the United States hindered the emancipation of the people of Indochina from their dependency on colonialism and large landowners. Since 9/11, on the other hand, American society has been forced to defend itself against the threat of terrorism. Only when the international community acknowledges that international terrorism is a shared threat will anti-Americanism recede in strength.

Only with this social background in mind can the shifting tides of public opinion be correctly interpreted. All German and international opinion polls indicate that, as of 2003, public sentiment has settled on the side of antipathy. The Frankfurt book fair of October 2003 brought to light a deluge of anti-American literature. Reading through this flood would only be worthwhile if it is taken as a model for cliched images of the world. Not a single book actually considers what anti-Americanism really is—a prejudice, an ideology, a distorted view, or an opinion even worthy of discussion? The mixture of anti-Americanism with anti-Semitism has had a particularly disastrous effect in German debates, since these debates do not take into account the special character of anti-Semitism or its particular meaning in post-1945 Germany. On the other hand, opinion polls treat both anti-Americanism and anti-Semitism as mere opinions. This downplays anti-Semitism and stretches anti-Americanism past the point of recognition. Well-founded rejection of a certain government's policies should in no way be judged as anti-American *per se*. Likewise, all criticism of Israel's government should not be considered anti-Semitic. However, it is this fact, *per se*, that must be emphasized. An integral aspect of anti-Americanism and anti-Semitism is the way in which they are camouflaged as mere opinions in order to garner the appearance of democratic legitimacy.

In this way, public debate seems more of a discussion of ghosts rather than of current alliances and conflicts between peoples. The public arena resembles show business as public figures jockey for positions on the issues. The blinding effects of public relations strategies collide with the grassroots voices that lurk beneath the surface of officially orchestrated opinion. Most political analysis, however, is satisfied with the merely superficial in terms of public and private opinion. Poorly designed public opinion polls stand in for empirical evidence. Public squabbles over the Iraqi campaign reveal more about the decline of the public sphere and public debate in the West than about the way that society thinks and behaves. To this end, polling science is too afraid of theory to really uncover anything. One of the rumors that will not fade away, even among spin doctors, is the ridiculous and unsophisticated assertion that the red–green coalition in Germany was reelected against the odds, and that Chancellor Schröder led a German-nationalist, anti-American election campaign. This explanation misjudges the demonstrable relationship between voter behavior and foreign policy. Whether one sees the war in the Middle East as right or wrong, the majority of the population views it differently from the peace activists. Most Germans see the war as something that is taking place far away from Europe. Therefore, the idea of German participation in a "war on terror" is not likely to win spontaneous approval in a country where the potential threat of terrorist groups has been dismissed. The situation was different 25 years ago when the Red Army Faction, who did not pose nearly as great a threat as Al Qaeda, was active. The trial of high-ranking terrorists in Frankfurt and Hamburg aroused a great deal less public interest than the sex and cocaine scandals of local figures, even though plans for a spectacular bomb attack on a Christmas market in Strasburg as well as for a poison gas attack on the Frankfurt subway were revealed.

The electoral success of the red–green coalition and its subsequent drop in the opinion polls has little to do with the rejection of the war in Iraq. Despite what spin doctors and election losers like to claim, voters are not a herd of sheep that can be easily manipulated. The foolish talk of elites, who supposedly cause wild fluctuations in public opinion so that they can be celebrated as masters of strategy, is simply a means by which professional political consultants create their own legends. Right now, Tony Blair is paying a harsh price for the illusion that anything that leads to success is justifiable. Foreign policy can only compensate for domestic problems, if there is a discernable foreign pressure, as there was in the era of détente. However, if the domestic situation is extremely serious, then foreign policy does not have this compensatory power. In the fall of 2002, the foreign policy situation was not ambiguous at all. The Bush administration had attempted to sell its intervention in Iraq as a continuation of the "war on terror." In order to accept the foreign policy strategy against the "axis of evil," a certain political worldview had to be shared—a worldview that even a majority of Americans did not share. For reasons of realpolitik, even this strategy was later disavowed in the case of North Korea, so that what emerged was a tangled web of interpretation-ripe strategies that involved power politics, harrowing scenarios about weapons of mass destruction, as well as political and moral justifications for a transfer of power from outside. The Bush administration did not succeed in representing this invasion as a necessary act in the fight against terrorism. By putting pressure on and manipulating the public, together with Blair's technique of asserting power, morality was employed as an instrument in the effort to gain domestic majorities. The loyalty of the American and British people toward the troops on the ground should not be mistaken as support for the war. Manipulation has been all too obvious and now that details are coming out about the way in which the occupation of Iraq was carelessly portrayed as a short-term affair, the British and American public have reacted with exasperation. A completely justifiable policy of regime change, which would aim at revolutionizing the entire Middle East, would require a 10–20-year presence of a substantially larger contingent of international troops than are now stationed in Iraq. Even with the best intentions, no American president would ever receive the support of a majority of Americans for an openly declared policy of long-term democratic intervention.

The credibility of American policies was put at stake in 2002. A "deeply rooted" anti-Americanism was hardly necessary to feel less than enthusiastic about these policies. In Europe, ambivalence is part of a self-perception that is shaped according to nation. In America, by contrast, the logic of power suits the social and psychological composition of the country. With this point in mind, it is easy to understand how criticism of American foreign policy slips into anti-Americanism. At first glance, the rhetoric of the "only remaining superpower" seems realistic. This rhetoric is a poor disguise, however, for a perspective of helplessness that Europe is loath to acknowledge. From this perspective, obvious differences in power are chalked up to being an integral component of the inequality and injustice that rules the world. Only when the past short century is viewed historically is it possible to understand that, despite the bipolarity of the political world order in the second half of the century, it was, in reality, an American century. The entry of the United States into World War I was the beginning of the end of Europe's centrality to world politics—a fact that the elites of old Europe accepted only begrudgingly. Even Sir Winston Churchill made sarcastic remarks about the ambivalent character of American help at a time when National Socialists were threatening Great Britain's very existence. The secular formulation of *translatio imperii*, which Dan Diner describes convincingly in his book *Das Jahrhundert verstehen*, could be either referenced ironically or taken as a red flag waved at a bull—something that seeks to fulfill its need for size and for significance. That is why President de Gaulle found supporters among

German politicians. They saw the possibility that German national traditions could live on in a Europe dominated by Germany and France. For Germany, on the other hand, the transatlantic relationship is distinguished by an imperative for social change that runs throughout the entire twentieth century. It could be called the American Promise, a promise for which post-1918 Germany was entirely receptive. While this seems completely forgotten today, this promise still permeates everyday life. An Americanism exists, which renews itself periodically, and, which plainly depends on the attractiveness of the "American Way of Life." The history of anti-Americanism can only really be understood if it is seen as an answer to a notorious Americanism, which has a long tradition in Germany. No less than Goethe himself wrote, "America, you have it better . . ." and this was also meant politically as a critique of European feudalism. The most German bildungsroman of all, Goethe's *William Meister*, offered up the song of the emigrant, whose destination is called America—a land in which fantasy and empire meet. After Europe's failed bourgeois revolution of 1848, America remained the land of the free. This stirred the imaginations of those who were left behind and who could not come to terms with the conditions in Germany. The America of their imaginations could be called a dream America. Already in the long nineteenth century, millions of Germans had this dream in mind as their real goal.

This dream of American life was revived more than once during the "short century". In the Weimar Republic, America was associated with the open-minded and the modern, with fashion, entertainment, and technical production. Even National Socialist ideology took into account German ambivalence toward American society. Despite the restrictive immigration policies that America introduced in the 1920s, Germans, especially in the lower classes, continued to believe in the American dream. The worldwide expansion of the entertainment industry also contributed considerably to America's popularity. In the fantasyland that was this dream, the English actor Charlie Chaplin became an American hero with whom the average moviegoer could identify. His film, *Modern Times*, created an image of the modern world that educated European elites could only begin to adopt in earnest after the fall of National Socialism. With *Les Temps Modernes*, French intellectuals, likewise, sent a signal that was also heard in Germany, that they would now turn toward a non-European version of the modern world. This prepared the ground on which the international *Movement of the Sixties* was built—a lifestyle revolution that turned its back on traditional Europe. Even international opposition against the Vietnam War developed on the basis of social relationships that had become Americanized. In no other country of Old Europe did this develop in such a strong or obvious way as it did in West Germany, where, in contrast to France or Italy, there was no communist party that could exist within the political public sphere. German protests against the Vietnam War also consciously followed the style, form, and content of the Civil Rights Movement in America. The Sozalistische Deustche Studentenbund (SDS) even got its name from its American counterpart, Students for a Democratic Society (SDS). The antiauthoritarian protest movement of the 1960s was social in motivation. In the final analysis, the protest movement could not come to terms with the pacifism of the post-National Socialist period and with the way in which pacifists adopted Germany's disarmament as if it were their own idea. Solidarity with the American soldiers who had deserted was still a priority, however, even in the midst of the anti-imperialist justifications of militant anti-Vietnam War protests. Not until the identity politics of the 1970s, which was a reaction to the failed attempt to transform society, were cultural elements mobilized to reject the United States, the superpower of the West. To this end, they gathered together a hodgepodge that included not only environmentalism and pacifism but also old attitudes of superiority and a more recently developed historical amnesia. In the late 1960s, this was incorrectly described as a generation gap. By the 1980s, emphasis on the generation gap disappeared when a generation-spanning consensus formed around the need for a new collective identity. The controversy was over *how* to build it. The *Historikerstreit* of 1985 became the most significant example of the new debates over German self-understanding. In this search for a new self-understanding, Germany looked to America for approval. This was demonstrated in the handshake between President Reagan and Chancellor Kohl at the graves of SS soldiers in Bitburg, where the chancellor used Germany's ambivalence as a means of blackmail.

The political classes of Europe can always count on the ambivalent attitude of the people toward the United States. Certainly, by the time NATO was established, American superiority in the Western alliance had become so obvious that the old relationships between the people and national identity were no longer sustainable. Under the rubric of national liberation from German occupation, Gaullists and the communist parties of the European continent were the most successful in maintaining a feeling of national continuity. England had meanwhile already fled into the unique role of the *special relationship*. Germany, on the other hand, had to turn away from its past in order to join either western or eastern alliances. This meant that at the end of the Cold War, no country in Europe was less prepared than Germany for the return of the national question. "Reunification" had attained the status of an ideology during the last 40 years of the short century. Although foreign commentators took the desire for unification as given, within Germany this was hardly the case. The dynamics of socialism's collapse created the longing for a national solution to the German question, even if the solution was intended more as a miraculous rescue of East Germany from the misery of "really existing socialism." While the worst aspects of a divided Germany could be projected upon the collapsed Soviet Union, the fact that the Allies divided Europe in reaction to Germany's attempted seizure of world power remained shrouded in memory. Gratefulness for Germany's prosperity during the Cold War is still invoked in pro-American terms but below the political surface and the commemorations that celebrate the Marshall Plan and the Berlin Air-Lift, lurks antipathy toward America. This antipathy is expressed in peculiar discussions about accusations of an allegedly collective guilt, or about the expulsion of Germans from previously occupied territories, or about bomb-filled nights. Then, the discussion is no longer about the German past, with its stereotypes of perpetrators and victims; it turns into debates over the influence of Jews on American policy. This merry-go-round of public debate has spun faster and faster since the Gulf War in 1992. The current, ill-considered characterization of allied troops in the Middle East as occupiers is linked in public memory with the occupation of Germany after 1945. In Germany, it is only reluctantly that the Jews and former concentration camps prisoners are conceded the right to see May 8 as a day of liberation. In the meantime, even this day has been sacrificed for the sake of national continuity.

In West Germany, the need for national continuity disappeared during the Cold War. Participation in the Golden Age of the *American Way of Life*, which stretched from 1949 to 1973, compensated West Germans through social progress for the nation's division. The American promise arrived. Even the protest and youth culture can be understood as a part of this desired and accepted Americanization. This was not the case in the East where, in the shadow of the Red Army, national continuity was monopolized in the face of the unwanted transformation of society to state socialism. The communist parties sought to curry favor with the *Volk*, especially after the painful experiences of June 1953 in East Germany, and then of 1956 in Poland and Hungary. In the Socialist Bloc, a dream America also existed. This dream was not as strong in East Germany as it was in Poland—with its

Greater Poland that included Poles who had migrated to America. In the GDR, the need for compensation on a national level prevailed over the societal shortages because, shoved between the GDR and the United States, the homeland of consumer capitalism, was the Federal Republic with its well-stocked West Berlin acting as a capitalist showcase. In the East, the collapse of the economy of shortage was thus experienced that much more as a *clash of culture*. Once the crisis-prone reality of West Germany, which in addition to internal problems also had to digest a collapsed East German economy, was recognized, the typical socialist idealization of western society quickly collapsed. In this way, the long-nurtured East German need for national continuity arrived at its anti-American destination. For many East Germans, the long awaited for modernization of society turned out to be an existential threat. Faced with this situation, claiming national membership seemed more important than trusting in the power of society to change. The eastern part of Germany made it through this process in the years 1989 and 1990 with breathtaking speed. No one longed for a new Germany, but rather for "reunification"—in other words, a reestablishment of the past national status quo. The dream America of "actually existing socialism" quickly transformed itself into the nightmare America of globalization.

To get a sense of the unique mixture of the old and new in German self-understanding, one has to grasp that united in one country are two different senses of reality that are products of two different social systems. For both parts of Germany, America remains, no matter what it does, a symbol of the new. Ambivalence toward the new is projected onto America: the more social life is experienced as prone to crisis, the stronger the fears over the new reality. In the summer of 2002, the worst flood in memory affected Germany. It was rightfully called the flood of the century. While the opposition candidate went on vacation, the chancellor entered the crisis like a strong, vigorous man who made promises for which he could be held accountable. Without a doubt, it was Schröder's behavior that was key to the spectacular and surprising success of the Social Democrats in the federal elections of 2002. The self-destruction of the FDP after they presented themselves as the "the fun party," allowed their adversary, the Greens, to appear more serious. At the same time, the Green foreign minister, Joschka Fischer, enjoyed unflagging popularity. Joschka Fischer did not become popular through anti-Americanism, however. Against the basic principles of his fellow party members, he pushed through—together with the chancellor who has faced similar problems in his own party—German participation in the war in Kosovo and in the "war on terror" in Afghanistan. The opposition was not able to distort his rejection of the Iraqi intervention as a contemptible brand of anti-Americanism, or to profit from it in any way, because it too is plagued by an ambivalent relationship with America. Indeed, it is from the opposition that the *Stahlhelmfraktion* comes. Composed of both members of the so called "wertkonservativ," value or traditional conservative, and voters, the *Stahlhelmfraktion* repudiates basic aspects of American society on account of its alleged permissiveness and supposed dictatorship of political correctness. They also maintain a specifically post–National Socialist brand of pacifism, which is always sounding the alarm, out of "their own experience," against the guerrilla wars that are possible in any intervention—as if the Nazi army marching toward Yugoslavia was the same as NATO troops trying to end ethnic cleansing. With their slogan "war is war," wisdom disappears, as does any real distinction between them and the neo-pacifist camp of the Greens. The Christian Democratic opposition, by comparison, would not have gained any votes by expressing unequivocal support for German participation in the Iraqi intervention. So they tried a zigzag course instead. At home, they portrayed themselves as moderately peaceful and in Washington, as the only reliable German ally of the Bush administration. This made them look untrustworthy and their foreign policy less than convincing. When the voters reject this brand of politics, it is hardly a sign of deeply rooted anti-Americanism.

Does anti-Americanism, to say nothing of a new anti-Americanism, exist at all then? At the close of 2003, anyone who pays attention to the German mass media, or listens to conversations in universities and public forums, or observes book publishing, where anti-American conspiracy theories do great business, would probably have the impression that a flood of anti-American sentiment is gradually reaching a high point. Personalities in the media and politics are trying to shape what they consider to be the people's consciousness. The sudden identification of a prevailing mood of pacifism and fundamentally anti-American convictions is integral to their own mainstream views— views that do not match reality. It is they who have interpreted the established ambivalence of the people toward politics and the media as an anti-American social psychology. This leads them to find anti-Americanism everywhere. Anti-American interpretations associate America in general, and George W. Bush personally, with the negative aspects of a widespread ambivalence toward power and violence. For reasons of realpolitik, rulers must, nonetheless, once again curb these voices, since no responsible European can be interested in an American disaster in Iraq. This results in making those who fanned the flames of anti-American opinion look unreliable, which in turn strengthens indifference toward politics. It is an old story. In all democratic countries, an antiwar mood predominates, even when, if not exactly when, elites, whether for good or bad reasons, act like war hawks. The assumption that the American people and their respective presidents lust for war is at the core of anti-American propaganda. With such a worldview in place, high moral status is awarded both to Germany's own peacekeeping policies and to the counterfactual conviction, which is especially popular in Germany, that violence is no way to conduct politics. In psychoanalytic terms, the anti-American worldview permits a narcissistic reevaluation. Moral superiority compensates for inferiority in the arena of power politics. Germans understand this mechanism especially well because they can pretend that this feeling of moral superiority is a historical lesson. Yet, it is a common European phenomenon that such a self-reevaluation comes at the expense of an imagined America. This is something that at least "Old Europe," as Donald Rumsfeld disparagingly termed it, had grasped. Politically, this sense of moral superiority is supposed to compensate Europe for the insecurity that accompanies its new role in world politics. It is in this state of insecurity, however, that the governing and the governed encounter one another.

The mystery of an omnipresent anti-Americanism in the post-1989 period can only be solved in social terms, since it is not only in a political sense that a new world emerged after the collapse of the socialist societies. Germany was overwhelmed by this transformation and has reacted by refusing to recognize it. The more idealistic expression "reunification" quickly gained acceptance over the more realistic expression, "unification." The internal dynamics of western societies, which could be termed their internal Americanization, has again led to a renationalization of Europe. This has not meant a return to old forms of nation-states, though. Nothing makes this clearer than the catchphrase "multicultural society," which has come to describe a society that is no longer ethnically homogenous. Even from this point of view, America appears like a role model to be both admired and feared at the same time. National–cultural conspiracy theories concerning 9/11 rationalize the attacks as an act of self-defense by a group of fanatical desert rebels who symbolize an essentially invented tradition of impotence. In Europe, ambivalence toward the process of social modernization has typically been expressed in anti-American terms. This response pattern dates back to the end of the nineteenth century, the age of the "invention of tradition." Anti-Americanism can best be understood as part of a *Weltanschauung*—a German word that gained international currency at the same time as *Kultur* began to be contrasted with *Zivilisation* in the German-speaking world. Anti-Semitism can also be a part of a *Weltanschauung* but its essential core consists of a practice that is directed against Jews and is violent in word and deed ("Jewish blood must flow"). The anti-American *Weltanschauung* commonly intersects with the consciousness of the average person who, in coping with the demands that society places on a sovereign citizen, elevates the everyday to the status of a kind of religion. In the magical square of work and exchange, power and violence, in which all members of society must find their way, the average person tries to find his or her orientation in the certainties of the everyday. These self-affirming certainties are meant to provide security in uncertain times. Thus, what many fear is that the unbridled, globalized economy of "neo-liberalism" will dismantle the welfare states of old-Europe—the kind that competed with socialism. Fears of poverty are bound up with the threats implicit in the fear-inducing expression, "American conditions" such as freezing homeless people in a New York winter—a terrible vision of Europe's future. The oil crisis of 1973–1974, brought the Golden Age to an end, ushering in a massive social transformation in western societies. This transformation brought new life to old patterns of interpretation. The paradigm of identity that was developed in academic circles in the 1970s, provided a way to interpret collective subjectivity in a new manner and set this new interpretation in a familiar framework. In this way, anti-American patterns of interpretation accomplish a genuine sociological miracle: one can feel like a member of a culture that is old, and thus superior to America, even though it is only recently that Europe has emerged as a political and social reality. Anti-Americanism has become, therefore, an ideological playing field in a self-proclaimed, post-ideological age.

NOTE

Translated by Raymond Valley and Michelle A. Standley.

5

AMERICA'S BEST FRIENDS IN EUROPE: EAST-CENTRAL EUROPEAN PERCEPTIONS AND POLICIES TOWARD THE UNITED STATES

Jacques Rupnik

On the eve of its long-heralded unification, Europe has been deeply divided. Less by the merits of the Iraqi crisis *per se* than by the perceptions of and policies toward American power. The transatlantic divide became an intra-European one with the countries of Central and Eastern Europe tipping the balance in favor of the American leadership. The letter entitled "United We Stand,"[1] a British–Spanish initiative signed by the leaders of Poland, Hungary, and the Czech Republic, became the symbol of that divide. It stressed the primacy of the "transatlantic bond guaranteeing our freedom." It was followed on February 5 by the letter of the "Vilnius Ten" (from Albania to Estonia) pledging their readiness to contribute to an international coalition to enforce the disarmament of Iraq.[2]

"I do not see Europe as being France and Germany. I think that's old Europe. If you look at the whole Europe its center of gravity has moved to the East," said the American secretary of defense adding that what is the characteristic of the "new Europe" is that "they are not with France and Germany, but with the United States." The undiplomatic bluntness of Donald Rumsfeld's statement or its debatable terminology (most of the capitals of Central Europe are, of course, just as "old" as those of Western Europe; as for new Europe, it is actually in the making through the enlargement of the European

Union [E.U.] to 10 new members) should not preclude the obvious element of truth it entails: all the countries that used to belong to the so-called Communist East—"from the Baltic to the Adriatic" to use Churchill's phrase from his famous iron curtain speech—have, with varying degrees of enthusiasm, pledged their support to the United States.

Hence the question: has the former Soviet bloc now become an "American bloc," the new backbone of the "American party" within an enlarged E.U.? Was the crisis related to the war in Iraq a temporary transatlantic disturbance, of which there have been many since Suez in 1956 to Bosnia almost 40 years later? Or was it a catalyst of deeper trends concerning European perceptions of and policies toward the United States? If the latter is the case and the transition period stretching from the end of the Cold War in 1989 to 9/11 is now over, then it is relevant to treat the contrasting responses to the crisis in the "core countries" of the E.U. and the East-Central European newcomers as part of a broader post–Cold War realignment. It also, therefore, justifies an attempt to briefly contrast the perceptions of America in the country now seen in the United States as the archetype of European anti-Americanism (France) with the perceptions of the East Europeans claiming to be "America's best friends" on the continent.

Several necessary caveats: first, one should use the term "anti-Americanism" with a degree of caution because of its diversities and ambiguities (the frequent combination of resentment of American power and the persistent attraction of the "American dream") and try, as much as possible, to distinguish the revival of an anti-American political discourse (when in doubt, blame the American "hyperpower") or expressions of alleged threats to a nation's cultural identity (*on se pose en s'opposant*) from the formulation of legitimate political differences over a wide range of political and economic issues or even the very nature of the "new international order." To express, as most European countries have done, opposition to the Bush administration over environmental issues (Kyoto) or even to the use of force without a UN mandate does not qualify as anti-Americanism (though both arguments might be used in anti-American discourse). When a London weekly runs a cover story entitled "Unjust, unwise, un-American,"[3] criticizing America's plan to set-up military commissions for the trial of terrorist suspects, it might be read in Washington as an illustration of an anti-American bias, until it is made clear that this comes from *The Economist* with impeccable "atlanticist" credentials and a tendency to identify the international role of the United States with its own free market agenda. Similarly, to argue that effective fight against terrorism implies a political effort focusing on the conditions that helped to bring about its emergence might be read in circles close to the present U.S. administration as "European pundit being 'soft' in the war on terrorism," or as giving excuses for anti-American terror if the author was no other than a former national security advisor to the president of the United States with strong connections to the new Europe going back to the Cold War era.[4]

No less importantly, to be put in a proper perspective, the study or the assessment of the intensity of European anti-Americanism should nowadays be conducted in parallel with, or at least taking into account, "Anti-Europeanism" in America.[5] The two phenomena are mutually reinforcing and have implications on the understanding of different attitudes among Europeans.

Second, an assessment of post-9/11 perceptions of America needs to be put in a historical perspective. Anti-Americanism in Europe has a history that suggests that it has been a cyclical phenomenon.[6] Post-war French anti-Americanism receded in the 1970s and 1980s with the parallel decline of Gaullism and communism in French politics, only to resurface in a new context two decades later. Similarly, to the extent that the current East European bout of Americanophilia is, at least partly, a reaction to decades of Soviet imposed domination justified by adversity with the United States, it is likely to change over time.

Third, there is a variety of perceptions of America in East-Central Europe, which is by no means a homogeneous bloc. Poles, Balts, and Albanians are clearly and for different reasons (opposition to Moscow for the former, opposition to Belgrade for the latter) the most closely identified with U.S. foreign policy. Hungarians, Czechs, or Slovenes displayed a more lukewarm support and concern for its implications on the European scene. Similarly, there is, as attitudes to U.S. military action in Iraq revealed, a great deal of differentiation between the political and intellectual elites on the one hand and public opinion on the other.

What used to be a French idiosyncrasy (the obsession with American power) has become a more broadly shared West European concern. The recent bout of anti-American feeling is at least as acute in Germany as it is in France. Never in the history of the Federal Republic had the chancellor lashed out so brazenly against its oldest ally, says Josef Joffe, the editor of the Hamburg weekly *Die Zeit*. More than Chirac's neogaullist posture, it was Schröder's open defiance of the United States that marked the end of the transatlantic consensus.[7] And it is precisely for that reason that Central Europeans, anxious to preserve it, started to compete for the title of the most devoted ally of the

United States. Both attitudes to the United States, thus, have to do with different responses to the post–Cold War realignments in Europe and post-9/11 assertion of American power on the international scene. The contrasting perceptions of America in Western and East-Central Europe can usefully be analyzed by focusing on the three main pillars not of wisdom, but of anti-Americanism in France with its three facets: fear (of power), resentment (of the American economic model and contempt (of mass culture)):[8]

1. Opposing attitudes toward the centrality of American power in the post–Cold War world. The differences over the future of NATO and its American leadership are among the extensions of that divide.
2. Contrasting attitudes toward the U.S.-led globalization drive and the relevance in that context of an "Anglo-Saxon" (i.e., free market) socioeconomic model seen as a threat to the continental European welfare state in Western Europe and as an inspiration for the dismantling of the legacy of communist *étatisme*, East of the Elbe.
3. There are also different responses to the penetration of American mass culture and lifestyles and its implications for the national (or European) identity.

AMERICAN "HYPERPOWER" OR THE "INDISPENSABLE NATION?"

After the end of the Cold War, small is beautiful, big is powerful, and medium size has become uncomfortable. That certainly seems to be the case of France, which has lost some of the room for maneuver it used to enjoy during the Cold War era. France found itself at odds with the "unipolar moment" as Charles Krauthamer described it, and pleaded, under Mitterrand as under Chirac, for a multipolar world. The Iraqi crisis simply accentuated a trend that was already well established. As an illustration, one can turn to the leaders (and more broadly to the editorial policy) of *Le Monde*. Its editor, Jean-Marie Colombani, the author of the famous "We are all Americans" in the immediate aftermath of 9/11, had earlier written a front-page piece entitled "Arrogances américaines"[9] where he defined some of the main features of French resentment of American power. First, "What was supposed to be a 'new international' order is nothing but a hegemony, the claim to a monopoly, that of the United States."

Second, American foreign policy, a mix of power and parochialism, "should avoid running the planet according to the whims of this or that lobby or the moods of Senator Helms."[10] Third, unilateralism and the reliance on force as opposed to negotiation and the legitimacy of the international community. The thought that the latter was effective sometimes thanks to the threat of the former (as the Balkan wars demonstrated) did not cross the mind of the director of France's leading newspaper.

The important thing here, however, is that the basic arguments against American unilateralism and the quest in the UN and in the E.U. of counterweights to it, pre-dates 9/11 and the Bush administration. It has gradually developed a European dimension through the E.U. countries' involvement in a number of multilateral efforts opposed by the United States. Among the most widely publicized were: the signing in December 1977 in Ottawa of the landmine treaty (opposed by the United States but also Russia and China), the Kyoto environmental treaty on the measures against global warming in 1998, the creation of an International Criminal Court, which is supported by all E.U. countries and opposed by the United States, demanding exemptions from prosecution for U.S. nationals.

The Iraqi crisis at the beginning of 2003 and the Franco-German opposition to the concept of a preventive war without the legitimacy of a UN mandate is to be understood in terms of the cumulative effect of accumulated grievances or both sides. The German chancellor's refusal to participate in any "adventure" (intervention in Iraq) and to write any checks to pay for it, and the European public's opposition to the war only emboldened the French to move one notch higher from Hubert Védrine's formula "amis, alliés, mais pas alignés."[11] The Franco-German partnership in opposing U.S. policy on Iraq seemed to give substance to the emergence of a "Euro-Gaullist" posture, an attempt to see Europe as a counterweight to U.S. power and leadership in matters of foreign and security policy. That is precisely where the East European newcomers to the Atlantic alliance parted ways with France and Germany.

Why are the Central Europeans "Pro-American?"

If the centrality of American power is a concern to "old Europeans" in France and Germany, it certainly is not seen as a problem by East-Central Europeans. They (particularly the Poles) consider that it was Ronald Reagan's confrontation with the "evil empire," rather than

West European emphasis on détente and Ostpolitik that contributed most to the demise of the Soviet system. The Cold War years have reinforced their commitment to the transatlantic bond, which, in contrast, is being eroded in West European perceptions since 1990. They feel European because they belong to the West,[12] while the French or the Germans belong to the West because they are Europeans. The two Europes are out of sync in their attitudes toward the implications of the end of the Cold War. In West European eyes, the Eastern Americanophilia is, at best, an anachronism. In East-Central Europe, Franco-German challenge to American leadership is seen as a reckless undermining of their security.

They closely associate their security with NATO and the U.S. presence on the continent. The French may be concerned about a unipolar world; the East Europeans have no nostalgia for a bipolar one. It stems from a certain reading of history that could be summarized as follows: after World War I, the United States had left the old continent, which did not bode well for Europe, particularly its Eastern part. After World War II, the United States stayed on, which allowed at least half of Europe to remain free and prepare for the emancipation of the Eastern part of the continent. In this way the United States can be seen as protecting Europe against the demons of its past.[13] In East-Central Europe, there is a widespread distrust of collective security and of pacifism identified since Munich with the appeasement of dictators. Paris would like to restrain American power, while Budapest, Prague, or Warsaw would point out that the UN failed to restrain anything in 1956, 1968, or 1981, let alone in Afghanistan or Bosnia. Among the three main modes of management of the international system (hegemony, collective security/multilateralism, and balance of power), the West Europeans nowadays tend to prefer the second while the East Europeans do not mind the first, so long as it is "benevolent." As for "balancing" American power with a Paris–Berlin–Moscow diplomatic axis, it is enough to raise Poland's fears of a "new Rappallo."

Beyond the lessons of history, there are the lessons from the Balkans. The Common Foreign and Security Policy of the E.U. was nowhere to be seen in the 1990s and it was eventually a U.S.-led military intervention under a NATO umbrella that put an end to ethnic cleansing in Bosnia and Kosovo. NATO, therefore, remains the only security guarantee in the eyes of the former Eastern bloc newcomers because it involves U.S. "hard security" capability. The E.U. is seen as a "soft security" institution; definitely not a substitute for American power. This act of faith is repeated all the more loudly as doubts have appeared in recent years over the American commitment to NATO. On the eve of its first enlargement in 1999 (Poland, Hungary, the Czech Republic), there were three main views about the future of the Alliance. The U.S. approach was summed up by the formula "out of area or out of business." The French priority was to build a "European Defense Identity." The Central Europeans wanted to "end the uncertainty"[14] about their geopolitical status, and would not have minded sticking to the old, well-tried formula of the first secretary general of NATO, who defined its purpose as "to keep the Americans in, the Russians out and the Germans down." Hence, the great anxiety on the part of the new members to see, after 9/11, the erosion of American interest in the Atlantic alliance. Partnership with Putin's Russia and coalitions of the willing became Washington's priority in the "war on terrorism." There, the French and other West Europeans saw a confirmation of the declining relevance of the Alliance. Fearing this and a strategic downgrading of East-Central Europe, the newcomers to NATO tried to compensate by an even closer alignment with the positions of the United States. That meant refitting NATO for the new U.S. strategic doctrine: "out of area" now meant "out of Europe,"[15] to follow America in the Middle-East in order to preserve its involvement in Middle Europe

In the contest for the most loyal ally of Washington—at the very moment when old Europe marked its distance—Poland was certainly difficult to beat. The Iraqi crisis provided the Bush loyalty test, which the French and Germans failed in contrast to the sometimes-overzealous East Europeans. When President Kwasniewski said, "If it is President Bush's vision, it is mine"[16] one could not help thinking that old habits of obedience die hard. Interestingly, the most committed to support the American leadership and the war in Iraq were the veterans of Soviet bloc communism such as Poland's premier, Leszek Miller and Romania's president, Ion Illiescu.[17] Interestingly enough, both (and their parties in Parliament) had opposed the U.S.-led intervention in Kosovo in the spring of 1999. They are now in office and, in the contest between old Europe and America, they chose, quite pragmatically, the most powerful. This provides a double advantage: the completion of the political laundering of the ex-communists as respectable democrats now receiving from Washington the title of the most trusted allies on one hand, and the prospect (at least the hope) of more tangible dividends on the other. Warsaw hopes that it might entice the Americans to move their military bases from ungrateful Germany to welcoming Poland. Romania and Bulgaria have provided their military bases on the Black Sea as a substitute for the defection of Turkey[18] and hope that they will become permanent. Whether or not the idea of the substitution of Germany and Turkey, the two major post-war pivot of U.S. political and military presence in Europe, with Poland and Romania is a wise move from the U.S. point of view, it certainly is seen as a major strategic asset in Warsaw and Bucharest.

Indeed, throughout the 1990s, Poland's policy has been gradually to "swing firmly into Washington's orbit."[19] The Polish foreign minister defined the goal as "strengthening Poland's position as the United States principal partner in the region and a major player in Europe as well. It is in our national interest to ensure continued U.S. presence in Europe and commitment to its affairs."[20] Historically, Poland's geopolitical predicament was between Russia and Germany. Now it is between the United States and Europe. It hopes, after a long eclipse, to have returned to the fore of the European political scene using its American connection (including an occupation zone in Iraq) as a leverage within the E.U. It is just possible that Poland has not fully measured the extent to which it was also being used by the United States not just for the purpose of "cherry picking" among Europeans but also explicitly for the purpose of dilution or even "disaggregation" of the European Union.[21] Such an outcome would, of course, be disastrous for Poland as for the other Central Europeans now joining the E.U. in the hope that it would do for them in terms of economic modernization, what it has so successfully done for Southern Europe in the previous two decades. In siding with the United States, the Central Europeans give primacy to what they see as a strategic priority but certainly not their long-term economic interests.

Beyond the foreign policy realignments of newly sovereign states and pure pragmatism of ex-communist politicians, there is another distinct brand of Americanophilia—that of the former dissident intellectuals. It recognizes America's "democratic mission" in bringing down dictatorships: just as the United States contributed to the downfall of communism, it can today contribute to that of other brands of totalitarianism.

In the 1980s, Timothy Garton Ash had in an essay defined Central Europe's new politics through three leading intellectual figures involved in the dissident movement: Vaclav Havel in the Czech Republic, Adam Michnik in Poland, and György Konrad in Hungary. Interestingly, the three adepts of nonviolent change in Central Europe have supported the American war in Iraq in the name of democratic "regime change." Havel signed the "letter of the eight" on his last day in office,[22]

Michnik joined the Washington-based Committee to Liberate Iraq, Konrad wrote in an article entitled "Why I support the war": "The bringing down of a bloody tyrant can only be sympathetic to former dissidents."[23] In reply to a German critic who saw in the three ex-dissident intellectuals' support for the war the latest illustration of the "betrayal of the intellectuals" (*la trahison des clercs*, to use Julien Benda's phrase), Michnik pleaded for the support of the United States as politically and morally justified. In substance, a new totalitarian threat had replaced Eastern communism—the Islamic fundamentalist terror.[24] Milan Simecka, a former Slovak dissident, now editor of the daily SME in Bratislava, called America a "dissident power" given its readiness to assert democratic values even alone against the rest of the world.[25] Veton Suroi, editor of *Koha Ditore* in Prishtina, Kosovo, drew a parallel between the way the United States was ready to use force against Milosevic and the military intervention that brought down Saddam's dictatorship.[26] For the former dissidents, America remains the "indispensable nation" because it has kept alive its democratic mission in the post–Cold War world. They do not seem to be deterred in their judgment by the shift from the concept of humanitarian intervention of the 1990s to the logic of power that prevailed after 9/11, from what Samantha Power called "liberalism without power" of the Clinton era to "power without liberalism" under George Bush.[27]

The fact that governments and intellectual elites have, to a large extent, provided support for the assertion of American power on the international scene should, however, be qualified by the diversity of views (the Soviet bloc has not been replaced by an American bloc) and by the great divide between elites and public opinion. This has been confirmed by a series of independent public opinion surveys, which show that East European candidate countries shared with the citizens of the member states a considerable reluctance to an American intervention in Iraq.[28] Interestingly, their reluctance was even greater than that of E.U. member in the case Weapons of Mass Destruction were found in Iraq and a UN resolution was reached.[29]

These data concerning the U.S. war in Iraq should be read against the background of other surveys conducted in 2002 and 2003 by the Pew Research Center. On the whole, the central Europeans share the goals of the post-9/11 fight against terrorism but not U.S. unilateralism. To the proposition "the U.S. take into consideration others" in the fight against terrorism, between 60 and 70 percent of central Europeans answered negatively (a much higher figure than among E.U. member-states). To the proposition "the world would be a more dangerous place if another country matched America militarily", old Europe (France, 64 percent; Germany, 63 percent) answers positively while Czechs (53 percent) and Poles (46 percent) seem less worried.[30] The view that "when differences occur with America it is because of (my country's) different values" (considered a key indicator for the assessment of anti-Americanism) is shared only by a third of the French and German respondents but by 62 percent Czechs.

In short, there is a striking difference in the response to the overwhelming primacy of American power on the international scene between Western and East-Central European governments and intellectual elites. But there seems to be a widespread transeuropean consensus among the peoples, thereby casting serious doubts on the depth of the old Europe versus new Europe divide vis-à-vis the United States.

GLOBALIZATION AND AMERICA'S SOCIAL AND ECONOMIC MODEL

The second dimension of American power that the French (and a number of other Europeans) are uncomfortable with is economic. Globalization and the promotion of the free market have been central to the perceptions about America, at least since the Reagan presidency. The American liberal model with high growth rates, high degrees of inequality combined with low rates of unemployment and low levels of social protection is seen as a major challenge to the continental "European social model" characterized by the welfare state, high levels of public spending, and high rates of unemployment. This is, in Michel Albert's terms, the opposition between the "Anglo-Saxon model" and the *capitalisme rhénan*[31] shared since World War II by West European Social Democrats as well as Christian Democrats. After the Reagan–Thatcher challenge to it in the 1980s, came the Clinton–Blair version under the banner of globalization and the "Third Way" as the only plausible adaptation to its challenges. Meanwhile, the continental welfare state model is in crisis, nowhere more so than in Germany and France, economically the "sick men of Europe." Thus, in the uneven debate between (French-led) "territorialists" and (American-led) "globalists," the post-communist Eastern Europe tended, rather predictably, to support the latter. There is a strong correlation in Western Europe (and France in particular) between critics of marketization/deregulation in the 1990s, not to mention antiglobalization protesters, and the resentment of America's economic power and influence.

In contrast, for the Central Europeans, the American free market model seemed doubly attractive in the post-communist transition. After half a century of state control over economic and social life, you do not want just to improve it but also to dismantle it. For that purpose, free market liberalism promoted by the United States and the myth of America as a society without a state seemed highly attractive.

For post-1989 East-Central Europe, America had the great advantage of never having had anything to do with socialism. To be sure, few (if any) in Warsaw or Budapest were familiar with Sombart's thesis explaining the "American exception" by the role of the frontier, and the impact of constant immigration flows. What they knew was Milton Friedman and the simple truth that, whether under Reagan or Clinton, America stood for the free market and got results while continental Europe (France and Germany) were contemplating a decade with almost zero growth and 10 percent unemployment. Hence the paradox: Chicago school economic liberalism was introduced in East-Central Europe under the banner of a trade union called Solidarity!

In the roll back of the post-socialist model, the American model appealed to economic and political liberals—to Klaus as well as to Havel. For the Central European free marketers in charge of the conversion to market economy in the immediate aftermath of the collapse of communism, the only debate was, as T. Garton Ash put it, between Hayekiens and Friedmanites. Most of them had American "gurus" to launch the "shock therapy." For Leszek Balczerowicz in Poland, it was Jeffrey Sachs, for Vaclav Klaus, it was Milton Friedman (and Margaret Thatcher). This enthusiasm for the American model subsided somehow when the political pendulum swung in Warsaw and Prague (and when Vaclav Klaus had to resign at the end of 1997 after it was revealed that that there was more than a "free lunch" worth of unaccountable party finances). But the main orientation remained with other countries joining in: Estonia the champion of free trade and post-Meciar Slovakia, inspired by George Bush's tax breaks, opting for a 19 percent flat tax rate for business and individuals (clearly out of step with continental Europe where the taxation rates are more than double).

The second inspiration for the "roll back of the State" comes from the human rights movement and political liberals. The dissident rediscovery of a language of rights and of the concept of civil society also pushed, albeit less explicitly, in the direction of the Anglo-Saxon model. "In facing a problem of some importance you'll find in France the State, in England a lord, in America a voluntary association"— Alexis de Tocqueville's observation is not entirely out of place in the

way post-communist Central Europeans approached their "problems
of some importance": the State was rolled back, the gentry is no more,
and a civil society, the only hope in town, is a long-term endeavor.
To the extent that both economic and political liberals converged in
considering the State as the enemy from whom freedom had to be
conquered, they shared what Isiah Berlin called "negative freedoms"
(to enjoy new freedoms, the State has to stop doing some of the
things it used to do). Hence also the attraction of the American model
of a minimalist State. An article in a Czech daily recently summed up
the perception of the latter as follows:

> In America all that is not forbidden by law is allowed. In Germany, all
> that is not allowed by law is prohibited. In Russia, all is forbidden to the
> extent that law permits it. In France, all is allowed even when law pro-
> hibits it. In Switzerland, all that is not forbidden by law is compulsory.

What matters here is, of course, not the accuracy of the statement
but what it reveals about a widespread perception: America associated
with individual freedom while continental Europe presents variations
of proliferating rules and regulations imposed (if not always implemented) by the State. This contrast is reinforced when related to the
comparison between Western and East-Central European concerns
and attitudes toward the U.S.-led process of economic globalization.
Is the E.U. a tool of that globalization or a way to cope with it and
shelter the newcomers against the adverse effects of globalization?
The post-1989 modernization of East-Central Europe is partly an
adjustment to the process of E.U. integration and partly the transformation of economies and societies under the impact of global U.S.
patterns. According to the Hungarian economist J.M. Kovacs: "By joining NATO, hosting multinational companies, introducing American-
style capital markets and welfare regimes or following global trends of
mass culture, some of the new democracies in Eastern Europe could
become in a few important fields different from the sociological
model(s) offered by Western Europe. All the more so because in the
takeover of global features the danger of producing peculiar hybrids
with communist legacies arises."[32]

The suggestion that East-Central European countries in transition were heading toward and "American" rather than a continental
"European" model deserves to be qualified as soon as one moves
from rhetoric to realities, from some of the initial impulses to the
current phase. The impact of American-style capitalism (ranging from
issues of corporate governance to social responsibility) is to some

extent related to the presence of American capital. The investment flows to East-Central Europe show, however, a formidable imbalance in favor of the E.U. In 2001, FDI (foreign direct investment) in Poland was 6.37 billion euros (compared to less than 37 million from the United States); in the Czech Republic, the EU investment was 10 times that of the United States (2429 millions compared to 249 millions). Similar differentials apply to the rest of East-Central Europe: Hungary 1247 against 10; Slovakia 888 against 28; Slovenia 391 against 21; Latvia 220 against 1; Estonia 228 against 0; Lithuania 171 against 0.[33] In short, whatever the rhetoric, the actual dynamics of economic integration links firmly the region to Western Europe rather than to the United States.

No less importantly, the differences in Europe on issues related to the economic model and globalization are not confirmed by public opinion surveys. The Pew Global Attitudes survey shows a fair amount of convergence between old E.U. members and new ones on main issues such as openness to the expansion of trade and rise in business ties.[34] The effect of globalization is seen positively by a similar number of Czechs and Slovaks (around two-thirds) as of West Europeans.[35] Only Poland shows greater reluctance with 38 percent positive opinions. A similar pattern emerges with the widespread acceptance of free markets combined with the need for a social safety net. Americans alone, according to the survey, care more about personal freedom than about government assurances of an economic safety net. Nearly six in ten value freedom to pursue individual goals without government interference while only a third think it is more important for a government to make sure that no one is in need. In contrast, the majority in all European countries believes the opposite.[36]

The only discrepancy between the current E.U. members and the newcomers from the East is public opinion attitudes toward anti-globalization protesters (often associating in their discourse U.S. influence with the negative view of globalization). While a significant number of West Europeans think that antiglobalization protesters are a "good influence" (Britain, 39 percent; France, 44 percent; Germany, 33 percent), only a handful of Central Europeans share such a view (Czechs, 18 percent; Bulgarians, 16 percent; Poles, 21 percent).[37] The contrast was particularly visible during the September 2000 World Bank/IMF summit in Prague where violent antiglobalization demonstrations were seen by the Czech population as a foreign import of anticapitalist/anti-American rhetoric and of a culture of violence and anti-Americanism without any echo in the domestic population.[38]

It can thus be argued that just as for attitudes toward the primacy of American power on the international scene, the attitudes toward American economic influence, often identified with the challenges of globalization, reveal a discrepancy between the political and economic elites dominant in the first decade after the collapse of the Ancien Régime and the public at large. The latter shares the basic perceptions and priorities of their West European counterparts, though it is less tolerant of some of the political excesses of the antiglobalization radicals.

THE "AMERICANIZATION" OF CULTURE?

The third dimension of anti-American *ressentiment* in France (and parts of Western Europe) concerns the penetration of American mass culture. Opposition to free-market globalization associated with the United States tends to be politically on the left. Opposition to the "Americanization" of culture tends to come from the nationalist right: the fear that modernity and mass culture destroy traditional values and dissolve national identities.[39] It tends to focus on two main issues. First, there is the opposition to the commercialization of culture, the idea that culture is to be seen (above all in the United States) as an industry just like any other, subjected primarily to the laws of supply and demand and of free trade. The argument widely shared by French elites is, in contrast, that art and culture cannot be treated as mere commodities; that culture and national identities related to it are too important to be left to the market forces, where economically weaker national cultures run the risk of being leveled by the all-powerful American steamroller.[40]

In this "cultural war," according to *Le Nouvel Observateur*: "America owes its domination of the world as much to its cultural hegemony as to its economic power."[41] Hence French defense of a "cultural exception" as a guarantor of diversity on one hand and of high culture threatened by mass culture and the powerful entertainment industry on the other.[42] France made these issues one of its priorities at the European constitutional convention and succeeded in introducing an amendment that gives countries veto power over cultural matters.[43] The cultural exception amendment means that a E.U. country could block trade deals with countries outside Europe in the field of cultural products, film, and music.[44] Nobody was under any doubt that this concerned the United States.

What then are some of the responses to the issue of the "Americanization of culture" in the countries that, historically, were cultural nations before they became political ones and where, until 1990, writers and philosophers were considered the ultimate rampart for a spiritual resistance to totalitarianism?

The conditions prevailing in the old days was described by the American novelist Philip Roth, after his return from a visit to Prague in the 1980s, as follows: "In the West, everything goes nothing matters, in the East nothing goes everything matters." Some in communist Europe had made a virtue out of necessity: the independent, samizdat culture was the last remnant of a noncommercial culture, with works of art "made with the only aim to appear" (to use H. Arendt's phrase) outside the consumer society. Hence the suggestion (from Kundera to Solzhenitsyn) that, paradoxically, the last refuge of high culture not corrupted by the American/Western commercialism, was precisely where it was threatened by "socialism that came in from the cold." Interestingly, a somewhat similar argument was made by the Polish Pope and the Catholic Church in Poland concerning the possible spiritual revival coming from the East to the decadent materialistic West.[45]

The legacy of communism and dissident counter-culture is more complex than this self-serving stereotype. The dissident "high culture" (samizdat translations, seminars) in pre-1989 Prague had more European than American influences (Heidegger, Arendt, Levinas, Ricoeur), but its counter-culture looked more to late 1960s and 1970s California and New York (Frank Zapa, Lou Reed, and the Velvet Underground[46]). Both had elements of a critique of dominant commercial culture. Vaclav Havel, the symbol of the "new" Central Europe clinging to common "atlantic" values was also a critic of modernity, warning against a world dominated by the logic of "impersonal megamachines" of which the Eastern communist version was the most extreme and most objectionable (though not the only) form.[47] In this, Havel and the Czech dissident intellectuals were influenced by the writings of Jan Patocka and Martin Heidegger. The latter had, after all, written of "Europe in a great pincers, squeezed between Russia on one side and America on the other,"[48] arguing that "from a metaphysical point of view, Russia and America are the same; the same dreary technological frenzy, the same unrestricted organization of the ordinary man."

Asked to comment on why such an author was considered so important by the dissidents (i.e., surely there were more reliable philosophical sources for thinking about democracy and the West), the Czech samizdat translator of *Being and Time* attributed it to Patocka's influence (his "master thinkers" being Husserl and Heidegger) and quipped that in those days "there was not much 'being,' but we had a lot of time. . . ."[49]

Both the Czech dissident intellectuals' critique of Western modernity (of which America was the most advanced incarnation) and the Polish Catholic assumption that Western democracy (of which America was the unquestioned leader) should be accompanied by a parallel spiritual renaissance in Europe have a somewhat hollow ring today. Poland is Europe's spiritual Piedmont because, as the Pope put it, "thanks to the experience of totalitarianism, it is Eastern Europe that has achieved greater maturity?" Well, we know what happened to that. We have seen, instead, after the collapse of totalitarianism and its economy of scarcity the unbridled triumph of consumerism and commercial mass culture associated primarily with America. "We have a new god: entertainment!," claims Czech writer Ivan Klima, commenting on the state of culture, 10 years after the "velvet revolution." In Vaclav Havel's words: "I am not sure if we are not catching up with the West precisely in the ways the West should be warned against."[50] The West, not just America.

Thus, although some Central European intellectuals have, in the 1990s, rediscovered the concerns of their French colleagues about the influence of (predominantly American) mass culture, they do not share the latter's defensive posture concerning the spread of English. The East Europeans have always known that few people will make the effort to have direct access to their language and culture and that learning the imperial *lingua franca*—which today happens to be American English—is a must for the small nations of the periphery. They are reassured to find themselves in the company of the Germans, the Italians, or indeed the French in this respect.

CONCLUSION

The contrasting perceptions and attitudes toward America's role as the only superpower, as a would-be model of democracy and open society, are not only related to different historical experiences and a different sense of one's own role. The French have difficulty adjusting to their current status as a medium size power while the small countries of East-Central appreciate America also as an equalizing factor on the European scene (correcting the imbalance with France or Germany). The different attitudes to America also have to do with Cold War legacies and, in the French case, to different perceptions of the peaceful revolutions of 1989. The French, at first, tried to see there a fitting contribution to the ceremonies of the bicentennial of the French Revolution. From a Central European perspective, 1989 was a very deliberate closing of the era opened by the French

Revolution (followed by the Russian Revolution of 1917) based on the idea that a better society can be brought about through violence. The year 1989 saw the triumph of the democratic idea over the idea of revolution and in that respect identified more easily with the legacies of the American Revolution or the American "model" of democracy.

The contrast between old and new Europe vis-à-vis America illustrated here in three different ways (American power, the socioeconomic model, mass culture) is by no means as clear cut as the current political circumstances would have us believe. It might be interesting to examine to what extent, in an integrated Europe, there might be an extension of some of the features of West European anti-Americanism to Eastern Europe. Conversely, it might be of interest to determine whether elements of American Europhobia or Francophobia are exported/adopted in East-Central Europe. A decade ago, the Paris-based Czech writer Milan Kundera wrote that he found "francophobe arrogance personally as offensive as the arrogance of big countries towards the small country I come from."[51] Not a widely shared view at the moment.

The current European divide about America might also suggest a misleading conclusion—that the ex-communist countries of East-central Europe are now at a crossroads, confronted with a choice between Washington and Brussels, NATO and the E.U. Nothing could be more removed from reality. Poland and the other East-Central European countries do not have the option of a "Puerto Rico status." Their future is in the European Union, not as the fifty-first state of the United States. Both sides in the transatlantic divide share a responsibility for confronting these countries with a choice they would have preferred to avoid.

Finally, the stark contrast outlined here concerns the political and intellectual elites more than public opinion in general. It is also likely to change over time. Meanwhile, the French might console themselves by thinking that the Central European infatuation with America's democratic mission is merely a phrase: "We are all Americans at puberty, we die French" (Evelyn Waugh).

NOTES

1. The letter was signed by five leaders representing member states of the E.U. (Britain, Spain, Italy, Portugal, and Denmark) and three candidate countries: Poland (Leszek Miller), Hungary (Peter Medgyessy), and the Czech Republic (Vaclav Havel). *The Wall Street Journal*, January 30, 2003.

2. "New Allies Back US Iraq Policy." *New York Times*, February 6, 2003. The letter was drafted in Washington by Bruce Jackson, a former Pentagon consultant and chairman of the U.S. Committee for NATO.

3. *The Economist*, July 12–18, 2003.

4. Zbigniew Brzezinski, "Confronting anti-American grievances," *New York Times*, September 1, 2002: "For America, the potential risk is that its nonpolitically defined war on terrorism may thus be hijacked and diverted to others ends. . . . If America comes to be viewed by its key allies in Europe and Asia as morally obtuse and politically naive in failing to address terrorism in its broader and deeper dimension . . . global support for America's policies will surely decline."

5. See Timothy Garton Ash, "Anti-Europeanism in America," in *The New York Review of Books*, February 13, 2003, pp. 32–34.

6. Thus, the American edition of a 1980s study of the phenomenon was published under the title, *The Rise and Fall of Anti-Americanism*, edited by D. Lacorne, J. Rupnik, and M-F. Toinet, (New York: St Martin's, 1990) and would now have to be revised as "the rise and fall and the rise again . . ."

7. Josef Joffe, "Continental divides," *The National Interest* (spring 2003), pp. 157–160 and "Round 1 goes to Mr Big," *New York Times*, February 10, 2003.

8. Ph. Roger's study of French anti-Americanism highlights this evolution in the nineteenth century from "antiaméricanisme du mépris" to an "antiaméricanisme de la crainte" after the Spanish–American War to what became later, after World War II, an "anti-américanisme du ressentiment." See, *L'ennemi américain*, (Paris: Seuil, 2002).

9. J.-M. Colombani, "Arrogances américaines," *Le Monde*, February 26, 1998.

10. This refers to the attempt by the U.S. Congress to decree who has the right to trade with whom. Although nobody would dispute the U.S. Congress' right to impose trade restrictions on American corporations, few Europeans would accept the idea that it has the authority to impose its laws on the trade of other nations.

11. H. Védrine (dialogue avec Dominique Moïsi), *Les cartes de la France à l'heure de la mondialisation* (Paris: Fayard, 2000), p. 72.

12. In the words of Andrei Plesu, the Romanian philosopher and former foreign affairs minister: "when we said West, it never crossed our minds that . . . Western Europe and Northern America were divergent entities." In "Who Do You Love The Most," TCDS Bulletin (New York: The Graduate School, New School University) (June 2003), p. 6.

13. The Nobel-Prize-winning Hungarian writer Imre Kertész considers that the European states opposed to the war in Iraq "forget that without the United States they could never have rid themselves of two dictatorships: that of Hitler and that of Stalin." I. Kertész, "L'Europe de l'Ouest a tort," *Courrier International*, no. 646 (March 20–26. 2003) (interview P. Dunai published in *Nepszabadsag*, Budapest).

14. "It's time to end uncertainty," address by Z. Brzezinski to the Conference of Central European Prime Ministers in Bratislava, May 11, 2001.

15. Ronald Asmus and Ulrich Weisser, "Refit NATO to move against threats beyond Europe," *International Herald Tribune*, December 6, 2001. R. Asmus was deputy assistant secretary of state between 1997–2000 in charge of NATO's enlargement and author of a study devoted to this subject, *Opening NATO's Door* (New York: Columbia University Press, 2002). See also Alexandr Vondra and Sally Painter, "No time to go it alone," *The Washington Post*, November 18, 2002. A. Vodra is deputy minister of foreign affairs of the Czech Republic.

16. David E. Sanger, "Alliances with Europe: Bush Redraws the Map," *New York Times*, January 24, 2003.

17. Andrei Plesu ironically comments: "We kissed and licked enough boots during our troubled history, and we'll know how to do it again. Don't even mention that from time to time we might be allowed to grab something, a bowl of warm soup, a political wedding, a funeral feast." *Art. cit.*, p. 6.

18. On the prospect of establishing permanent U.S. bases in Bulgaria, see the statement of the Bulgarian foreign minister, S. Passy, in *Novinite*, March 5, 2003 and that of the defense minister, N. Svinarov, in *Bulgarian News Digest*, March 24, 2003. Hungary already has a U.S. base at Taszar, cf. "Une base magyare au service de la guerre contre Bagdad," *Le Courrier International*, no. 632 (December 12–18, 2002).

19. Daniel Michaels, "Who helps the US in times of trouble? Poland, of course," *Wall Street Journal*, January 8–9, 1999.

20. W. Cimoszewicz—remarks at CSIS, Washington, December 14, 2002—*Polish Embassy Post*, Washington (spring 2002), p. 4. N.B.: in March 1999, the same Mr. Cimoszewicz, with 162 MPs of the Polish Sejm, voted against NATO military intervention in Kosovo. The same MPs in 2003 voted for U.S. action in Iraq.

21. The idea that the United States should pursue in Europe "coalitions of the willing," "disaggregating" the E.U., which was being "diluted" by enlargement in any case, was formulated by Richard Haas, then head of Policy Planning at the State Department, at a conference with European interlocutors held at Brookings, Washington, D.C. April 3–4, 2003.

22. In a little-publicized speech, made on the eve of the NATO summit in Prague, the Czech president, Vaclav Havel pointed out that his country, in his lifetime, went through two experiences with far-reaching consequences, which Czechs bear in mind when considering support for a military intervention. The first is Munich in 1938 and the capitulation of European democracies facing Hitler's threat "supposedly in the interest of peace." The second is the Soviet-led invasion of Czechoslovakia in 1968 when "in the name of value that ranked higher than national sovereignty" (i.e., socialism) Soviet "brotherly help" was provided. "It is always necessary to weigh on the finest scales whether an envisaged action would really be an act helping people against a criminal regime and protecting human kind against its weapons, or whether, by any chance, it would not be another variation of the 'brotherly help,' though more sophisticated than the Soviet version back in 1968." Opening speech

of President Vaclav Havel at the Aspen Institute conference, "The Transformation of NATO," Prague November 20, 2002.

23. *Frankfurter Allgemeine Zeitung*, February 27, 2003.
24. Adam Michnik, "Nous, les traîtres de l'Europe," *Libération*, April 8, 2003.
25. Speech at a conference devoted to "T.G. Masaryk and America," Washington, D.C., September 19, 2002.
26. Veton Suroi, "Les tyrans ne tombent que sous les bombes," *Le Monde*, February 15, 2003.
27. Samantha Power, in *The New Republic*, February 2003.
28. This apparently applies even in the Baltic countries whose governments were, next to the Polish one, the most favorable toward the support of the United States: 74% in Latvia opposed toppling the Iraqi regime by military force and Prime Minister Einars Repse's ratings dropped from 70 to 40% after his expressing support for the U.S. position, cf. E. Tomiuc, "Eastern Europe: do citizens of Vilnius 10 support action against Iraq. Or only their governments? In Radio Free Europe features," February 7, 2003.
29. A Gallup-Europe poll conducted in the last week of January 2003, see Ch. Châtelot, "Les pays de l'Est justifient leur fidélité aux Etats-Unis," *Le Monde*, February 1, 2003.
30. The Pew Global Attitudes Project, "What the world thinks in 2002," The Pew Research Center, Washington, D.C., December 2002, p. 58. The data from the survey are also presented in *The Economist's* special report "Living with a superpower," January 4, 2003, pp. 18–20. See also Tony Judt, "The way we live now," *The New York Review of Books*, March 27, 2003.
31. Michel Albert, *Capitalisme contre capitalisme* (Paris: Seuil, 1991).
32. J.M. Kovacs, "East European trajectories in times of integration and globalization," *IWM Newsletter*, no. 4 (fall 2001), p. 11.
33. Eurostat data presented by Jacques Moris, "Une nouvelle Europe . . . celle de D. Rumsfeld?," *Bulletin de l'AFTS*, no. 4 (2003), p. 5.
34. The Pew Global Attitudes Project, *View of a Changing World*, June 2003, The Pew Research Center, Washington, D.C., p. 71.
35. Ibid., p. 85.
36. Ibid., p. 105 (the more East and South-East one goes, the less "liberal" public perceptions of globalization are).
37. Ibid., p. 97.
38. Another difference concerns the peasant movements' protests. In France, the Confédération paysanne led by José Bové overtly attacks American symbols as part of their campaign against globalization. In Poland, Leppers's "Self-defence" peasant movement is anti E.U., not anti-US.
39. There are obviously left-wing variations on the theme as well. It tends to associate the fear of "Americanization" of French society with the segmentation of culture, and multiculturalism, which undermines the universalistic and integrating ambitions of the French "republican model."

40. For a lucid analysis of the issues and some of the economic data concerning the production and the dissemination of culture, see Denis Olivennes, "La fin de l'impérialisme culturel américain," in *Le Débat*, no. 119, March 2002, pp. 108–114.

41. "La guerre cultuelle," *Le Nouvel Observateur*, March 4, 1998.

42. Former French minister of culture, Jack Lang used the phrase "la machine à raboter les cultures." Alain Finkielkraut author of *La défaite de la pensée*: "La barbarie a fini par s'emparer de la culture. C'est l'industrie des loisirs, cette création de l'âge technique qui réduit les œuvres de l'esprit à l'état de pacotille ou, comme on dit en Amérique, d'entertainment." *Ibid.*

43. E. Schwarzenberg, "Le conflit entre les Etats-Unis et l'Europe s'étend à la culture," *Le Figaro*, May 17–18, 2003; Thomas Fuller, "Paris wins amendment in new EU constitution," *International Herald Tribune*, July 11, 2003.

44. There is a reservation, however, such a veto exists only when a trade deal "risks prejudicing the Union's cultural and linguistic diversity." Ibid.

45. Lech Walesa on the occasion of his first visit to France stated: "You have material goods, we have spiritual values."

46. After his debate with President Clinton at CUNY, Lou Reed gave a concert for President Vaclav Havel on his last official visit to the United States.

47. See, in particular, his 1994 essay "Politics and Conscience" published in Vaclav Havel, *Essais politiques* (Paris: Calmann-Lévy, 1989), pp. 221–248. In a recent interview, he spoke of a "totalitarianism of consumption" associated with globalization. Interview with J. Rupnik, *Politique Internationale* (winter 2003), p. 22.

48. Martin Heidegger, *An Introduction to Metaphysics* (New Haven: Yale University Press, 1959), p. 37.

49. Conversation of the author with Ivan Chvatik, translator of *Byti a cas*, on the occasion of its publication by Oikumene (Prague, 1996).

50. Vaclav Havel, speech at the tenth anniversary of *Gazeta Wyborcza* (Warsaw, May 1999).

51. "Car la francophobie, ça existe. C'est la médiocrité planétaire voulant se venger de la suprématie culturelle française qui a duré des siècles. Ou bien, peut être, est-ce, au-delà de notre continent, une forme de rejet de l'Europe." Milan Kundera as cited in *Paris-Prague, les intellectuels en Europe*, edited by F. Mitterrand and V. Havel (Prague: Institut Français, 1994), p. 94.

6

THE SPECIAL RUSSIAN WAY: THE ORIGIN AND EVOLUTION OF RUSSIAN PERCEPTIONS ABOUT THE UNITED STATES

Nikolai Zlobin

When I was a student at a Moscow elementary school, one of my class duties involved the preparation of so-called political information for my classmates. Political information took up 10 minutes of our daily class time and was devoted to global events of the past 24 hours. My tasks were: to make a list of the daily presenters and to remind them about it the night before; to supply the information if someone fell sick; and finally, to make sure that 90 percent of the news was devoted to exposing "American imperialism."

Exposing it was never a problem—practically everything we read in the papers about America had an extremely negative tone. My job was merely to supply the required amount of criticism. Despite our young age, we knew this to be another element of the propaganda machine, whose rules we had to obey. Moreover, we were sure that American kids were doing the same thing. We just couldn't understand what for.

We never placed much trust in what we read about America. I'll cite as evidence, two typical children's jokes of the time. In the first, a Russian and an American are playing chess. The American makes a move and says, "You have no meat in your country." The Russian makes his move and responds, "Your country oppresses blacks." The American counters the move and says, "But *your* country has no meat." The Russian while making his move says, "But *your* country oppresses blacks." The American thinks about it, makes a move, and says, "We'll steal Brezhnev from you." The Russian's response: "Then *you* won't have meat."

In the second, a boy comes home from school and says, "Tomorrow I have to bring a ruble to class for the starving people in America." The father says, "I'm not giving you any money—I don't know for a fact that America has starving people." The next day the son comes home again and says, "I have to bring a ruble for the homeless people in America." The father responds, "No, I need evidence that America has homeless people." On the third day, the son says, "I need to give a ruble to the American Communist party." The father immediately takes out three rubles: "Here you go—if the US has a Communist party, I'm sure it has plenty of homeless and starving people." The cynicism acquired under communist rule, instilled in us a critical approach to reality and prevented us from developing real anti-American sentiments.

But to this day, there is still no complete understanding of the colossal differences that separate Russia and the United States. The more Russia integrates with the West, the more it faces the incompatibilities of mentalities, psychologies, lifestyles, and systems of values between the two countries. This is leading Russia to an inevitable psychological breaking point. No one knows what price it will have to pay for this integration—not from a military, political, or economic point of view, but in terms of having to adapt its own cultural and spiritual values. The growing awareness of this inevitability complicates the Russian–American/Western dialogue and amplifies anti-American sentiments in a significant portion of Russian society.

The Russian perception of America can be distinguished by two mindsets. The first is based on deep-seated notions within Russian culture, history, religion, and mentality. These perceptions have been shaped over centuries, and, depend to a great extent, on how Russia has viewed herself and her place in the world, and on how she relates to other countries and cultures, particularly the West and the United States. This perception is a fairly stable assortment of views and judgments, where changes take place slowly and painfully.

Even anti-American propaganda, which the USSR was subjected to over the course of several generations, could not influence this perception decisively. In many ways, its nature is objective. It includes, for instance, the Russian dislike of America's religious pluralism (as Vasily Klyuchevsky wrote, "the West has a church without a God, Russia has a God without a church"[1]), the doctrine of privacy,[2] and the rule of law. As in a mirror, we can observe fundamental changes occurring within Russia herself in incremental steps. This perception relates to America's own evolution to a much lesser extent.

The second way or altered mindset toward the United States is related to superficial phenomena, ephemeral factors that encompass a wide spectrum of issues—from business and politics to sports and fashion. The changes here are more rapid, influenced by events, news, and political campaigns. Stereotypes and emotions reign supreme, as do personal subjective motives and the manipulation of public opinion. In this category, everything is, to a large extent, connected to events in America, its actions around the world, and how these actions are interpreted by the Russian media and political elite. One example is the reaction to the judging scandal at the Salt Lake City Winter Olympics, which practically the entire Russian society took as an anti-Russian campaign, an insult to the entire nation, and an attempt to denigrate Russian successes in sports. The State Duma devoted a special session to examining the possibility of withdrawing the team from international competition, and President Putin was forced to produce several statements.[3] In other words, we have here a subjective perception, that has little to do with the first, deeper, cultural perception.

The Russian perception of America, at any given moment, is always a combination of these two elements. Each time, the combination is different, and the two elements do not play equal roles. On a day-to-day basis, the subjective factor has more influence in forming Russian perceptions, which leads to political miscalculations on both sides of the Atlantic. This happens not only because people tend to react more sharply and emotionally to the contemporary events that have a direct bearing on their life, but also because, first of all, the objective elements of percieving America deal with fundamental Russian values rather than with America proper, and are therefore turned inward rather than outward. The United States is a mirror into which Russia constantly gazes.

Second, because of various factors, Russian society knows exceptionally little about America, but thinks otherwise. Much of this knowledge has a twisted, fragmented, and sometimes-falsified character. This is especially true for such fundamental issues as America's political evolution, the American system of values, their morals and style of thinking, the logic of democracy, and capitalist markets. To be fair, the average Russian knows more about America than the average American knows about Russia. But the Russian is certain that he knows enough to draw his own conclusions. This forms the basis for a large number of stereotypes and false judgments, widespread in Russia, that bloom tumescent after each individual incident, preventing a rational examination of it.

Third, several times over the course of the last century, Russian society was forced to fundamentally change its system of values and

moral priorities. Each time, the state forced people to reorient themselves toward new ethical and ideological systems, which were modified
to suit the political needs of the time. The ideology of "building communism" was based on a rejection of the past. Schoolbooks were
constantly rewritten, and history was falsified on a colossal scale. This
rejection of history was partially successful—the ties between ages and
generations were nearly severed. People's cultures and worldviews
were, to a significant extent, removed from their historical roots, and
grounded instead in communist ideology, with its perpetual political
campaigns that took the form of "the struggle against . . ." It could
be against "rootless cosmopolites," "warmongering capitalists," the
kulaks, the "doctors-killers," cybernetics, "dilettante corn-growing,"
or Stalinism. Since the end of the 1980s, Russia's *Weltanschauung* has
experienced catastrophic shifts. Moreover, anti-American propaganda
during the Cold War imposed a firm negative image of the United
States in the minds of a part of society. But a more objective perception
of America in the mass consciousness has always existed and continues
to exist and the events of 9/11 did not change that.[4]

Taking all this into account, let us briefly try to analyze the contemporary content of the first objective element of the Russian
perception of the United States.

Those who have read *War and Peace* may recall the highly
Franconized Russian *zeitgeist* at the time of the Napoleonic war—
French manners, ideas, fashions, literature, art and education formed
a significant part of Russian society. The novel begins with a conversation at a ball, spoken in French. The upper and middle classes spoke
only in French, treating it as "the language of progress." Russian was
for the servants. And yet, all of the protagonists express a sincere
hatred toward Napoleon, and toward French politics in general.

Curiously, all of the novel's characters—regardless of class, income,
or education—treat the French ("the frogs") and indeed all foreigners
with a sense of slight condescension, a feeling of vague superiority, an
awareness of possessing some higher knowledge denied to all non-
Russians. This sentiment can be observed in the characters of Anton
Chekhov, Nikolai Gogol, and others. France stood for a concentrated
expression of the West in general.

In today's Russia, this perception applies to America. Just like the
victory over Napoleon or the Russian Army's March 1914 entrance
into Paris did not create a shift in the perception of France, neither did
the events of 9/11 cause a noticeable change in "the hearts and
minds" of Russians. For contemporary Russians, the United States is
the new concentrated expression of the West. In his time, Peter the

Great called upon Russia to catch up with Europe, an idea that Nikita Khrushchev later reformulated with his slogan: "Let's match and surpass America." As the malnourished Russian citizens joked surreptitiously, "Khrushchev never said we'd be fed on the way."

But Khrushchev, unlike Peter, promoted victory over the United States, not integration with it. In Soviet times, the United States became the catch-all for the negative traits and stereotypes of the West. Negative perception of the United States became loaded with all the "detrimental Western traits"—spiritual death, aggressiveness, individualism, narcissism, egoism, mercantilism.[5] Western Europe was always seen as coupled with the West, and ceased to be a "full-fledged West" outside of that coupling.[6]

The United States became the newest, more powerful source for the traditional split in Russian society's perception of the West.[7] On the one hand, Russia's status as a perpetual straggler caused a feeling of jealousy toward the United States, as well as feelings of admiration, desire to imitate, respect and fascination. But on the other hand, aversion toward the American experience and lifestyle strengthened a sense of moral and intellectual superiority. In other words, the powerful inferiority complex was at least counterbalanced, if not replaced, by the no less powerful complex of spiritual superiority.[8] Even in today's political circles in Moscow one frequently encounters the view that in the alliance between Russia and the United States, the latter should be the purse and the fist, while the former the brain.

In "Public Readings on Peter the Great," Sergey Soloviev noted that since Russia was poorly defended by geography and was subject to enemy invasions, "the lack of defining physical boundaries was replaced by the Russian people with spiritual boundaries—religious differences in the west and south, inter-denominational differences in the west. Within these boundaries the Russian national consciousness fortified itself, maintaining its uniqueness and independence."[9] In that respect, America is perceived as the complete opposite. On the one hand, her territory was securely guarded by natural boundaries, which has always been a cause of jealousy for the Russians. "Not possessing any enemies around herself," wrote Nikolai Danilevsky 130 years ago, "she could economize on everything that others spent on sovereign existence. If we look at what it cost Russia having to arm herself at the time of the Vienna peace congress, these expenditures alone would comprise billions that Russia, like America, could have spent on building a web of railroads, a merchant fleet, and all sorts of technological improvements for manufacturing and agriculture."

In the United States, "a long-term economizing on the country's assets, not spent on national defense, accumulated immense riches, which could not have appeared otherwise."[10] Russia, on the other hand, always had to devote tremendous resources to defense— primarily against the West.

On the other hand, America, in the Russians' perception, is a country without spiritual unity, without the originality in which Russia takes so much pride. The "melting pot" mentality, tolerance, religious pluralism, the neglect of ethnic roots—all of it considered inferior to and in contradiction with the Russian system of values.

The Americans' national character, with its pragmatism, optimism, and openness, has always been one of the most irritating features for Russians, who see pragmatism as the opposite of spirituality, and tolerance as a form of permissiveness and lack of moral boundaries.

These antithetical worldviews are one of the major sources of Russian anti-Americanism. That is precisely why, at the end of the Cold War, many Russians had become more anti-American despite the elimination of the threat of military conflict with the United States. In democratization, they saw a danger to their system of values, their way of life, and spiritual uniqueness. For many, defending their country's borders consisted of defending those intellectual and spiritual riches, in the narrow sense of the word.

Throughout the course of Russian political culture, there is a great pull toward isolation, inside the fortress keep, into the "outer shell."[11] Nikolai Gogol thought that Russia should be a monastery. In *The Brothers Karamazov*, Fyodor Dostoyevsky sets up the conflict between Zosim and Alyosha as Russia's conflict between the doctrine of the monastery and the doctrine of the world that surrounds it, and, consequently, between two different value systems.[12] Integration with the West is today seen by many in Russia as the rejection of isolation, a rejection of Russian uniqueness and the acceptance of foreign—that is, American—norms and values. Lev Gumilev once worried about the fact that an inescapable consequence of integration will be "a complete rejection of homeland traditions followed by assimilation."[13] The United States cannot change this outlook, because it is rooted in the Russian mind.

Accepting their country's uniqueness as fact, Russians also accept the uniqueness of their main historical opponent—the United States. This raises themselves in their own eyes. Over a hundred years before the Cold War, Russian philosopher V. Pecherin prophesized that Russia and the United States would begin a new era of world history.[14] But American uniqueness has a pejorative connotation for Russia.

If Russia is unique in its depth and complexity, culture and spirituality, then the United States is unique in its simplicity, lack of spirituality, primitivism, and dogmatism. Everything good in the United States originates from the outside. There is even a Russian joke that asks why American presidents aren't known for their intellect. It is because to be president, one has to be born in America.

Russians are constantly comparing themselves to Americans. If there is something in which Russia is better, faster, stronger, be it ice-skating or spaceflight, the Russian's heart fills with pride and satisfaction. They do not take other countries into account. Many are convinced that Americans are also constantly comparing themselves to Russians, that there is some sort of a historical contest between the two societies. And, therefore, an exceptionally strong stereotype dwells in the mass consciousness—what's good for Russia is bad for America, and vice versa. The possibility of mutual interests is perceived by the masses with great difficulty. It is difficult to overestimate the political consequences of such a perception.

Russians are deeply convinced that the United States never does anything to damage itself, or to altruistically help others. "American Messianism" consists of spreading its own values and ideals to other societies. For this reason, America will not do anything good for Russia unless it receives something better in return. In contrast, "Russian Messianism" is always done for the benefit of others. It is believed, for example, that the Russian Army's involvements over the past few centuries, including the Italian and Swiss missions of Alexander Suvorov, the anti-Napoleonic wars, the First and Second World Wars, conflicts in Africa and Asia, wars in Spain and Afganistan, etc., were always done for the benefit of outside interests rather than its own—in order to help others who were deprived of rights, oppressed, and treated unjustly. Paraphrasing the words of Sergey Soloviev's famous poem: "What sort of country, Russia, do you choose to be— the land of Xerxes or the land of Christ?"; it could be said that Russia assumes it has always chosen Christ.[15]

Supporting the international communist movement was perceived as a self-sacrifice in the name of others. The USSR was an empire where the center lived worse than the periphery, and where sacrifices were always made to improve life in the provinces—the Soviet republics and the countries of Eastern Europe. In other words, in the Russian consciousness, their country is a beacon unto other nations, which saves them by preserving their culture, language, customs, and sovereignty, while the United States "enlightens" by Americanizing other countries's native culture and politics, forcing the English language upon them, and subordinating them to her economic interests.[16] The United States, in other words, is the land of Xerxes.

Conspiracy theories against Russia have always been widespread, and it is from this angle that American actions are frequently assessed. This is why, for example, American efforts to assist the establishment of Russian democracy and private markets are seen by a significant part of the population as an "American conspiracy" to enslave Russia. Sergey Soloviev, describing Peter the Great's efforts to Westernize Russian society, noted that the masses who protested against the replacement of the Russian style of dress with a foreign one "do not pay attention to the fact that the change taking place is a replacement of the old-style dress not with a dress of some foreign nation, but the dress of all Europe. . . ."[17] Similarly, the fact that, today, not only America but the entire civilized world lives with democracy and free markets does not prevent Russians from focusing all their suspicions upon the United States. The average Russian does not believe in the purity and honesty of American intentions, but sees only a clandestine goal to attain political or economic profit.

There is a duality in Russian mass political culture. On the one hand, it is believed that Russia is at the center of world events, that everything is in some way connected with it. America, meanwhile, is trying to push Russia into the periphery. It follows, then, that America cannot be believed or relied upon, because it will use Russia, then betray, and discard her. The good intentions of Washington cannot be believed, because they are pure hypocrisy. On the other hand, there is sincere surprise expressed at the fact that America doesn't trust Russia.[18] The juxtaposition of profound suspicion toward America and the no less profound resentment for not being trusted by America is a traditional trait of the Russian mentality. Russians are so worried the United States may be trying to deceive them that they attempt to deceive them first.[19]

French Slavist Georges Nivat noted that he was constantly urged to be baptized while in Russia. His objection that he was already a baptized Protestant was waved off.[20] Even today, a Western Christian (Catholic or Protestant) is, in the eyes of the Russian Orthodox Church, "improperly baptized," an inferior Christian, even worse than representatives of other religions. Religious pluralism is therefore another serious source of divergence with the United States.

Russia did not have in its history a period of state secularization, involving the separation of church and state, and school from church. Until 1917, the tsar was the head of the Orthodox Church. The "holy law" was a mandatory part of primary education, and Russian nationality was determined solely by belonging to the Orthodox religion. For centuries, administrative power and ideology stemmed from the same source—the upper echelons of the political system. Both sides profited tremendously from such a union—the church always had a government-like character, while the state, through the church, controlled and formed public sentiment. There would be no *gustibus non est disputandum*.[21] The administrative–ideological union of the church and the state meant that any sign of dissent was punished by both sides. Someone protesting the Orthodox Church immediately became a state criminal, while an opponent of the government was also considered a heretic. The Decembrists were declared to be heretics, for example, while Lev Tolstoy and Alexander Pushkin were saved only by their fame. In other words, unlike the United States, which was based on the ideas of the Reformation, Russia never even underwent such a reformation in the first place.

This led to an undeveloped tradition of free thought in Russia. Society became uncompromising and intolerant. The slogan of the Socialist Revolutionaries at the beginning of the twentieth century, "Those not with us are against us," reflected this perfectly. Soon afterward, the communists followed through on that principle by eliminating not only the Socialist Revolutionaries but all other parties as well. "The floor is yours, Mr. Pistol," wrote Vladimir Mayakovsky at the time. The large majority of intellectuals emigrated first to Europe, and later to the United States. The emigration began long before the communists. Sergey Soloviev wrote that not one (!) person sent abroad to study by Peter the Great ever returned home,[22] while great Russian patriots Alexander Herzen and Piotr Chaadaev spent their lives abroad.[23] Russian society learned and grew accustomed to living in conditions where ideology, spiritual values, faith, and ethics all "trickled down" from the top through the administrative organs. The central administration, the state, Russian federal agencies were always "masters of the mind" and this proved to be an important trait of the political culture.

Even the arrival of the communists in 1917 changed only the content of the system. Karl Marx replaced God, *The Communist Manifesto* replaced the Bible, and the party meeting replaced the sermon. Faith remained, except the state became communist instead of Christian Orthodox, and Marxism–Leninism began to be taught fastidiously in schools. The Siamese twins—no longer church and state, but state and party—continued to coexist in a mutually beneficial union. Mayakovsky has a poem about a Petersburg tram that was moving under capitalism, but on October 25, 1917 suddenly found itself under socialism. The tram didn't change, nor did the conductor, the rails and the passengers remained the same, but the tram now simply moved in a different political system.

Russian society was never able to develop its own system of norms and values, one that was independent from the state.[24] It was always an object of ideological manipulation by the central powers.[25] Vasily Klyuchevsky called it "the national education aspect of power" in Russia, with its main "pedagogical tool"—the infamous "tsar's cudgel" of Peter the Great.[26] Unlike in America, in Russia the state always told people how to think, specifying, in the words of Mayakovsky, "what is good and what is bad."

After the collapse of the Soviet Union, many Russians complained about the lack of an ideological compass, a system of values brought down from above without which they felt lost, and society began to crumble. Mikhail Gorbachev is seen by many in Russia not only as a man who destroyed the ideology of communism, but as a state criminal. That tram of Mayakovksy was suddenly riding in a democracy. That is why the search for a system of values and a new national idea is so important for Vladimir Putin—a search that wins him high levels of personal popularity.

Ideological dependence on the state results not only in great challenges toward creating a civil society, but also toward the average Russian's difficulty in comprehending the separation between state and society, and between the public and the private, that exists in the United States. America is viewed through the actions of the White House, and American society is seen as an object of direct manipulation by the federal government. Coming from their political culture, the Russian cannot comprehend, for instance, how the president of the United States may be limited in his powers. The story of the rejection of the infamous "Jackson-Vanick" trade agreement, when three consecutive presidents called for its annulment and were all rejected by Congress, makes no sense to him.

Russian writer Sergei Dovlatov, who immigrated to America in the 1970s, recalled that only there did he realize the "impotence of Mr. Reagan. You cannot force. You cannot command. The most inconsequential issues are put to a vote. And most importantly, everyone gives advice. And you must listen, or be branded as authoritarian."[27] The Russian, on the other hand, knows that all one must do is get to Putin, and the problem will be solved. Russian politicians who visit Washington spare no effort to get into the White House, assuming that it is the "American Kremlin." As they leave, they spread their hands in wonder, saying, "Why couldn't I do it? The president himself said that he agrees."

In his famous book *The Russian Idea*, Nikolai Berdyaev wrote that "the Russian moral consciousness is very different from the moral consciousness of Westerners; it is more Christian in form. Russian moral judgments are determined in relation to the person, not abstract law of property or government or the vague greater good. They search less for an organized society and more for a community, and have few pedagogical features."[28] Not laws and rules but trust should form the basis of a contract. Relationships between people are more important than what is written on paper, more important than procedure.[29] "God is not in strength but in truth"—words of Alexander Nevsky that are known to every Russian, meaning that not strength, law, or norms—America's strong points—should determine the order of things and relations between people but something spiritual, subjectively personal.[30] "Russian life does not acknowledge any laws," concluded Vasily Klyuchevsky.[31] Not the rule of law, but the rule of something that is just and proper. It is no accident that in answering the question, "What does the American lifestyle mean to you?" Russians put wealth, drive to succeed, and high quality of life at the top of the list, and justice, compassion, and humanity at the bottom.[32]

The restructuring of relations between the government and society, between the public and the personal is seen by Russians as destructive to the state, a betrayal of "what generations of Russians fought for," an abandonment of the Motherland. Russian history teaches that as soon as the institution of government is weakened, Russia is faced with issues of national independence and sovereignty. Gorbachev and Yeltsin destroyed that institution and in doing so put Russia on her knees in front of America. In 1999, only 7 percent thought that Gorbachev played a positive role in the country's history, while 34 percent considered it negative. Yeltsin was judged positively by 2 percent of the respondents, and negatively by 30 percent. The leaders judged as contributing the most positive things to Russian history were Leonid Brezhnev and Joseph Stalin, at 19 and 15 percent, respectively.[33] An independent Russia means a strong, powerful, well-armed state. Many think that its restoration should be the primary goal today, not human rights, elections, or freedom of the press. A strong society can only be a result of actions by a strong government. The American way—a strong government arising out of a strong society—is incompatible with the Russian situation, and its insistence by the United States upon Russia, in the form of democracy, is destroying the Russian state.

I could mention a whole number of other objective factors that influence the formation of the American image in Russia—from America's racial and ethnic characteristics to the deep divisions in the understanding of privacy and personal freedom. They have a fundamental, historical character, and depend little on Russia's political system or changes in American society. The events of 9/11 did not change these factors.[34] But on that day, the war on international terrorism had a major influence on the subjective perception of America. In that respect, since the end of the 1980s, two tendencies, which are at first glance contradictory, may be observed.

The first is that anti-American sentiments in Russia were either increasing or remaining stable at high levels. This period was marked by a feeling of national humiliation as a result of Russia's rapid decline relative to the USSR of the 1980s. Ideas of a conspiracy against Russia (this time, executed successfully by Washington) began circulating widely in Russian society, as did notions of hostility of foreign interests to Russia and the humiliating Russian dependence on the United States. In 1998, approximately a third of Russians believed in the "international conspiracy against Russia."[35] Many American stereotypes, instilled into the public's consciousness by communist propaganda, began to self-perpetuate. For example, 25 percent of Russians believed that Russia is doing badly precisely because its failure is beneficial to foreign countries.[36]

The society experienced growing disenchantment with the new sociopolitical realities. The economic crisis was directly reflected in the quality of life and the Russians' social security net. A noticeable portion of the population began forming a view that the major political triumphs of the period—a free press, democratic elections, and a reform of the government—were not worth so much suffering.[37] The United States was seen as the catalyst of this suffering, pushing the Russian government in that direction. The economic aid it provided to Russia was seen not only as a national humiliation, but a desire of the American corporations to position themselves in the Russian market. For example, in 1999, 75 percent of Russians believed that Russia is too dependent on the West.[38] From 1990 to 1993, the number of people who thought Russia was threatened with "the selling off of national riches to foreigners" increased from 48 to 73 percent.[39]

The exponential growth of contacts between the two societies should be judged as extremely positive. Yet, this contact became a sort of a "reality check," strengthening some mutual stereotypes and even creating new ones. When people who think they know each other start to live together, they often discover that they think differently, get in each other's way, and degenerate into petty but endless squabbles.[40] Their differences become more apparent. The initial period of embrace in the years of perestroika could be called a honeymoon. Continuing the metaphor, it could be said that both societies brought into their "marriage" the old problems and stereotypes.[41]

American passiveness toward Russian corruption and organized crime also contributed to the increase in anti-Americanism. The policies of privatization and the shock therapy undertaken by Yegor Gaidar with the recommendations of American economists, put most of the population on the brink of poverty while enriching a select few—primarily government officials and local bureaucrats.[42]

Yeltsin's team became a symbol of corruption, which did not prevent Washington from extending its enormous assistance, seeing a greater threat in the opposition—the communist Gennady Zyuganov. The presidential elections of 1996 were the apotheosis of this support. Half of the Russians, at the time, considered American allies to be Russian enemies, and more than a third were convinced of the threat of an American military invasion of Russia.[43] Many believed that Yeltsin was a tool of Washington, since he was working under their control to complete the extermination of their recent opponent.[44]

The loss of Russia's global influence was another factor of animosity toward the United States. For the people of Russia—the inheritor of the USSR, which achieved a status of a superpower by paying a hefty price of blood and sacrifice—the loss became a profound psychological trauma. The Americanization of former republics and allies, who sought to distance themselves from Russia, take up anti-Russian stances, and reorient themselves to the West with Washington's support, were seen as an especially negative development. Russia lost access to international markets, including those for arms, which were immediately taken over by American corporations. The number of Russians who thought that their country always provokes the hostility of other states grew from 42 percent in 1994 to 56 percent in 2000.[45]

A feeling that democratization was yet another method of undermining Russian influence in the world and subjugating Russia's former estates was fomenting. In response to the question, "Who should Russia strengthen its ties with?" in 1999, 16 percent pointed to Asia, and only 13 percent pointed to the United States. A year before that, 18 percent thought it necessary to strengthen ties with the United States, and only 9 percent with Asia.[46] That is, if on the question of America's role in Russia's domestic issues they were ambiguous, in trade and international matters they did not see the United States as a friend and ally. In April 1999, 48 percent of Russians considered the

United States an enemy in the international arena, while two years prior, only a third thought so. The number of people who saw China as Russia's enemy decreased six-fold, and, in 1999, fell to 3 percent.[47]

The second tendency in Russian society during the 1990s was related to the fact that the United States ceased to be some abstract "force of evil." America became more a nation of regular people in the form of tourists who visited Russia or seen by Russian tourists visiting it. American news agencies, government organizations, and NGOs began to display an active presence in Russia. Russians began traveling to the United States, buying products made there, and getting their share of American popular culture. Cultural and scientific exchange facilitated an evolution of perceptions. America was less and less "the government of America" of the Cold War and more of "the country of America," which could be judged in simple human terms. In 2001, the number of those who considered the United States an enemy state decreased from 52 to 43 percent, while the number of those who saw her as a friend grew from 32 to 43 percent. Sixty-five percent judged friendly relations with America as a positive development, while only 12 percent saw this as negative.[48]

Russians felt the responsibility for world order out of sheer inertia. The concept of "peaceful coexistence" between two major military powers continues to influence public sentiment.[49] It is understood that the United States has the same responsibility and, therefore, cannot be interested in weakening Russia, because no one needs a weak partner. That is, the suspicion toward American politics or the conviction of her aggressiveness did not abate, but human contact and common sense led many in Russia to see a chance for creating new relations that would be acceptable for both sides.

The Russian reaction to NATO actions in Yugoslavia in the spring of 1999 is a good illustration of this. They shocked Russian society. At the beginning of the bombing, the percentage of people responding favorably to America fell from 57 to 14 percent, while the number responding unfavorably grew from 28 to 72 percent.[50] The aggression, as the Russian press called the action, was considered a direct threat to their nation by 70 percent of Russians.[51] Sixty-one percent responded favorably to Evgeny Primakov's response, who, when he learned of the attack *en route* to the States on an official visit, turned his airplane around and went home.[52] Sixty-three percent placed the blame for the events on NATO, and only 6 percent on Yugoslavia.[53] Relations with the United States worsened (51 percent), the number of people opposing the relationship increased.[54] Twenty-seven percent thought that the United States had benefited as a result of the war, while only 1 percent thought the Kosovar Serbs did.[55]

But, on the other hand, the explosion of anti-Americanism ran head-first into the well-defined boundaries of realism—namely, the desire to avoid a military conflict with the United States at all costs. Eighty-six percent thought Russia should not engage itself in such a conflict; only 13 percent supported shipping arms to Yugoslavia, 4 percent supported sending volunteers, and 3 percent supported severing diplomatic ties with the United States. Two months after the start of the bombings, a more balanced assessment could be observed. The number of people who blamed the West for the conflict decreased from 63 to 49 percent, while the number of those who supported strengthening ties with the United States increased from 26 to 59 percent.[56]

Similar tendencies could be observed during the U.S. Iraqi campaign in the spring 2003. From the campaign's very beginning, the Russian media mounted an unprecedented anti-American attack. In the March of 2003, according to VTsIOM data, 83 percent of Russian citizens responded with indignation to American actions in Iraq, and only 2 percent approved of these actions. Fourteen percent of the people characterized relations between Russia and the United States as tense, against 6 percent in August 2002. From November 2002 to March 2003, the number of Russians who expressed negative or extremely negative sentiments toward America rose from 29 to 55 percent.[57] Seventy percent considered America as a conqueror, not a liberator of Iraq. In March 2003, 70 percent said that their feelings toward Saddam Hussein were either positive or neutral. The number of people who thought that the United States played a positive role in the world dropped sharply, from 23 percent in August 2002 to 14 percent in March 2003.[58]

The anti-American hysteria in the Russian media continued until April 2, 2003, when President Putin stated that Russia is not interested in an American defeat in Iraq. The tone of the Russian press changed immediately. Pragmatic considerations began to take over. The number of people who expressed positive sentiments about Saddam fell from 23 percent in March to 10 percent in April, while those who expressed negative sentiments more than doubled—from 14 to 29 percent.[59] At the end of April, according to FOM data, the number of respondents who felt positive about the United States was over 50 percent, and 70 percent supported maintaining close relations between the two countries. Only 5 percent backed the contrary stance.[60]

Approximately the same reaction can be discerned in other uneasy moments of the Russian–American relationship—NATO's eastward expansion, U.S. withdrawal from the ABM treaty,[61] differences over Chechnya, the Winter 2002 Olympics, and trade wars over steel and poultry.[62] On the one hand, anti-American sentiment grew, but on the other, an orientation toward a union with the United States remained strong.

Anti-American phobia, skepticism, disillusionment, and suspicion were counterbalanced to an increasing extent not only by the "humanizing" of America, but also by practical considerations. If the United States wants to strengthen ties with Russia for its own selfish purposes, Russia should use the situation to its advantage. In the mass consciousness, the idea of integration with America and the West picked up speed during the 1990s. In 1999, 63 percent thought that strengthening relations with the United States was important for Russia.[63] Rapprochement with America was becoming an independent Russian priority. More and more people saw in this a necessary pre-condition for Russia's economic and political renaissance, and its full entry into global civilization. In the summer of 2001, 73 percent of respondents said that they viewed the United States in a positive light, while 22 percent viewed it as negative; 77 percent noted that they felt positive toward the American people, while only 9 percent viewed them negatively.[64]

In the period between the Yugoslavian crisis and the events of 9/11, one could observe a decrease in both negative and highly positive judgments of the United States, with the concurrent increase in neutral assessments. Since then, this tendency has stabilized. In September of 2001, 46 percent were neutral in their feelings toward the United States. Polls from March 2002 and February 2003 showed the same results.[65] That is, the emotional approach to the issue waned while a pragmatic approach became more prevalent. Emotional indifference is a necessary component for a rational–pragmatic perception.[66] President Putin, while making a strong political statement by announcing his unconditional support for the United States in the wake of 9/11, was not contradicting the evolution of his country's public opinion.

The position of the Russian elite proved to be a greater obstacle for Putin. Throughout the 1990s, this elite had been the driving force for the Westernization of Russia. One of the main methods that the new generation of politicians used in fighting the old Soviet *nomenklatura* was the deliberate, *accuratissime*[67] Americanization of life and culture, which corresponded to their sociopolitical and economic agenda. To be "pro-American" at the time, in the eyes of a casual participant, meant being a progressive liberal, a proponent of the free market, a free press, and human rights; that is, to have an image that was in direct opposition to that of the representatives of the old communist ideology. Orienting toward the United States brought political power.

But the situation gradually changed. On the one hand, as compensation for the national humiliation, the disillusionment with the new social ideals and a demand for a return to the old social and political ways, which were thought to have been discarded, returned. Thus, in the winter of 2001, to the question "Did the democrats of early perestroika bring Russia more harm than good?," 47 percent said "more harm," and only 2 percent said "more good." Sixty-six percent said that reforms of the Gaidar administration were unnecessary and destructive, and 50 percent were willing to return to the pre-perestroika USSR.[68]

The idea of a Russian "special way" began gaining popularity. In the spring of 2000, 60 percent of respondents said that Russia should go its own way, and 18 percent that it should use the path taken by the USSR.[69] Debates about the Russian "national idea"[70] and the nature of Russian government began heating up, while the political role of the Russian Orthodox Church increased.[71] The belief in the inability of Western analytical tools to comprehend Russian society, as well as the concept of Russian uniqueness and its incompatibility with Western sociopolitical norms received mass support.[72] There was a movement to buy domestically made products, and nostalgia for the cultural values of the Soviet times: films of the 1950–1970s gathered huge television audiences, and radio stations playing Soviet-era music gained record numbers of listeners. The change in mood was reflected in the elite, parts of which took on extremely anti-American positions.[73]

On the other hand, further Americanization for certain Russian circles was a fraught with the possible loss of comfort, of transparency in the decision-making processes, the opening of financial flows, the battle against corruption and favoritism, the rule of law, and respect for human rights and ethnic minorities. Americanization went too far—the elite began losing control over the news agencies, which it had only recently been using in its own interests to Americanize the country and prevail over communist bureaucrats. In other words, the further popularization of the American theory and practice became, in its own way, a *censor morum*, and undermined the strength and omnipotence of the new Russian authorities. They couldn't allow that to happen.

The Russian elite began to feel first-hand the consequences of the fall in international influence and the loss of choices for their country. A sense of jealousy toward the American elite began to increase—not material jealousy (most Russian politicians have more wealth and assets than their American counterparts), but "geopolitical jealousy" of America's military, political, and diplomatic choices, jealousy toward their ability to fulfill their agenda. At the beginning, the new elite naively assumed that it would play the same role in the world as the Soviet elite once did, that is, *idem et caeteris*.[74] The realization that this was not to be turned into anti-Americanism among the new ruling elite.

By the end of the 1990s, Russia began transforming itself into a country with a pro-American or neutral population, and a political elite that viewed the United States with skepticism, suspicion, and hostility.[75] Yet, a small but powerful pro-American group also formed in the elite—one that after 9/11 began to be associated with President Putin and his inner circle.[76] Speaking in front of Russian diplomats in July 2002, Putin declared that the Russian–American relationship was based on "a new reading of the national interests of both countries, as well as a common understanding of the nature of global threats." He called for the development of a "trusting partnership between Russia and the US."[77]

The terrorist acts of 9/11 became events of historic magnitude, altering many global processes. It is too early to speak of their influence on the Russian citizens' objective perceptions of the United States. Not enough time has passed for emotions to cease playing a defining role. The uniqueness of the Russian reaction is tied to the fact that the event that started a new epoch happened not in Russia, as it did 10 years ago, but on the territory of a former foe, which had defeated Russia in the Cold War. Many Russians saw this as the true end of that war, because both countries now had common priorities.[78] Thus, 40 percent believe that the terrorist threat is a global one, and that the attack could have occurred in Europe or in Russia. Yet, 63 percent believed that this was payback for America's foreign policy.[79]

Immediate reactions to the terrorist attacks were extremely emotional. "Pity and compassion" were named by 50 percent of the respondents, "fear, anger, and shock" by another 36 percent, "indifference" by only 2 percent. Seventy-nine percent said they condemn the people who celebrated the attacks. If before the terrorist acts only 20 percent thought that the United States played a positive role in the world, while 58 percent thought it played a negative role, the numbers after the attack changed to 26 and 48 percent, respectively. The number of those who saw America as an unfriendly state decreased from 52 to 43 percent, while the number of those who saw it as a friend increased from 32 to 43 percent.[80]

The 1990s saw the development of the unchallenged and undeniable power of the United States. But on September 11, "a nameless and omnipotent evil not only destroyed the power of the US, but called into question the possibility of the existence of a power that can withstand such evil."[81] For Russians, who, in the words of an old remark by Winston Churchill, respect and fear nothing more than power, the blatant vulnerability of America was an important psychological factor. There was a reassessment of the concepts of "us" versus "them." Gradually, in both countries, an understanding emerged that our differences, for all their relevance, are immeasurably smaller than traditionally thought. It could be said that after 9/11, a real long-term basis for strategic union, one that isn't politically adversarial, could be created. In many ways, it is still a *tabula rasa*. But Putin's course of rapprochement with America began receiving widespread support. After George Bush's visit to Moscow in May 2002, Putin's rating rose another 7 points and reached 75 percent. Many judged the meeting itself in a positive light as well.[82]

The popularity of Putin's foreign policy is based on the fact that he doesn't go for concessions, but demands "equal cooperation"—so think 50 percent of Russians. Twelve percent think he received unilateral concessions from America, and 13 percent think he makes concessions to America. By comparison, 42 percent think that Gorbachev made unilateral concessions to America, 46 percent think Yeltsin did so,[83] and neither put "a trusting partnership" with America as one of their goals. In public opinion, Putin's pro-Americanism does not contradict his image as a protector of Russian interests.

The number of people who condemn America for something regularly exceeds 50 percent, while 70 percent of Russians are for "Russia and the US having a closer relationship." Many think that the terrorist acts helped America understand Russia. This gives Moscow a chance for a substantial increase of its global influence—not at the cost of American influence, but in tandem with it. America can effectively respond to the threat it was given and carry the burden of global leadership only in a union with Russia, accepting Russia's just and uncompromising stance on battling global terrorism. So think 60 percent of Russians.[84]

Russia is an example of a country where there is a perpetual distinction between the deep-seated objective perception of America and the public sentiment at any given time. That is why it is so easy to make a mistake, to build a political trajectory, or make decisions on the basis of the latest opinion poll. By the time the decisions are enforced, the moods will change and the policy will be dissonant with the sentiment. Such miscalculations, on the parts of both Russian and American elites, are not uncommon. On the other hand, to construct an agenda based on fundamentals is also dangerous, since public opinion could the politician's popularity shift dramatically, thus calling into question. But in a Russian–American relationship, only such an approach will be strategically successful. Such was Putin's decision, for example, to support America after 9/11.

Alexander Pushkin once noted that he was annoyed by many Russian attitudes, but became even more annoyed when foreigners pointed them out. Even today, many Russians would concur with the words of their great poet. Isn't "Love it or leave it!" a famous American expression? The evolution of Russian perceptions about America reflects a centuries-old Russian conflict between a tendency to integrate with the Western world and a desire to maintain its uniqueness. No one really knows if this conflict will reach a solution, but we can be sure that the United States will remain a yardstick by which Russians continue to measure themselves.

NOTES

The author wishes to thank Leon Aron, director of Russian studies at the American Enterprise Institute, and Barbara Friedman from the University of Missouri for valuable comments made during the preparation of this chapter.

1. Vasily Klyuchevsky, *Сочинения в девяти томах*, vol. 9 (Moscow: Mysl', 1990), p. 386.
2. Suffice it to say that the Russian language has no word for "privacy"—evidence, in my opinion, of the existence of two widely divergent principles of society in Russia and the United States.
3. As a February 2, 2002 survey by Russia's Public Opinion Fund (hereafter POF) showed, the Olympics sharply changed Russian opinion of the United States. Only 17% of Russians called the United States a friendly nation, while 71% thought it hostile. As a result of the Olympics, the number of Russians who viewed the United States positively decreased sharply by 12%, which equaled the increase in the number of people who thought that the United States was Russia's enemy. By comparison, before the Olympics, 29% of people saw America unfavorably, and 32% favorably. A few weeks after the Olympics, the surge of anti-Americanism began to decline once again. The United States was viewed favorably by 49%, and unfavorably by 41%. See http://top.rbc.ru/index2.shtml for 03.07.2002 and 04.01.2002.
4. See A. Oslon, "Реакция на 11 сентября в российском общественном мнении," in *Америка: взгляд из России. До и после 11 сентября* (Moscow: POF, 2001), p. 31.
5. See *Dominant*, no. 6, 19, 23, 37, 47; 2002, no. 6,19 (Moscow: POF, 2001).
6. See G. Diligensky, *«Запад» и российское общество* (Moscow: POF, 2001), July 12, http://www.fom.ru/reports/frames/d012541.html.
7. See Alexander Zinoviev, *Запад* (Moscow: Tsentrpoligraf, 2000).

8. Alexander Block formulated this forcefully in his poem "Scythians."

9. Sergey Soloviev, *Чтения и рассказы по русской истории* (Moscow: Pravda, 1990), p. 439.

10. Nikolai Danilevsky, *Россия и Европа* (Moscow: Kniga, 1991), p. 498.

11. Ibid., pp. 68–69.

12. This conflict unfolds in *War and Peace* as well. For this reason, the traditional English-language translation of the title may confuse the reader. In Russian, the word "mir" can mean both "world" and "peace." A more correct translation would probably be "War and the World."

13. Lev Gumilev, *От Руси до России: очерки этнической истории* (Moscow: Svarog and K, 2002), p. 217.

14. Memoirs of V. Pecherin, *Замогильные записки (Apologia pro vita mea)* were published in the book *Русское общество 30-х годов XIX века. Люди и идеи: Мемуары современников* (Moscow: Nauka, 1989), pp. 148–311. Pecherin propounded the idea of rejecting "the tyranny of materialist civilization," and thought that humankind's salvation lay in religion, not science. Pitirim Sorokin thought that Russia and the United States are bound to have a binding peace, since they have similar systems of values and institutions. See Pitirim Sorokin, *Россия и Соединенные Штаты* (New York: Chekhov Publishing, 1944).

15. An interesting related fact is that in the initial drafts of his novel, *The Idiot*, Fyodor Dostoyevsky calls his protagonist Count Myshkin "a Count of Christ." See F. Dostoyevsky, *Собрание сочинений в 10 томах*, vol. 6 (Moscow: State Literature Publishing House, 1957), p. 709.

16. This idea is widespread in Russian culture. Recall that in *Crime and Punishment*, Dostoyevsky brings together Raskolnikov and Sonya Marmeladov, juxtaposing pragmatic reason with emotion. Sonya is also a criminal, but she criminalizes herself for the sake of others. It is better to be the victim, the object of aggression, rather than the aggressor, says Dostoyevsky.

17. Soloviev, *Чтения и рассказы по русской истории, op.cit.* pp. 493–494.

18. In trying to understand the origin of Russian anti-Americanism, I often see a double reflexive emerging: we don't like them because we think that they don't like us.

19. Russia's biggest modernizer, Peter the Great, once said to his circle of advisors, "We need Europe for a few more decades, and then we can turn our back on it." See Klyuchevsky, *Сочинения в 9 томах*, vol. 8, Articles, p. 397. Since then, in moments of improvement in relations between Russia and the West, such talk is regularly heard among the Russian political establishment.

20. Georges Nivat, "Расхожее мнение, что у нас на Западе царит безверье, ошибочно . . ." *Kontinent*, no. 112 (2002), pp. 247–248.

21. One can't argue about taste (lat.).

22. Soloviev, *Чтения и рассказы по русской истории*, p. 447.

23. Contemporary emigrant poet Igor Guberman wrote about this once: "The muted Russian soul / eschews associations / and takes on foreign

languages / with glossaries and detestations. / How queer the hue of Russian life / composed o'er so many centuries / its conscience talks to Russia / albeit in foreign languages." I. Guberman, *Гарики на каждый день* (Moscow: EMIA, 1992), pp. 221–222.

24. Dostoyevsky's *The Idiot* is interesting in that respect. Dostoyevsky tries to prove that the necessary basis for public life is not the law or the state, but the moral authority of the church, and that Russians can develop successfully only within a framework of the ideals of the Russian Orthodox Church. His protagonist Count Myshkin is, in the words of Saltykov-Schedrin, a man who had attained "a complete moral and spiritual balance."

25. Interestingly, the eminent sociologist Pitirim Sorokin thought, on the contrary, that the political and economic roots of the democratic system are identical in Russia and the United States, having grown out of a peasant system of values. See Pitirum Sorokin, *Россия и Соединенные Штаты* (New York: Chekhov Publishing, 1944), pp. 38, 64, 75, 88–89.

26. Klyuchevsky, *Сочинения в 9 томах*, vol. 8: Articles pp. 378, 383–384.

27. Sergei Dovlatov, *Проза*, vol. 2, p. 135

28. Nikolai Berdyaev, *Русская идея: Основные проблемы русской мысли XIX века и начала XX века* (Paris: YMCA Press, 1971), p. 243.

29. Nikolai Berdyaev writes that "rationalism is the fatal sin of the West . . . Russia is free of the sin of rationalism, which binds one to necessity." See *О России и русской Философской культуре*, (Moscow: Nauka, 1990), pp. 81–82. Alexander Herzen sharply criticized the idea of a parliamentary democracy and thought the *русский мужик* will save the world.

30. One recalls the history of a judicial error in Lev Tolstoy's novel *Воскресение* and the fate of its heroine Katyusha Maslova.

31. Klyuchevsky, *Сочинения в девяти томах*, vol. 9 с. 424.

32. ФОМ. *Американский образ жизни.* 05.31.2001; http://www.fom.ru/survey/dominant/203/517/1746.html.

33. http://www.fom.ru/survey/finfo/579/1316/4569.html.

34. According to an POF survey from October 2001, 80% of Russians said that their perception of the United States had not changed after the attacks. www.fom.ru/survey/dominant/290/721/2358.html.

35. *Современное российское общество: переходный период* (Moscow: Institute of Sociology RAN, 1998), p. 22.

36. *Мониторинг общественного мнения: экономические и социальные перемены.* Journal of the All-Russian Center for the Study of Public Opinion (hereafter—ACSPO), 1997, no. 1, с. 12; no. 2, с. 21.

37. As an example, I could cite a POF survey from the fall of 1999. To the question "Which were the hardest years of your life," 65% said 1996–1999, 33%—1991–1995, 5%—1986–1990, while only 6% chose the years of World War II, and 3% the first post-war decade. See http://www.fom.ru/reports/frames/t906402.html. On the question of which years were the best, 27% said 1976–1980, another 27%—1981–1985, and 20%—1971–1975. See http://www.fom.ru/reports/

frames/t906401.html. Answering to the question of when, if ever, they wanted to emigrate to the West, 57% said they desired to do so during Yeltsin's rule. See http://www.fom.ru/reports/frames/t907309.html.

38. ФОМ-ИНФО. Moscow: POF, 1999, no. 45.

39. *Мониторинг общественного мнения: экономические и социальные перемены*. Journal of ACSPO, 1994, no. 1, с. 16.

40. Sergei Dovlatov recalled what irritated the Russians who met Americans for the first time: "Americans are naïve, callous, heartless. One cannot be friends with Americans. They drink vodka in microscopic doses. It's like drinking from toothpaste caps. They are not concerned with global problems. Their main slogan is 'Look at things simply!' And no ecumenical grief! When they divorce, they go to a lawyer. (Instead of pouring out their hearts to colleagues.) They describe their dreams to psychoanalysts. (Instead of calling a friend in the middle of the night.) The country is in disorder. Gas is getting expensive. The blacks are everywhere. Most importantly—democracy is threatened. If not today then tomorrow it will stagger and collapse. But we will save it!" Dovlatov, *Проза*, p. 135.

41. One amusing but typical example of the persistence of stereotypes is a magnum opus prepared in the years of perestroika by a large collective of leading Americanists and published under the editorship of Yevgeny Primakov, G. Arbatov, and others: *Современные Соединенные Штаты Америки: Энциклопедический справочник* (Moscow: Political Literature Publishing House, 1988). In it, the chapter devoted to the Communist Party of the United States is longer than the space devoted to the rest of the political parties combined, including the Democratic and the Republican. (pp. 94–101). American foreign policy is described as unambiguously aggressive, militaristic, and conducted in bad faith (pp. 262–271), the economy is described as constantly in crisis (pp. 136–140), and the mass media are characterized as having a "propaganda complex" (p. 404).

42. An interesting fact related to this is that the number of Russians who are against American investment into their regional economy grew from 32% in June 1995 to 40% in October 1998 to 46% in June 1999. See http://www.fom.ru/reports/frames/t905314.html.

43. *Современное российское общество: переходный период*, p. 22.

44. In August 1999, 44% considered the United States as the biggest source of threat for a nuclear conflict. http://www.fom.ru/reports/frames/of19993406.html.

45. *Общественное мнение-2000. По материалам исследований* (Moscow: ASCPO, 2000), p. 86. A POF survey from April 1999 showed that from August 1997 to April 1999—the month of the NATO bombings in Yugoslavia—the number of people who thought Russia had foreign enemies grew from 44 to 73%. See http://www.fom.ru/reports/frames/short/of1999160.html.

46. http://www.fom.ru/reports/frames/of19992704.html.

47. http://www.fom.ru/reports/frames/of19991601.html.
48. www.fom.ru/survey/dominant/310/761/2510.html.
49. Incidentally, such an approach has remained popular after 9/11; 40% assess Russian–American relations from this point of view. www.fom.ru/survey/dominant/310/761/25510.html.
50. http://www.fom.ru/reports/frames/of19991503.html.
51. http://www.fom.ru/reports/frames/o904402.html. The same tendency can be observed in surveys conducted by VTsIOM. See www.wciom.ru/vciom/new/press/press020909_22.htm
52. http://www.fom.ru/reports/frames/t904209.html.
53. http://www.fom.ru/reports/frames/of19991703.html.
54. http://www.fom.ru/reports/frames/of19991802.html.
55. http://www.fom.ru/reports/frames/t905406.html.
56. http://www.fom.ru/reports/frames/t904208.html; http://www.fom.ru/reports/frames/of19993003.html; http://www.fom.ru/reports/frames/o904803.html; http://www.fom.ru/reports/frames/o904402.html; http://www.fom.ru/reports/frames/of19991503.html; http://www.fom.ru/reports/frames/of19991703.html; http://www.fom.ru/reports/frames/of19991802.html; http://www.fom.ru/reports/frames/t905406.html. It must be noted that this didn't prevent public opinion from accusing Yeltsin of inaction and the betrayal of fellow Slavs, and led to his popularity falling to its lowest point.
57. VTsIOM Press Release #9, March 25, 2003; www.wciom.ru/vciom/new/press030325_09.htm. Press Release #9, April 30, 2003; www.wciom.ru/vciom/new/press030430_13.htm.
58. FOM, April 24, 2003; www.fom.ru/survey/finfo/804/1616/6992.html.
59. FOM, May 5, 2003; www.fom.ru/survey/dominant/810/1629/6251.html.
60. FOM, April 24, 2003; www.fom.ru/survey/dominant/806/1620/6216.html.
61. Only 8% of Russians judged the U.S. withdrawal from the treaty in positive terms, and only 5% thought that it may positively reflect on Russian–American relations. See http://www.fom.ru/reports/frames/of014901.html.
62. According to a POF survey from March 2002, 79% of Russians supported a ban on the import of U.S. poultry. As main reasons for their support, they said that it would be a response to the limitations on Russian steel exports to the United States, the judging scandals at the Olympics and the appearance of American military inspectors in Georgia. The poultry ban, in the opinion of the majority, demonstrated "Russian independence from American and even an ability to oppose it." See http://www.fom.ru/reports/frames/d021130.html; http://www.fom.ru/reports/frames/d021108.html.
63. http://fom.ru/survey/finfo/578/1315/4564.html.
64. www.wciom.ru/vciom/new/press/press020909_22 htm.

65. CDI Russia Weekly # 243 February 7, 2003.

66. Interestingly, according to surveys conducted in France and Russia in the summer of 2002, Russians and French hold similar opinion of America; i.e., Russian perceptions have shifted closer to the European ones. See http://www.wciom.ru/wciom/new/public/public_own/020909_usa.htm.

67. Thorough (lat.).

68. *Общественное мнение-2000. По материалам исследований*, p. 82.

69. Ibid., pp. 81–82. Since the 1990s, the great majority of citizens support "the special Russian way." See L. Gudkov, *Русский неотрадиционализм*. In the journal *Мониторинг* (Moscow: ASCFA, 1997), no. 2, pp. 5–8; G. Dilegenskiy, *«Запад» в российском общественном сознании*, in the journal *Общественные науки и современность* (Moscow: INION, 2000), no. 5, pp. 71–89.

70. The Eurasian idea has once again begun gaining popularity in Russian society. Its intellectual elaborator has become the "Eurasia" party, with Alexander Dugin at the helm. See A. Dugin, *Евразийский путь как национальная идея* (Moscow: Arktogea-Center, 2002). It contends, in part, that "Russia either has a Eurasian future or none at all. Our task is to comprehend and triumphantly solidify around the world the Russian Eurasian truth" pp. 15, 17.

71. Danilevskii showed in his famous book *Россия и Европа [Russia and Europe]* not only Russia's uniqueness, but even the uniqueness of the Slav people, to which, in the words of philosopher Nikolai Strakhov, "belongs an exclusive position among other nations, to which history has no adequate equal," Nikolai Strakhov, *О книге Данилевского «Россия и Европа»*, In Nikolai Danilevsky, *Россия и Европа* (Moscow: Kniga, 1991), p. 515.

72. See Fyodor Tyutchev: "You cannot reason Russia out / you cannot measure it with tape / It is a wholly different state / With Russia, you should just have faith." This famous poem was used as a traditional form of self-justification for Russians, not only for the West, but even more frequently for themselves. I could cite a poem of Mikhail Lermontov, which is also frequently used to justify Russia's "uniqueness": "I love my land, but with a curious love / My reason cannot conquer it / No glory bought with blood / No calmness filled with prideful trust / No cherished oaths of cloudy pasts / Can stir within me pleasant dreams."

73. As an extreme example, I could cite an article by the editor-in-chief of a popular newspaper *Завтра* Alexander Prokhanov, author of the novel *Господин Гексоген*, which received the most prestigious Russian literature award in 2002: "Once again the dreadful starred-and-striped cobra is rising across the ocean on its sinister tail, suspended over the world, fixing its merciless reptile gaze toward Iraq. America, gone mad on Yugoslavian and Afghani blood, drunk from its unpunished acts, delirious with world dominations, is continuing to control the history of the world, fixing its course with its super-smart weapons, with its spent uranium cores, its vile provocations comparable to the Gulf of Tonkin incident, or the

destruction of its own skyscrapers in Manhattan. Americans are disgusting to everyone. Nations look with repulsion upon the transatlantic boor, who has only one ally—Israel, the yellowest, most six-sided star on the American flag, which will inevitably fade with the next sunrise. 'Dear Lord, bring ruin upon America,' "—pray people on all the continents at the dawn and dusk of their days. A. Prokhanov, *Ирак, брат мой*, in *Завтра*, August 20, 2002, Even more picturesque is the opinion of the leader of LDPR, vice-speaker of the state, Duma Vladimir Zhirinovsky: http://www.compromat.ru/main/zhirinovskiy/bushu.htm.

74. Same for others (lat.).

75. In May of 2001, POF asked this question of the Russian elite: "Do you think the majority of Russians see America favorably, unfavorably, or neutrally?" Surprisingly, the answers were the opposite of the masses' opinion: 20% thought the Russians see the United States favorably, 40%—unfavorably. See Oslon, *Америка: взгляд из России. До и после 11 сентября*, p. 31.

76. It's interesting to note that Putin's support for the United States in the immediate wake of 9/11 increased his rating in Russia. See Oslon, "Реакция на 11 сентября в российском общественном мнении," in *Америка: взгляд из России. До и после 11 сентября*, p. 34.

77. *Выступление президента Российской Федерации В. В. Путина на расширенном совещании с участием послов Российской Федерации в МИД России*, July 12, 2001, http://www.president.kremlin.ru/text/appears/2002/07/17449.shtml.

78. It must be said that the majority of Russians (60% in the summer of 2002) did not think that the Cold War was over, and among those who did think it was, the ending date was "when Yeltsin began drinking with the Americans." See http://www.fom.ru/reports/frames/d022233.html.

79. Oslon, *Америка: взгляд из России. До и после 11 сентября*, pp. 27, 167.

80. Ibid., pp. 31, 137, 166, 201. It should be noted that according to surveys by the ASCPA, a year after the tragedy, the Russians' opinions did not change significantly—52% continued to believe that the Americans got what they deserved and that "now they know first-hand how the people in Hiroshima and Nagasaki, in Iraq and Yugoslavia felt during the bombings"; 42% did not believe so. See http://gazeta.ru/print/2002/09/11/vrossiinezal.shtml.

81. Oslon, "10 тезисов о Новой Эпохе", in *Америка: взгляд из России. До и после 11 сентября*, p. 10.

82. http://www.wciom.ru/vciom/new/public/public_own/020909_usa.htm; http://www.wciom.ru/vciom/new/press/press020517_12.htm.

83. http://www.wciom.ru/vciom/new/public/public_own/020507_politru20.htm.

84. http://gazeta.ru/print/2002/09/11/vrossiinezal.shtml; *Америка: взгляд из России. До и после 11 сентября*, pp. 50–54.

7

SAUDI PERCEPTIONS OF THE
UNITED STATES SINCE 9/11

F. Gregory Gause, III

There is no bilateral relationship that was more affected by the 9/11 attacks than the Saudi–American relationship. On the American side, the reason is obvious: of the 19 hijackers of the 4 planes that crashed into the World Trade Center, the Pentagon, and a field in central Pennsylvania, 15 were from Saudi Arabia. Osama bin Laden, the leader of the group behind the attacks, also is from Saudi Arabia. As Americans learned more about the hijackers, bin Laden, and the more general *salafi* movement, popular anger against Saudi Arabia grew. According to a poll by Zogby International, in January 2001, 56 percent of Americans polled viewed Saudi Arabia favorably and 28 percent unfavorably. In December 2001, those numbers had basically reversed, with only 24 percent viewing Saudi Arabia favorably and 58 percent unfavorably.[1] Much of the American political and media elite, which had generally accepted the U.S.–Saudi relationship—an exchange of security for oil, to simplify—began to question the value for the United States of a close relationship with Riyadh. While the Bush administration has asserted since 9/11 that the relationship with Saudi Arabia remains solid, there is no question that the unprecedented public focus on Saudi Arabia (even greater than during the 1973–1974 oil embargo, I would argue) has shaken the foundations of the bilateral relationship.

A similar process took place in Saudi Arabian public opinion after the 9/11 attacks. Popular disaffection with the United States was already substantial before the attacks. American policy on the Israeli–Palestinian conflict and on Iraqi sanctions was generally unpopular. Bin Laden and other Saudi dissidents had successfully raised the issue of the American military presence in the Kingdom. Reacting to the intense media scrutiny on Saudi Arabia in the United States that followed the attacks, the Saudi government took a number of steps to distance itself from the United States. These moves, in effect, opened the door to more open expression of anti-Americanism in Saudi Arabia than is usually permitted. The Saudi government, perhaps taken aback by the vigor of those sentiments, began, in the spring of 2002, to send signals that there are limits to the anti-Americanism that it will tolerate at home. While this was happening, a vigorous debate emerged within Saudi *salafi* circles about the appropriateness of even considering dialogue with the West in general and the United States in particular.

This chapter will consider the question of Saudi views toward the United States from these various perspectives, with special attention to how the government's policy is both affected and affects general public opinion and the debates within the *salafi* trend.

THE SAUDI GOVERNMENT AND PUBLIC OPINION POST-9/11

The first response of officials in the Saudi government to the attacks of 9/11 was to deny any Saudi responsibility for them, even to deny that any Saudis were involved (carefully noting that bin Laden, stripped of his citizenship in 1994, was no longer a Saudi).[2] The focus on Saudi Arabia in the American media led a number of Saudi officials, including Crown Prince Abdallah, to complain publicly that the Kingdom was being targeted in a "campaign" against it.[3] The Saudi government very publicly denied American forces the right to use Saudi bases for the air campaign in Afghanistan, even while quietly allowing the U.S. to use the command and control center at Prince Sultan Airbase, south of Riyadh, to coordinate that campaign.

Public disquiet over the course of events after 9/11 led Crown Prince Abdallah to hold a series of meetings with Saudis from a number of sectors (educators, police and security officials, army officers, religious scholars and officials) in October and November 2001 to explain his policy and the state of U.S.-Saudi relations. In one of these meetings, he revealed that, in August 2001, he had sent a letter to President Bush complaining of the American stand on the Arab–Israeli issue. In that letter, he said that differences between the two countries on that issue had grown so great that "from now on, you have your interests and the Kingdom has its interests, and you have your road and we have our road."[4] The context of Abdallah's public revelation of tensions with the United States was actually a defense of the value of the U.S.-Saudi relationship for the Palestinians. He went on to say that, because of his letter, the Bush administration shortly thereafter announced public support for the idea of a Palestinian state.[5] However, the fact that a Saudi leader publicly acknowledged such a dispute with the United States, undoubtedly, was meant to demonstrate that Riyadh was reflecting the views of its citizens on this issue.

These signals from the top of the Saudi ruling elite that all was not well in its relationship with the United States were taken by the Saudi media as a green light for criticism of the American response to the attacks of 9/11. Saudi accounts of the "media campaign" against the Kingdom in the United States accused the American media of practicing "psychological terrorism" against Saudi Arabia, emphasized that such criticism was inspired by "Zionist" elements, and called into question the "real" goals behind the American "war on terrorism."[6] Saudi newspaper coverage of the war in Afghanistan highlighted civilian deaths due to American bombing. The Saudi press published a number of stories about Saudis detained in the United States, some of which accused American authorities of mistreating those detained. During a visit to Saudi Arabia in January 2002, when I saw these stories in the local Saudi press, I was asked by a young Saudi journalist why the United States had a deliberate policy of mistreating Saudis in custody. When I questioned both the logic and the evidence underlying his assumption, he responded, "This is what is being said in the streets."

Public opinion polling in Saudi Arabia after 9/11 confirms widespread disagreement with, even hostility toward, the United States. A Gallup poll, conducted in late January–early-February 2002, reported that 64 percent of Saudi respondents viewed the United States either very unfavorably or most unfavorably. Majorities in the poll associated America with the adjectives "conceited, ruthless and arrogant." Fewer than 10 percent saw the United States as either friendly or trustworthy.[7] A Zogby International poll, conducted in March 2002, reported similar results. Only 30 percent of the Saudis polled supported American-led efforts to fight terrorism, while 57 percent opposed it; and only 43 percent had a favorable opinion of the American people, and 51 percent an unfavorable opinion—the highest unfavorable rating of the 8 Muslim countries in which the poll was conducted. The Zogby poll focused on specific sources of Saudi public antipathy toward Washington. Majorities looked favorably upon American science and technology (71 percent), American freedom and democracy (52 percent), American movies and television (54 percent), American education (58 percent). However, fewer than 10 percent viewed

U.S. policy in the Arab world or the Palestinian issue in a favorable light. Of those polled, 64 percent said that the Palestinian issue was either the most important or a very important political issue to them, and 79 percent said that they would have a more favorable view toward the United States if it "would apply pressure to ensure the creation of an independent Palestinian state."[8]

Anecdotal evidence supports the general impression left by the polling data that Saudi public opinion has been distinctly anti-American in the period following 9/11. Prince Nawwaf ibn Abd al-Aziz, the head of the Saudi foreign intelligence bureau (al-'istikhbarat), told the *New York Times* in January 2002 that the vast majority of Saudi young adults felt sympathy for bin Laden's cause (which parts of the bin Laden agenda his "cause" included is not made clear), even though they rejected the attacks on New York and Washington. The paper reported that a Saudi intelligence survey conducted in October 2001 of educated Saudis between the ages of 25 and 41 concluded that 95 percent of them supported Mr. bin Laden's cause.[9] While it is difficult to judge their effectiveness, there have been a number of grassroots initiatives in Saudi Arabia urging the boycott of American products and American franchises since 9/11.[10]

The upsurge of Israeli–Palestinian violence in April 2002, with Israel reoccupying major West Bank towns, saw popular demonstrations in the Kingdom, very unusual events in this tightly controlled political system, in support of the Palestinian cause and in protest of the strong American–Israeli relationship. One of the demonstrations was held in front of the American consulate in Dhahran.[11] While a large part of the general anti-Americanism evident in Saudi public opinion comes from *salafi* and other Islamist political quarters, it is not restricted to the Islamist tendency. The April 2002 Israeli–Palestinian violence, led about 70 Saudi public intellectuals, many identified with more liberal interpretations of politics and of Islam, to issue a very anti-American statement, including the following lines: "We consider the United States and the current American administration to be the nursemaid of international terror. It forms with Israel the real axis of terror and evil in the world."[12]

Saudi public opinion anger toward the United States over the Palestinian issue is relatively easy to document, given the Saudi government's willingness to allow its citizens to express themselves on this issue. It is harder to gauge how important other parts of bin Laden's "cause"—his objection to the presence of American military forces in Saudi Arabia, to the American position on Iraq, to American support for undemocratic regimes in the Arab world, including

Saudi Arabia—are in accounting for anti-American sentiment in the Kingdom. Undoubtedly, all play a role, but it is difficult to tell how much of a role. What is unquestionable, however, from both anecdotal and more scientific methods, is that anti-Americanism in Saudi Arabia since 9/11 has been a substantial public opinion force.[13]

THE DEBATE IN *SALAFI* SAUDI CIRCLES ABOUT 9/11 AND THE UNITED STATES

Much of the public opinion discourse on the United States, as on any political issue in Saudi Arabia, is driven by religious circles—both the official Islamic establishment supported by the Saudi state, by dissident *salafis* both at home and abroad, and by an interesting group of *salafi* Islamists who float in between those two groups. It is these circles that have had a monopoly on state-permitted discourse in Saudi Arabia, and in turn been promoted by the Saudi state both at home and abroad, for decades. They, therefore, have access to the institutional resources to be heard, even when what they are saying might discomfort the Saudi rulers. They certainly do not encompass the entire universe of opinion in Saudi Arabia, but they represent the most important (though very possibly not a numerical majority) and organized public opinion tendency in the Kingdom.

The official religious establishment in Saudi Arabia, closely allied to the state, denounced bin Laden and the attacks of 9/11 from the outset, and in unambiguous terms. The Mufti of Saudi Arabia, Shaykh Abd al-Aziz Al Alshaykh, on September 15, 2001, issued a statement saying the attacks "run counter to the teachings of Islam," characterizing them as "gross crimes and sinful acts."[14] One day earlier, the chairman of Saudi Arabia's Supreme Judicial Council, Shaykh Salih bin Muhammad Al-Ludhaydan, termed the attacks a "barbaric act . . . not justified by any sane mindset, or any logic; nor by the religion of Islam. This act is pernicious and shameless and evil in the extreme." He also condemned those who commit "such crimes" as "the worst of people."[15] Both statements also cautioned against blaming Islam, or Muslims in general, for the attacks. Some months after the attacks, when Al Qaeda's responsibility had been acknowledged by Saudi authorities; the Saudi minister of Awqaf and Islamic affairs, Shaykh Salih bin Abd al-Aziz Al Alshaykh told *al-Hayat*: "It seems to me that Al-Qaeda's thought and approach, from what I have heard of it, is based on two things: first on declaring as apostate (takfir) governments, and second on the necessity of jihad against unbelievers (al-kufar) and governments, and inflaming massacres in order to announce jihad.

These things, from the perspective of shari'a, are in error and a deviation in the understanding of shari'a." He went on to say that "whenever religiosity (al-tadayyun) increases without proper knowledge, deviation will increase."[16]

The Saudi authorities also indicated to the clerical establishment that they would not tolerate any of the state clergy contravening the government line in the crisis atmosphere after 9/11. In November 2001, Crown Prince Abdallah met with leading members of the 'ulama, and told them in no uncertain terms that there should be no "going beyond the boundaries" in religion (la ghulu fi al-din).[17] Reports that some mosque preachers had taken "leaves of absence" because of their differences with the government over post-9/11 policy can also be seen as an indication of the government's control over the religious establishment.[18] Those who even indirectly questioned that arrangement were quickly rebuked. During the November 2001 meeting with Crown Prince Abdallah, a senior religious functionary, Abd al-Muhsin al-Turki, the secretary-general of the Muslim World League, apparently made a comment to the effect that the 'ulama shared with the Al Sa'ud family the responsibilities of rulership in the country. In January 2002, two senior members of the ruling family, Prince Talal bin Abd al-Aziz and Prince Turki Al Faysal, both known for their liberal views, wrote newspaper articles refuting this claim, forcefully reiterating the fact that the rulers ruled, and the 'ulama advised the rulers.[19]

Given this strong control by the state over the religious establishment, it is not surprising that the credibility of the religious pronouncements condemning bin Laden and the 9/11 attacks from that establishment were called into question by many in the *salafi* trend. To fill this "credibility gap," the Saudis were able to mobilize the support of a number of past critics of the regime, notable *salafi* dissidents of the early 1990s, many of whom had spent time in Saudi prisons. These *salafi* dissidents condemned bin Laden and supported the government's handling of the post-9/11 crisis.[20] Shaykh Salman al-'Awda is a good example. A fiery critic of Saudi policy in the Gulf War, he was jailed in 1994, and subsequently held under house arrest until 1999. Since 9/11, he has condemned extremism in the Muslim world, calling it a "deviant understanding" of Islam, or a "deviant application of legitimate teachings."[21] Another example is Shaykh 'Ayd al-Qarni. Al-Qarni had been banned by the government from conducting religious and proselytizing activities for some time, but after 9/11, he returned to the field. He asserted in an interview that his return was with the permission of the Saudi rulers, with whom he shared the view that they had to "unite ranks, unify Muslim discourse, call to God and avoid exaggeration" in religion (using the same words that Crown Prince Abdallah had earlier used in his November 2001 meeting with the *'ulama*). Al-Qarni criticized the rush to jihadist activities among Muslim youth, cautioned against anything that would threaten national unity in Saudi Arabia and reminded Saudis of their obligation to loyalty to their rulers.[22]

This coming together of the Saudi leadership and its former Islamist critics is the most interesting development in Saudi politics since 9/11. It certainly signals some decline in the credibility of the official *'ulama*, as the regime clearly has seen the necessity of reinforcing the official condemnations of bin Laden with support from religious figures who have more credibility in *salafi* circles. It also could indicate that Saudi Islamist thinkers and activists realize that, in the new world atmosphere of rejection of religious extremism, they need to trim their sails and seek the protection of the Saudi rulers. It could simply be that these activists disagree with bin Laden. But one thing that this phenomenon does prove is the continuing ability of the Al Sa'ud to rally support around them in a time of crisis.

However, this entente between the Saudi rulers and their former *salafi* critics does not imply any change in the views of those critics toward the United States. A -Awda, while calling for mutual respect between Islam and the West, is extremely critical of Western society philosophically and of American policy in the Middle East specifically. While he condemned the attacks of 9/11 as "a horrible thing born of arrogance," he labeled them "the bitter fruit of a tree planted by America, for American has succeeded brilliantly in making enemies for itself."[23] Al-Qarni called the United States after 9/11 "an oppressor in the guise of an oppressed," and accused it of using the pretext of 9/11 to initiate wars that it had previously planned. He called Israel "a cancer in the body of the Islamic world, which will not be healed except by tearing it out from its roots."[24] In some measure, the regime has been able to garner support from its *salafi* critics because of the Saudi perception that the United States is conducting a campaign of criticism and pressure against its rulers since 9/11. How long this entente will last, as the Saudi government now seeks to repair ties with the United States, remains an open question.

There are elements within the Saudi *salafi* movement that were not reconciled to the Saudi government in the post-9/11 period. Saudi *salafis* in exile, represented by Sa'd al-Faqih and the Movement for Islamic Reform in Arabia (www.miraserve.com), continued their criticism of the government and their opposition to the U.S. role in the Middle East. Al-Faqih, the most credible spokesman for the *salafi*

exile opposition, never criticized the attacks of 9/11 and continued to
refer to bin Laden as "Shaykh" in the MIRA publications, emphasizing
his leadership role and putative religious credentials.[25] He has also
been very critical of the *salafis* who did reconcile with the Saudi government after 9/11.[26] In Saudi Arabia itself, some *salafis* opposed
the government's stance indirectly, either by refusing to rally to the
regime or by speaking out against specific government policies. One
'alim, Shaykh Humud bin 'Uqla' al-Shu'aybi, published an incendiary
fatwa early in the crisis condemning any Muslim government that
cooperated in any way with the United States.[27] While the Saudis were
able to maintain control over the violent *salafi* tendency in the country
in the immediate post-9/11 period, they were not able to eliminate it.
On May 12, 2003, suspected Al Qaeda sympathizers attacked three
residential compounds in the city of Riyadh with car bombs, killing
34 people, including 9 Americans. The perpetrators were believed to
be linked to a group of 19 Saudis who were being sought by the government for their involvement in a suspected terrorist plot disrupted
by Saudi police just days before the May 12 bombings. Sa'd al-Faqih's
website published selections from what purported to be a statement
by the 19 suspects on May 12, the same day as the bombings. That
statement accused the Saudi regime of having lost whatever Islamic
legitimacy it once had because of its cooperation with the United
States "in making war on the Muslims of Afghanistan and Iraq." It
went on to say that killing Saudi leaders was legitimate, because they
"were in the line of the Jews and the Christians."[28]

A telling sign of divisions within the *salafi* movement is the debate
that emerged within Saudi Arabia over an overture by some *salafis*
toward "dialogue" with Western intellectuals. The genesis of this
overture was a statement published by a number of prominent American
intellectuals shortly after the attacks of 9/11 entitled "What We're
Fighting For."[29] It set out a defense of Western liberal values and the
right of self-defense in the face of the 9/11 attacks. In response, Saudi
intellectuals, including many prominent *salafis* (e.g., Safar al-Hawali,
'Ayd al-Qarni, Muhammad al-Fawzan, Muhsin al-'Awaji) published a
response entitled "How We Can Coexist."[30] The signatories "welcome
dialogue and exchange," and acknowledge that there are "mutually
beneficial relationships and common interests between the Muslim
world and the West." However, the bulk of the statement is highly
critical of American (and, more generally, Western) policies, not only
with regard to Israel but more generally in the region. The signatories
contend that "policies of conflict in the West are bringing about
the destruction of civil security throughout the world in the fame of

fighting terrorism . . . [I]t is important for the West to realize that civil security in the Islamic World has not seen stability for decades and a lot of the impediments to civil security have come about under the umbrella of Western policy and quite possibly due to the direct actions of the West."

This was hardly a statement of common ground with American policy toward the Middle East and the Muslim world. However, the signatories were criticized by some Saudi *salafis* for being too willing to engage in dialogue with the West. In a statement entitled "The Alternative Statement" circulated in the Kingdom, the attacks of 9/11 were justified on the basis that, from Hiroshima through Israel's response to the Palestinian intifada through sanctions on Iraq, American policy has deliberately targeted civilians for attack. The "Statement" said that it was the obligation of Islam to dominate the world, and that conflict between Islam and the West is inevitable: "those who wish to turn this confrontation into a peaceful dialogue will not succeed." The Statement viewed the attacks of 9/11 as an effort to redress the imbalance of forces in that confrontation. It concluded saying that it would take another such attack for the United States to learn its lesson. The only course by which dialogue is possible with the "West" is if the United States reverses its policies in the Middle East, apologizes for the past and pays compensation to Muslims for its past crimes.[31]

With the American focus on confronting Iraq, which accelerated in the fall of 2002, those in the Saudi *salafi* trend advocating dialogue with the West became even more critical of American policy, and implicitly of the Saudi relationship with the United States. In November 2002, 209 Islamist activists published a petition in the London-based Arabic newspaper *al-Quds al-'Arabi* condemning American policy toward Iraq. Of the 209 signatories, 160 were from Saudi Arabia, including Salman al-Awda and Muhsin al-'Awaji. Much like the earlier "How We Can Coexist," this document did not posit an unalterable confrontation between Islam and the West, or support a bin Laden interpretation of jihad. The signatories called on Muslim youth to avoid violence, and on religious leaders to "spread moderation in the *'umma*, and the middle way (al-tawassut) and tolerance based on the correct interpretation of the message of Islam." They made a special plea to those in the United States "who are supporters of justice, lovers of peace and opponents of war" to stand against American policy.

However, their criticism of the American stand on Iraq was harsh. They said that "the insistence of the American administration on using force and hostility toward the states of the region brings to mind the Crusader campaigns and the era of colonialism . . . Just as those ages opened the gates of jihad and just resistance and ended with the destruction of the hostile Crusader forces of evil, so any form of aggression against the 'umma or contempt for it will open the gates of jihad and legitimate just resistance which will end in the destruction of the attacking Crusader and Zionist forces of evil, by the will of God." They saw American aims as going far beyond Iraq, to "destroy the Muslim identity of the 'umma, spread American culture in the region, control its oil and non-oil resources" as well as support Israel and put an end to the Palestinian intifada. The signatories called on Muslim government to oppose the American intervention, and to build stronger relations with the countries of Europe and East Asia as an alternative to reliance on the United States.[32] Even among those who accept the need for dialogue with the West, opposition to American policy in the region continued to grow as the crisis of 9/11 led to the crisis over Iraq.

It is difficult to judge the extent of support within Saudi Arabia, or even within the *salafi* trend there, for either the call for dialogue with the West or the criticism of it. We know the outline of the debate, but not the relation of forces on either side of it. It is also important to recognize that the *salafi* trend is not the only factor in political discourse in the Kingdom. While much less organized than the *salafis*, and with access to fewer institutional resources, there are other currents of thought in the country, almost all of which are more open to the "dialogue of civilizations" than the *salafi* critics are (though many are very critical of U.S. policy in the Middle East themselves).[33] In fact, there was something of a popular backlash against the religious establishment in the spring of 2002, following a fire at a girls' school in Mecca in which a number of the students died. Saudi religious police reportedly impeded rescue efforts, to prevent the girls from being seen unveiled. They were severely criticized in the Saudi media, and the event led the Saudi government to remove control of the female education system from the Special Presidency for Girls' Education, dominated by the religious establishment, to the Ministry of Education. The May 2003 bombings also elicited a considerable number of denunciations of the Islamist monopoly on political discourse in the country from more liberal Saudis.

Conclusion: Does it Mean Anything?

All indications point to relatively high levels of anti-American feeling in Saudi Arabia in the period after the attacks of 9/11, with the prospect of war against Iraq serving to intensify those feelings among many in the country. The roots of these feelings vary considerably, from a relatively simple rejection of American support for Israel to a deep-seated, religiously based rejection of dialogue with non-Muslims. But the widespread nature of these feelings cannot be denied. The Saudi government itself recognizes this fact. Saudi officials from Crown Prince Abdallah down have emphasized repeatedly that they see the Saudi–American relationship as solid and unshakeable. The Saudi government has taken a number of steps aimed at improving the atmosphere in the relationship, from the Crown Prince's peace initiative on the Arab–Israeli front (revealed to *New York Times* columnist Thomas Friedman, a harsh critic of Saudi Arabia after 9/11) through his visit to President Bush's ranch in Texas and his open letter to President Bush on the first anniversary of the attacks, to his January 2003 initiative in the Arab League to put the organization on record in favor of greater political and economic openness in Arab countries. While these steps are largely aimed at improving the public view of Saudi Arabia in the United States, they are also a signal to Saudi public opinion that there are limits to the amount of anti-Americanism at home that the regime will tolerate. Elite intellectuals close to the regime have picked up on these signals, with a number of articles appearing in August 2002 arguing that a complete break with the world's only superpower will not serve Saudi, Arab, or Muslim interests.[34]

The question then presents itself: do these widespread public feelings of anti-Americanism make any difference on the policy level? I argue they do, but indirectly. The Saudi regime is sufficiently insulated from public pressures that it would not abandon its ties to the United States simply in reaction to public opinion. In a situation where it saw its own direct interests threatened, the Al Sa'ud would ignore public opinion and cooperate openly with the United States, as was the case with the Iraqi invasion of Kuwait in 1990. However, the Al Sa'ud realize better than outsiders that their public is increasingly educated, urban, and informed about the world, and thus more readily "politicized" than might have been the case in the past.[35] In cases where there immediate security is not at risk, the Saudi leadership will pay more attention to that public opinion. The fact that the leadership so publicly disassociated itself from the immediate American reaction to 9/11, by denying the United States the right to use Saudi bases for attacks on Afghanistan (at least publicly), and from American policy on Arab–Israeli questions is an indication that public opinion, while not determinative, is increasingly important in the Saudi policy process.

The tensions between the United States and Saudi Arabia since 9/11 have highlighted an uncomfortable truth about the relationship that dates back to its very beginnings. On neither side is there a strong public constituency for the relationship. It is a relationship between elites, based on very clear understandings of mutual interest. There is no sentiment in it. The myths propagated by those whose business it is to maintain the relationship ring hollow once exposed to public scrutiny. Each country is the perfect foil for publicists and propagandists in the other country, culturally and politically. Will the relationship end soon? No. Those interests that tie the elites together are very strong. But public opinion trends on both sides constrain the relationship. It will not get closer. More likely, it will revert to something like the level of the pre-1990 period: close and cooperative, but less publicly close on the military level, with greater political distance between Riyadh and Washington. It is on oil that the relationship began, and it will be on oil that the relationship will, in the future, revolve. If there comes a breaking point between Saudi Arabia and the United States, it will not be from public opinion pressures on either side, but rather on fundamentally different conceptions of how the Saudis should use their "oil power" in the world market.

NOTES

1. Poll cited in Dr. James J. Zogby, "New poll shows damage done," December 24, 2001. Accessed via "GulfWire," e-newsletter, www.arabialink.com.

2. As late as December 2001, Saudi Interior Minister Prince Na'if ibn Abd al-Aziz Al Sa'ud told an American reporter: "Until now, we have no evidence that assures us that they [Saudis on board the airplanes] are related to Sept. 11. We have not received anything in this regard from the United States." Douglas Jehl, "Saudi minister asserts that bin Laden is a 'Tool' of Al Qaeda, not its mastermind," *New York Times*, December 10, 2001. It was not until February 2002 that Prince Na'if publicly admitted that Saudis were involved in the attacks. "15 of 19 Suicide Hijackers were Saudi," *Associated Press*, February 6, 2002.

3. For one example, see Karen DeYoung, "Saudis seethe over media reports on anti-terror effort," *Washington Post*, November 6, 2001.

4. The quote is taken from a long article about Abdallah's letter and U.S.–Saudi relations before 9/11: Sulayman Nimr, "qisat al-rasa'il al-mutabadil bayn al-amir abd allah wa bush," *al-Hayat*, November 6, 2001, p. 7. For the first account in the Western press of Abdallah's discussion of Saudi–American tensions before 9/11, see James M. Dorsey, "Saudi leader warns US mideast policy may force kingdom to review relationship," *Wall Street Journal*, October 29, 2001.

5. This is the interpretation put forward in the Saudi account of the meeting conveyed in the *al-Hayat* article referenced above.

6. For an account of such comments from a number of Saudi newspapers, see " 'amrika wa 'al-'irhab al-nifsi' wa 'ahdaf al-hamla al-'askariyya," *al-Hayat*, October 16, 2001, p. 6.

7. Richard Burkholder, "The U.S. and the West—through Saudi eyes," Gallup Tuesday Briefing, August 6, 2002, www.gallup.com/poll/tb/goverpubli/20020806.asp.

8. "The 10 nation 'Impressions of America' poll report," Zogby International, August 7, 2002, www.zogby.com/news/ReadNews.dbm?ID=610.

9. Elaine Sciolino, "Don't weaken Arafat, Saudi warns Bush," *New York Times*, January 27, 2002.

10. An anecdotal account of such boycotts can be found in Neil MacFarquhar, "An anti-American boycott is growing in the Arab world," *New York Times*, May 10, 2002. American exports to Saudi Arabia in the first half of 2002 were 30% lower than in 2001, the lowest level in 12 years. Roger Hardy, "Saudi-US trade plunges," BBC, August 23, 2002, http://news.bbc.co.uk/2/hi/world/middle_east/2213250.stm. Given the downturn in oil prices in the months immediately following the 9/11 attacks, it is difficult to determine how much of the decline in American exports to Saudi Arabia is the result of consumer boycotts and how much is the result of more general economic factors.

11. "Back Palestinians with words, not deeds says Naif," *Arab News* (Jidda), April 6, 2002.

12. The petition was published in *al-Quds al-'Arabi* (London), April 20–21, 2002, p. 4.

13. A similar conclusion was reached by seasoned Middle East observer Eric Rouleau after his visit to the Kingdom following the attacks. See his "Trouble in the Kingdom," *Foreign Affairs*, vol. 81, no. 4 (July/August 2002).

14. "Saudi Grand Mufti condemns terrorist acts in U.S.," September 15, 2001, www.saudiembassy.net/press_release/press_release00.htm.

15. Statement by H.E. Shaikh Salih bin Muhammad Al-Luheidan, Chairman of the Supreme Judicial Council of the Kingdom of Saudi Arabia, "Condemnation of Terrorism," September 14, 2001, www.saudiembassy.net/press_release/01-spa/terrorism-01.htm.

16. "al-minhaj al-salafi didd al-tayarat al-mughaliyya wa takfir al-'afrad wa al-hukumat laysa min al-'islam," *al-Hayat*, February 18, 2002, p. 10.

17. "wali al-'ahd al-sa'udi li kibar rijal al-din wa al-'ulama: fi hadhihi al-'ayyam al-'asiba 'alayna al-ta'ani wa tawdih al-haqa'iq," *al-Hayat*, November 15, 2001, p. 8.

18. The leaves of absence were reported in James A. Dorsey, "Saudi leader seeks to rein in clergy," *Wall Street Journal*, March 14, 2002, pp. A9, A12. The London-based Arabic newspaper *al-Quds al-'Arabi* reported in an article published on February 1, 2002 that a number of imams had resigned their positions. That article was translated and published in *Middle East Economic Survey*, February 18, 2002, vol. 45, no. 7.

19. Prince Turki's article appeared in *al-Sharq al-'Awsat* on January 20, 2002, in the religion section. See www.asharqal-awsat.com/pcdaily/ 2001-2002/religion/religion.html. The article by Prince Talal was referred to in *al-Hayat*, February 6, 2002, p. 2.

20. On the phenomenon of *salafi* political activism and opposition in Saudi Arabia in the 1990s, see F. Gregory Gause, III, *Oil Monarchies: Domestic and Security Challenges in the Arab Gulf States* (New York: Council on Foreign Relations Press, 1994), pp. 31–44, 94–98; Mamoun Fandy, *Saudi Arabia and the Politics of Dissent* (New York: Palgrave, 1999); Joshua Teitelbaum, *Holier Than Thou: Saudi Arabia's Islamic Opposition*, Policy Paper No. 52 (The Washington Institute for Near East Policy, 2000); Gwenn Okruhlik, "Networks of dissent: Islamism and Reformism in Saudi Arabia," *Current History*, January 2002.

21. See in particular his article on "al-tatarruf wa al-tatarruf al-mudad" [Extremism and counter-extremism], December 12, 2001, on the web-site http://www.islamtoday.net. On that same site, one can find in English his condemnation of the 9/11 attacks and the full text of his interview with *New York Times* correspondent Douglas Jehl, which was the basis for the *Times* article of December 27, 2001.

22. See his interview in *al-Hayat*, February 4, 2002, p. 15.

23. For his criticisms of the philosophical underpinnings of Western notions of freedom, see his "al-'islam wa al-gharb: mudakhala ma'a fukuyama fi harb 'fashia al-qarn al-hadi wa al-'ashrin," *al-Hayat*, January 18, 2002, p. 10. For his specific criticisms of American policy, see his English-language statements at www.islamtoday.net.

24. "al-qarni: tazayud 'adad al-harakat wa al-madhahib al-fikriyya al-'islamiyya 'alamat marad," *al-Hayat*, February 4, 2002, p. 15.

25. See, for example, nashrat al-'islah number 317, June 3, 2002 (www. miraserve.com/monitors/amt.htm) for al-Faqih's analysis of the "future of the battle between bin Ladin and America"; and nashrat al-'islah, no. 311, April 22, 2002 (same URL) for his analysis of the future prospects of bin Laden's confrontation with the Al Sa'ud.

26. See, for example, his criticism of Safar al-Hawali in nashrat al-'islah no. 287, October 22, 2001; and his criticism of other *salafi* dissidents in nashrat al-'islah no. 290, November 12, 2001 (both at www.miraserve. com/monitors/amt.htm).

27. For that *fatwa*, see http://www.aloqla.com/mag. On al-Shu'aybi, see Douglas Jehl, "For Saudi cleric, battle shapes up as infidel vs. Islam," *New York Times*, December 5, 2001.

28. nashrat al-'islah number 366, May 12, 2003 (www.miraserve.com/ monitors/amt.htm).

29. The statement and list of signatories can be found at www. propositionsonline.com/html/fighting_for.htm.

30. I found an English-language version at www.islamtoday.net/english, which is the website of Shaykh Salman al-'Awda, in the section entitled "Special Articles."

31. I obtained a copy of "The Alternative Statement" via fax from a source in Saudi Arabia in June 2002. There were no signatures attached to it, so it is difficult to determine how widespread these sentiments are. However, the debate over the original statement and this response has been discussed by Sa'd al-Faqih in nashrat al-'islah no. 317, June 3, 2002 (www. miraserve.com/monitors/amt.htm). He reports that a number of signatories of the original call for dialogue with the West were forced by the negative reaction to issue a "clarification" of their views. Those retractions were confirmed in interviews in Saudi Arabia in January 2003, though I have been unable to find texts of the "clarifications."

32. The text of the petition and the signatories can be found in *al-Quds al-'Arabi* (London), November 22, 2002, p. 2.

33. Anecdotal evidence can be found in Neil MacFarquhar, "A few Saudis defy a rigid Islam to debate their own intolerance," *New York Times*, July 12, 2002 and in the newspaper columns of prominent Saudi writers like Turki Al Hamad, who writes in *al-Sharq al-Awsat*, Da'ud al-Shiryan, who writes in *al-Hayat*, and Jamal Khashogji, who is now editor of *al-Watan*. One can also discover this fact by talking to Saudis.

34. See the article by Ghazi al-Qusaybi, until recently Saudi ambassador in London and now the minister of Water in the Saudi cabinet. Al-Qusaybi had been very critical of the Bush administration in the past. "laysa min salih al-sa'udiyya dukhul muwajaha ma'a 'amrika," *al-Hayat*, August 21, 2002, p. 9. See also Muhammad bin Abd al-Latif Al Alshaykh, "man al-mustafid min ta'miq al-sharakh al-sa'udi-al-'amriki?," *al-Hayat*, August 23, 2002, p. 9. For an account of Saudi fears that the backlash in the United States against the kingdom might be permanently damaging U.S.-Saudi relations, see Dawud al-Shiryan, "al-'alaqat al-sa'udiyya-al-'amrikiyya fi mahkamat al-ra'i al-'am," *al-Hayat*, August 18, 2002, pp. 1, 6.

35. I examine these social changes in Saudi Arabia and their potential consequences for Saudi politics in earlier articles: F. Gregory Gause, III, "Political opposition in the Gulf monarchies," European University Institute Working Papers, RSC No. 2000/61, 2000; and F. Gregory Gause, III, "Be careful what you wish for: the future of U.S.-Saudi relations," *World Policy Journal*, vol. 49, no. 1 (spring 2002).

8

THE PALESTINIAN PERCEPTION
OF AMERICA AFTER 9/11

Camille Mansour

It is difficult to say anything new about Palestinian perceptions of America after 9/11; all what can be done is to rearrange, to categorize, to compare. One way to categorize is to say that Palestinians do not all have the same perception of America, and that it is necessary to distinguish between different Palestinian groups according to certain criteria. These would include socioeconomic class; political affiliation; whether people are from an urban environment, a village, or a refugee camp; whether they are long-time residents of the West Bank and Gaza, "returnees" arriving after the signing of the Oslo accords, or refugees living outside Palestine in Lebanon, Syria, or Jordan. I cannot pretend to be able to describe the perceptions of each group or sub-group, but perhaps such a systematic enquiry, while important as a research project, is not necessary for our purposes here. Rather, it seems to me that our purpose is determined by *why* we are interested in Palestinian perceptions, in other words, what is at stake as far as these perceptions are concerned. Since perceptions of the "other" are linked to perceptions of oneself (in many ways being a kind of self-affirmation), I think that the answer lies in what these perceptions say that is meaningful about future trends as seen by the perceiving actor (in this case, the Palestinians), about actions they might undertake, about the object perceived (in this case, America), and finally about how these images, mirror-images, and counter-images might affect the policies of the various actors (in this case, the United States, Israel, and the European and Arab countries).

If the study of perceptions has such a functional relevance, then this chapter can be restricted to dealing only with those Palestinians who appear to have the greatest influence on the Palestinian internal

debate and policy, that is, those who live in the West Bank and the Gaza
Strip. Similarly, I will limit myself to the following categories only: the
Palestinian street, the Islamists, Leftist and secular (including Fatah)
activists, and the leadership. I will conclude with the Palestinian internal
debate and its relation to the image of America.

THE PALESTINIAN STREET

By "Palestinian street," I mean the spontaneous, knee-jerk reactions
and outlook of the broadest spectrum of the population, encom-
passing, for example, Islamists, secularists, the elite, and so forth. How
is America after 9/11 (and in many respects, before 9/11) perceived
by these people? It is interesting to note, from the outset, that people
differentiate between U.S. official policy and American society and
culture. While the attitude toward the former is overwhelmingly negative, as we shall see, the latter are viewed with a kind of fascination.
In a survey conducted in March–April 2002 in five Arab countries
(Saudi Arabia, Egypt, Kuwait, Lebanon, and the United Arab Emirates)
by Zogby International, Arabs who were polled "had strong favorable
attitudes toward American 'Science and Technology,' 'Freedom and
Democracy,' 'Education,' 'Movies and Television,' and also had largely
favorable attitudes toward the American people."[1] Everything points
to the fact that the Palestinians share this positive Arab outlook: this
is attested by the sheer numbers (several hundred thousand) of
West Bank and Gaza Palestinians who have visited or emigrated to the
United States, or who wish to do so.

On the perception of official America, the Zogby International
study reveals "extremely negative attitudes toward U.S. policy vis-à-vis
the Arab world, Iraq and most especially toward Palestine."[2] A broader
survey weeks later by the same organization (this time adding to the
five Arab communities cited above three more groups: Morocco,
Jordan, and the Arabs in Israel) on the overall impression of America
and other selected countries, indicates a very low "favorability score"
for America. This does not imply, the author of the survey asserts,
"an anti-Western sentiment at work," because Canada and France, for
example, receive a "consistently net positive rating."[3] Other polls in
Arab and Islamic countries conducted during 2002 all indicate a
dramatic deterioration of the global image of the United States.[4]
Specifically concerning the Palestinians living in the West Bank and
Gaza, a survey commissioned by the British Council (which also
covered other countries) in February–March 2002 found that the
United States attracted a very high "unfavorability."[5]

The following, in my view, are the main perceptions held by Palestinians concerning America, which explains their negative attitudes toward it:

1. The United States is fundamentally anti-Arab and anti-Muslim. People do not find any other explanation for its double-standards approach toward Israel and other countries, such as Syria.
2. The United States considers itself above international law and international obligations.
3. The global antiterrorism campaign after 9/11 is a pretext to tighten U.S. domination over the Arab–Muslim world.
4. The United States is blindly pro-Israel; the ties that bind these two countries are unshakable. Israel represses the Palestinians with American weapons. There is "a total subjugation of American decision making to the priorities and policies of the Israeli government."[6]
5. U.S. foreign policy seems double-faced: "Human rights, the great Wilsonian concept of the people's right to self determination seems to stop when the subject of discussions are Palestinians."[7]
6. The U.S. characterization of all forms of Palestinian military struggle as "terrorism" (not only suicide operations against Israeli civilians, but also operations against the Israel's occupying army) is a cover whose aim is to give Israeli Prime Minister Ariel Sharon a free hand in the Palestinian territories. For the Palestinian in the street, the reoccupation of the entire West Bank in spring 2002, the death of hundreds of people, the demolition of thousands of houses, the uprooting of tens of thousands of trees, would not have been possible without American approval.
7. The Palestinians are asked to accept whatever the U.S.-Israel alliance offers them in the framework of a peace settlement. Neither international law nor the Palestinian struggle may be legitimate factors in such a settlement.
8. The campaign against Iraq is not only an American design. Israel has played an important role in pushing for such a campaign. "In the eyes of the prime minister [Ariel Sharon], the war in Iraq is an opportunity to change the balance of power in the area. Sharon proposes a division of labor: Israel will take care of Arafat. America will smash the sources of Arab power."[8] Ordinary Palestinians concur with this assessment of Sharon's motives made by many in the Israeli press, and even fear a scenario whereby a mass expulsion of Palestinians outside the West Bank is provoked.

It is important to stress at this point that Palestinian perceptions of America have been exacerbated by the intensity of the Palestinian–Israeli confrontation since September 2000, almost a year before 9/11. The Palestinian street considers that they have paid a heavy price because of U.S. policy. The exacerbated character of Palestinian perceptions of America has sometimes led to defiant attitudes, such as raising portraits of Osama bin Laden or Saddam Hussein during demonstrations. At certain times, the more Palestinians have been accused of terrorism because of suicide operations, the more they have supported them. Some commentators have argued that in so doing, the Palestinians have fallen into Sharon's trap. This may be true, but the issue here is the spontaneous reactions of the people, not the rational choices made by policymakers.

One question that emerges from this overview of the Palestinian negative perception of America is whether it fuels organized mobilization and action against the United States? To answer this question, it is time to consider those groups whose behavior—contrary to the spontaneity of the street—is marked by a measure of organization and intentionality.

THE ISLAMISTS

As stated earlier, the Palestinian Islamists, that is, Hamas and Islamic Jihad, share the Palestinian street's negative perception of America and its role in Palestine and the region. Interestingly, however, they appear to be very keen on avoiding statements that could be seen as going beyond the vague anti-Americanism of the street. Thus, Palestinian Islamists, as of spring 2001, have announced that Israeli military actions in the West Bank and Gaza, including the killing of Palestinian civilians and extra-judicial executions of activists, would be met by suicide operations against civilian targets in Israel. Dozens of such operations have, in fact, taken place since then, but in the one or two instances where U.S. citizens were among the casualties, the Islamists were quick to declare that Americans had not been targeted. The question is, why this concern?

It seems to me that Hamas and Jihad consider themselves to be Palestinian organizations, and not worldwide Islamic organizations. Their focus is the Israel–Palestine arena, and they appear to gear any support they get from other Islamic groups or countries toward their Palestinian agenda. To use Farish Noor's terms, the Palestinian Islamists do not "localize" the anti-American struggle but try to "universalize" their local anti-Israeli struggle. The enemy is at home and can be targeted, so why look to an enemy who is far away? A symbolic example can illustrate the point. During 2002, there was a call to boycott American products in several Arab countries as a response to the U.S. administration's support of Israeli policy. This call was effective in many instances, but in the West Bank and Gaza it was practically absent: what would be the point of boycotting American products when people have no alternative but to buy Israeli products? Clearly, Palestinian Islamists give priority to the anti-Israeli struggle over an anti-American or an anti-Western perception: in Olivier Roy's words, the Palestinian case illustrates the "nationalization of Islamism."[9]

I will conclude this section with the following paradoxical observation. While Palestinian Islamists have dissociated themselves from campaign against the United States, the United States has associated itself with the Israeli campaign against the Islamists. By outlawing Hamas and Jihad under its antiterrorism fight, and cracking down on financial support from American Islamic organizations to Palestinian Islamists, the United States has upgraded local "terrorist" groups to the rank of "global" ones, which, however one looks at it, is neither a deserved honor nor a justified stigma.

THE LEFT AND SECULARIST ACTIVISTS

The anti-Americanism—however mild—of the Palestinian Islamists is clearer in comparison to the more accommodating line taken by the secularists, including Fatah cadres, and those on the left among Palestinian activists. It is interesting to note here that this was not the case historically. In the 1960s and 1970s, the Palestinian resistance organizations considered themselves as part of the third world anti-imperialism. Some of these organizations, like the PFLP, argued that instead of hitting the protégé, it was more efficient to hit the head. Hijacking, anti-American operations, and operational alliances with other movements, took place. Three important characteristics of the earlier period should be noted:

1. The Palestinian armed organizations were not inside Palestine, but in the neighboring Arab countries; this means that there was as much incentive to strike Israeli or U.S. targets all over the world, such as planes and embassies, as to carry out operations against Israeli-controlled territory.
2. The Soviet Union, while distancing itself from the modus operandi of the Palestinian armed organizations, was not, in most cases, disturbed by their anti-imperialist, anti-American drive.

3. Jordan and later Lebanon provided a safe haven, or sanctuary, for Palestinian armed organizations, insofar as the host state was incapable of controlling them. A similar situation evolved much later in Afghanistan, when the Taliban government, far from being able to control Al Qaeda, was controlled by it. Jordan in the late 1960s, Lebanon in the 1970s, and Afghanistan in the 1990s show that transnational political violence by non-state actors can only be sustained when these actors operate from a territory that is not sufficiently controlled by its government.[10]

For the Palestinian left and the secularist activists, however, the situation in the 1990s bore little resemblance to the earlier decades. The three characteristics of the regional and international environment that helped explain their recourse to transnational violence no longer existed. First, Palestinian resistance organizations no longer had a sanctuary after their withdrawal from Lebanon in 1982, not even in Syria (simplistic propaganda notwithstanding). Second, anti-American and anti-imperialist slogans became obsolete after the demise of the Soviet Union. Third, the Intifada and the Madrid-Oslo process made the West Bank and Gaza—rather than Amman, Beirut, or Tunis—the center of the Palestinian polity. While the secular activists, including the Fatah, and part of the left were among the first returnees, many PFLP and DFLP cadres, who had opposed the Oslo agreements from Damascus, gradually became reconciled to the new situation and arranged for their return to the Palestinian territories. Thus, both the push and pull factors of the 1980s and 1990s worked against Palestinian political violence outside the Israeli–Palestinian territory and in favor of integration into a process conducted by the Palestinian leadership and involving a will to settle the conflict with Israel through peaceful negotiations and American assistance.

However, as we shall see in the next section, the hopes placed in the Oslo process faded in the late 1990s. With the outbreak of the Palestinian–Israeli confrontation in September 2000, secularist and leftist activists were progressively drawn from participating in unarmed popular demonstrations against the Israeli army, to shooting against the Israelis, and finally to suicide attacks inside Israel. Not only was hitting U.S. interests off their agenda, but they—and the governing elite—now had a pragmatist, instrumental approach to the potential role of the United States in the Palestinian–Israeli accommodation.

THE PALESTINIAN LEADERSHIP

The Oslo process and the establishment of the Palestinian authority in the West Bank and Gaza have had important effects on Palestinian-U.S. relations. The Oslo agreements opened the way for Israel to sign a treaty with Jordan and to establish ties of differing importance with a number of Arab countries. The centrality of the Palestinian question in the Arab world became, perhaps, more operational than ideological. Whatever the ups and downs of Palestinian–Israeli relations between 1994 and 2000, Palestinian–American contacts intensified. For the Clinton administration, relations with the Palestinians became an important component of U.S. policy in the region and acquired a strategic dimension because of their impact on Israel's place in the region. This relationship, likewise, compensated for any negative effect that U.S. policy toward Iraq could have on Arab perceptions.

As for the Palestinian leadership, now that it had gained American recognition and an open door to the White House, nurturing the relationship became vital. This does not mean that it had any illusions about weakening U.S.-Israeli ties, but, at least, it thought that by maintaining intensive contacts with the U.S. administration, it could involve Washington in the minutiae of the Palestinian–Israeli relations in such a way as to give the administration a stake in a successful outcome of the final negotiations. Certainly, the Palestinian left would have argued that it was unrealistic to count on American pressure to get Israel to halt settlement building, for example, but neither the Palestinian left nor the intellectuals criticized the development of Palestinian-U.S. ties. A positive image of the United States emerged on the Palestinian street, and this reached a climax in December 1998 with President Clinton's visit to Gaza.

It is possible that Bill Clinton became so entangled in the minutiae of Palestinian–Israeli negotiations that he came to want a successful outcome by the end of his term (January 2001) at any price. And success at any price meant ignoring the situation that had developed on the ground in the West Bank and Gaza: expansion of the settlements, mounting Israeli restrictions on Palestinians in their daily lives, Palestinian loss of confidence in a fair negotiated outcome, and so on and misrepresenting the gap between the negotiating positions of the two sides. It was on this basis that he hastily convened the Camp David summit in July 2000 in the conviction (or at least the hope) that the weaker party, the Palestinians, would bend to pressures. When this did not occur (though there was a real narrowing of the gap), Clinton immediately put the blame on the Palestinian side. This signaled the start of the downward slope in U.S.-Palestinian relations.

This is not the place to analyze the reasons behind the failure of Camp David negotiations in July 2000[11] or to deal with the unfolding Palestinian–Israeli confrontation, which broke out in September 2000.[12] I will deal only with those elements that are necessary to understand how the Palestinian leadership, in the conduct of its affairs, perceived the role of America, first in the transition between the Clinton and George W. Bush presidencies, and then after 9/11. During the last three months of the Clinton administration, when the Intifada consisted mainly of popular demonstrations against the Israeli military (which already, during that period, exacted a heavy toll in Palestinian lives), the Palestinian leadership tried to get Washington to recognize Israel's responsibility for the confrontation and requested the establishment of an international commission of enquiry. The Palestinian objective was to improve their negotiating position on the final status issues and to internationalize the path to a settlement by involving other actors than Israel and the United States. In November, Clinton acceded to the demand concerning the commission by constituting a watered-down fact-finding committee under U.S. auspices and the chairmanship of George Mitchell. Shortly thereafter, in December, he presented to the two sides his "Parameters" for a final settlement, which significantly improved, from the Palestinian point of view, what was on the table at Camp David. However, in terms of the internal calendars in Washington and Tel Aviv, it was too late. Bush replaced Clinton in January 2001 and Sharon was elected prime minister in early February.

Initially, the Palestinian leadership was not unhappy with George Bush's election as president. Encouraged by the Saudis, the Palestinians thought that Saudi influence could be brought to bear on an administration whose pillar was the pro-Republican oil lobby. Very early, however, it became clear that the Republicans, who had an interest in the Gulf area, were driven by the idea that as long the Palestinian–Israeli confrontation did not spill over into the region, there was no reason to intervene. The Palestinians also soon realized that the neoconservatives, the other pillar of Bush's administration, were against any "nation-building" intervention as a matter of general principle and had a pro-Sharon bias. Finally, the Palestinian leadership could not help noticing that both groups wanted the new administration to differentiate itself from its predecessor's active approach. This was expressed by the Administration's formal abandonment of the Clinton peace parameters no later than two days after Sharon's election, its insistence that Arafat make a 100-percent effort (impossible to measure in any case) to end Palestinian violence as a condition before any meeting with the American president, and its support of Israeli Prime Minister Sharon's definition of violence and conditions for a ceasefire after the publication of the Mitchell Commission's Report in April 2001 (thereby condoning, in effect, the Israeli battering ram tactics against the Palestinians).

It is necessary, at this point, to summarize the Palestinian leadership's attitude toward the militarization of the Intifada, because this is intimately related to its relations with the U.S. administration. I have explained elsewhere[13] that the leadership—because of the constraints imposed by its dual nature (a quasi-state structure and a national liberation movement), the restrictions on its territorial jurisdiction, and fears for its own survival—acted as the "overseer" of the uprising rather than as its "general staff." This meant, from a declarative standpoint: asserting that the root of violence lay with Israel even while carefully refraining from referring to Israel as the enemy; remaining silent when actions by different Palestinian groups were undertaken against the Israeli occupying army, while condemning suicide operations and reiterating each time its opposition to the killing of civilians, whether Israeli or Palestinian. From a practical standpoint, the overseer approach meant arbitrating between different Palestinian activist groups, letting things happen, and seriously intervening in favor of a cease-fire only when absolutely necessary and when significant backing from the Palestinian population could be expected. The reasoning behind the approach was that as long as Israel (or at least Washington) did not compensate the Palestinian leadership with a tangible reward relating to the peace process, the Palestinian leadership would not be in a position to control the street.

The Bush administration's lack of interest in an Israeli–Palestinian peace process, its permissiveness concerning Israeli military measures in the West Bank and Gaza, and the gap between the administration and the Palestinian leadership on the cause of the violence show that a low ebb in Palestinian–American relations predates the 9/11 attacks on New York and Washington. However, when the attacks occurred, the Palestinian leadership very quickly understood their implications: on the one hand, fears that the neoconservative argument describing all forms of Palestinian struggle against occupation as "terrorism" (and thus lumping it indiscriminately with Al Qaeda) would be strengthened, and, on the other hand, hopes that the viewpoint of Secretary of State Colin Powell would prevail, according to which America would need calm in the Middle East and Arab support in order to focus on identifying, locating, and pursuing those directly responsible for the attacks. At this delicate juncture, Arafat hastened to line up behind Washington and tried to calm the situation on the ground. He was keen to show that he held one of the keys for American access to the Middle East (in terms of influencing how America is seen in Arab opinion) and that he knew how to use this key positively and unhesitatingly (ahead of Egypt's Mubarak, for instance, who was far more reticent). This approach seemed to bear some fruit, as testified by the administration's displeasure with an Israeli attempt to escalate in the two or three days following 9/11, considered as a cynical exploitation of the tragedy, pressure on Tel Aviv for a cease-fire, and hints that there would be movement toward a Palestinian state.

In mid-October, the Palestinian leadership could claim that its status in Washington, while lagging very much behind its level during the Clinton era, was better after 9/11 than it was before. However, several factors quickly shattered this optimism: the seemingly easy victory against the Taliban and bin Laden's forces in Afghanistan, thus silencing those in Washington who claimed that America needed the support of Arab and Islamic countries; the tilt in the internal power struggle in favor of the neoconservatives; the affirmation by the latter, now virulent unilateralists allied with Christian fundamentalists, of an arrogant imperial America ready to fashion regimes sympathetic to America and to combat terrorism everywhere, especially in Muslim-inhabited areas. In the Palestinian–Israeli arena, the triggering event that gave the upper hand to the alliance between American neoconservatives and Ariel Sharon was the assassination (October 17) of an Israeli minister of the extreme right, Rehavam Ze'evi, an outspoken advocate of transferring the Palestinians outside Palestine, by members of the PFLP in retaliation for Israel's assassination of their leader, Abu Ali Mustafa. From that point on, Palestinian–U.S. relations witnessed an aggravating deterioration whose tempo appeared closely linked to the deterioration on the ground: targeted assassinations of Palestinians by Israel, suicide operations against civilians in Israel, closure of Palestinian towns and villages, shooting at Israeli soldiers and settlers, land grabs by and for Israeli settlers, and, finally, reoccupation of the entire West Bank and parts of the Gaza Strip.

Many observers have argued that the Palestinian leadership, whatever the merits of its case, failed to grasp the gravity of the 9/11 shock on America and the almost absolute American tendency to view any Palestinian violence as terrorism, and thus failed to take all the measures necessary to stop all Palestinian attacks. The reality, however, is more complicated. A year after the start of the Palestinian–Israeli confrontation, the Palestinian leadership had become technically and politically incapable of controlling the diverse Palestinian activist groups (control that even the Israeli military with all its might has not been able to do following its reoccupation of the whole West Bank) and was thus paying the price of its overseer approach. Technically, the fact that Israel, after each attack (usually undertaken by Islamist groups), chose to destroy the infrastructure (buildings, communications, chains of command) of Palestinian security forces made the latter less and less efficient. Politically, even if the leadership was technically capable of dismantling Palestinian armed networks, it was caught between the danger of provoking a Palestinian civil war and the prospect of American condemnation and Israeli reprisals.[14] Obviously, it chose to avoid civil war and risk being weakened and delegitimized in Washington. It is known that delegitimation has taken the form of an American call to replace Arafat and reform the institutions of the Palestinian authority, including the security apparatus, as a precondition to any discussion of the establishment of a viable Palestinian state called for in President Bush's "vision" (June 2002). I will now tackle the issue of reform in the framework of the Palestinian internal debate.

THE PALESTINIAN INTERNAL DEBATE AND THE IMAGE OF AMERICA

It would be inaccurate to restrict the Palestinian internal debate to the question of institutional reform and to assume that the debate began only at the end of spring 2002. Soon after Oslo, many issues came to be debated in the Palestinian public space: models for building state institutions, the relationship between Islam and the state, the rule of law, the place of the judiciary vis-à-vis the traditional modes of societal conflict resolution, the role of civil society, the respective roles of public and private sectors, the economic model for Palestine, strategies toward Israel for ending the occupation (negotiations, popular resistance, armed resistance), and so on. After September 2000, other issues were consecutively added to the debate: whether or not to go beyond popular resistance and militarize the Intifada; whether or not to extend operations inside Israeli territory, to conduct suicide operations, to end suicide operations completely. With the reoccupation of towns and villages in 2002 and the impasse facing the Intifada, the debate has become more introspective and centered on the question: what went wrong? The actors already enumerated in this article were involved in many of these issues, but with further sub-categorization, such as, within Fatah, between returnees and "veterans" of the first

Intifada and, within the leadership, between different circles around Arafat. Obviously, many others have participated in the debate such as political parties, NGO activists, journalists, intellectuals, business people, and civil servants. Given the U.S. weight in Israel and the Middle East, it is not surprising that those taking part in the Palestinian internal debate have positioned themselves on many issues according to the way they perceive America's conduct with regard to the peace process and Israeli security, how they understand America's choices in funding certain Palestinian programs and not others (through USAID assisting, for instance, the training of judges and the police forces), or how they see America's influence on the choices made by other international institutions active in the Palestinian territories (such as the World Bank and IMF in the arena of devising the Palestinian legal framework for a market economy).

It is not my purpose here to tackle all issues and actors of the Palestinian internal debate and to connect each issue and each actor to the perception of America. I will focus only on the question of reform. Given Arafat's strategy to allocate preference to the establishment of the State over institution-building and his patrimonial approach as a means of internal control, criticism was voiced very early on against the way the Palestinian authority institutions were being established. But, given the U.S. interest in encouraging the Palestinian security forces to repress anti-Israeli operations by Islamic activists, the Clinton administration did not want to weaken the Palestinian authority by applying pressure on the issue of the rule of law: for example, the establishment of state security courts was not criticized. Palestinian human right groups could not but notice that what governed U.S. policy in the Middle East was not universal principles such as human rights and peoples' self-determination, but whatever expediency that support for Israel required at any given time. The sudden conversion of the administration to reform during the spring of 2002 confirmed, for people in the street, and particularly for those who had not ceased advocating reform since the mid-1990, that Bush's call was another expediency, a tactic aimed at delaying serious resumption of the peace negotiations, which would have required a steady involvement from Washington and pressures brought to bear on the Israeli government to stop seizing land in the West Bank and Gaza, to end the closures of towns and villages, withdraw from areas occupied since September 2000, and accept a fair basis for a Palestinian–Israeli accord.

At a time when the Palestinian authority apparatus had lost control over the territories that were under its jurisdiction before September 2000, many Palestinians felt that even if it became "the perfect government," it still would be no more than an empty shell in the grip of an occupying army, which would go on insisting that whatever reform measures were adopted would be insufficient. Palestinian skepticism concerning reform was confirmed when the U.S. administration's attitude on Palestinian elections began to change: while the administration had advocated such elections in June 2002, it very quickly retracted when it realized that Arafat would pass the test at the polls. Many Palestinians would have subscribed to the words of a Hamas leader in Gaza in a harsh article on reform: "Whoever implements the policy of America and Israel is acceptable to them no matter how repressive he is against his own people. Whoever rejects the policy of America and Israel is branded by them as undemocratic, no matter how popular he is and even if he got his position through fair and democratic elections."[15]

As for the beleaguered Palestinian leadership, and whatever its misgivings about U.S. intentions, it had no other option than to face the issue of reform, because its very survival was at stake. Once the issue was imposed on the political agenda, it became a football in the internal power struggle rather than a road map to the perfect government. And as is the case in all power struggles in the world, the first to jump on the reform bandwagon were the pragmatists around the leadership who had something to gain in the power struggle (in this case, mainly the various Fatah factions) and those already in the leadership (mainly individuals loyal to Arafat) who had something to lose. Consequently, these last made some concessions, for example, in accepting the creation of a prime ministerial post, and were prepared to move ahead with other reform measures so as not to give the United States or Israel the excuse to proceed to another stage in the dismantling of the Palestinian authority and allow Israel to remove Arafat himself. Ironically, those who showed the least interest in the reform agenda were precisely those who had always advocated it with no thought of personal gain, as well as members of opposition groups who felt they had no chance in the present power struggle and the weary and disenchanted Palestinian street.

To conclude, it is fair to say that the Palestinian perception of America is not devoid of ambiguities and contradictions, not only among the various groups and forces, but also within each individual, because the image of America, unavoidably, has a bearing not only on their future but even on their self-image. For many Palestinians in the street, for intellectuals, the negative image of U.S. policy is mixed with admiration for American achievements. For the governing elite, the negative image is mixed with the pragmatic and existential need to deal with the only remaining superpower, the only country in the world that has any influence on Israel and that since 9/11 claims to impose its vision on the Middle East through the military campaigns against Afghanistan and Iraq. Thus, whatever the ambiguities and contradictions, the attitude of most Palestinians toward America appears to be more a consequence of America's dominant status than an expression of the so-called clash of civilizations.[16]

NOTES

1. James J. Zogby, *What Arabs Think: Values, Beliefs and Concerns* (Utica, NY: Zogby International and Arab Thought Foundation, 2002), p. 63.
2. Ibid.
3. Ibid., pp. 62–63.
4. For example, the Gallup poll conducted in December 2001–January 2002 in nine Arab and Muslim countries, Andrea Stone, "Many in Islamic world doubt Arabs behind 9/11," *USA Today*, February 27, 2002; the poll conducted late summer and early fall 2002 in 44 countries by the Pew Research Center in association with the *International Herald Tribune*, see Brian Knowlton, "A rising anti-American tide," *International Herald Tribune*, December 5, 2002.
5. British Council, *Connecting Future Research: Palestinian Territories Summary Report* (London: British Council, 2002), p. 2.
6. Hanan Ashrawi, "Image and reality: the role of the U.S. in the Middle East," in www.miftah.org/display.cfm?DocId=167.
7. Daoud Kuttab, "America is a great country but," in www.amin.org/eng/daoud_kuttab/2001/13sept2001.html.
8. Aluf Ben, "The celebrations have already begun," *Haaretz*, February 20, 2003.
9. Olivier Roy, *L'Islam mondialisé* (Paris: Seuil, 2002), p. 33. The fact is that little has been heard about individual Palestinians being members of bin Laden's Al Qaeda (see ibid., p. 23). So far, nobody (whether Palestinian Islamists, Israeli, or American spokespersons) has claimed a link between Palestinian Islamic organizations and Al Qaeda.
10. Some would argue, here, that states can be secretly behind sustained transnational political violence and that some Arab states have been involved in this kind of practices. But are there states among world or regional powers that are immune from the accusation? The difference between non-state actors and states conducting transnational violent operations is that the latter can be deterred, punished, or even submitted to by other states, while the former can only be dealt with through providing the conditions (not only military but also political and economical) that will allow the reconstruction of the hosting state's authority over its territory.
11. See Hussein Agha and Robert Malley, "Camp David: the tragedy of errors," *The New York Review of Books*, August 9, 2001; Akram Haniyyé,

"Ce qui s'est réellement passé à Camp David," *Revue d'études palestiniennes*, no. 77 (automne 2000).

12. For example, Menachem Klein, "The origins of Intifada II and rescuing peace for Israelis and Palestinians," in www.fmep.org/analysis/klein_origins_of_intifada_II.html.

13. "The impact of 11 September on the Israeli–Palestinian conflict," *Journal of Palestine Studies*, no. 122 (winter 2002), pp. 10–12.

14. See also Graham Usher, "Facing defeat: the Intifada two years on," *Journal of Palestine Studies*, no. 126 (winter 2003), pp. 29–33.

15. Ibrahim al-Maqadmah, "The American–Zionist reform," in www.amir.org/views/ibrahim_almaqadmeh/2002:oct19.html. Note that al-Maqadmeh was assassinated by the Israeli army in March 2003.

16. For field study validating the "anti-dominance" explanation over the "clash of civilizations" explanation, among a sample of students at the American University of Beirut, see: Jim Sidanius et al., *Why Do They Hate Us? The Clash of Civilizations or the Politics of Dominance*, New York: Russell Sage Foundation, Working Paper no. 187, 2002.

9

ANTI-AMERICANISM IN PAKISTAN

Mohammad Waseem

INTRODUCTION

The context for the present chapter is the post-9/11 wave of anti-American feelings in Pakistan, especially after the U.S. war on Taliban as well as the electoral victory of proto-Taliban groups in the October 2002 elections in the Pakhtun belt of the two provinces of Pakistan, NWFP, and Baluchistan. To understand the ambivalent and hostile attitudes toward the United States, or more precisely anti-Americanism in Pakistan, one needs to inquire about:

- other strands of negative feelings in Pakistan, which can be compared and contrasted with feelings against the United States;
- the sources of these feelings;
- the strength or weakness of these feelings in terms of their potential for transformation into public action, diplomatic profile, or policy structure;
- the relevance of these feelings for the future shape of events.

Attitudes toward America developed in Pakistan out of a variety of patterns of interaction between the two countries over the last half-century. However, most typically, this interaction has been characterized by the one-way flow of American influence and much less, if at all, the other way round. There were both positive and negative factors involved in strengthening the Pakistan–American relations. At the heart of the former was the American capital and technology, which Pakistan direly needed and which the United States was ready to make available to a significant level. As for the latter, the two countries were relatively free of any baggage from the past in terms of hostile relations, being as they were geographically distant and historically and politically irrelevant to each other, especially as Pakistan emerged as a distinct entity only in 1947. That means that Pakistan–American relations operated essentially from a pragmatic perspective. As opposed to this, relatively rigid ideological perspectives about certain other countries such as India, Israel, and the USSR-Russia characterized the national goals for most of the post-independence period in Pakistan.

The remoteness of the American public and private life from the experience and imagination of Pakistanis in general lent a peculiarly reductionist character to attitudes toward that country. At the bottom of it lay a state-to-state relationship, which was understood by Pakistan in terms of its security and economic development. Pakistani perceptions about Washington often took a turn for the worse in the wake of the latter's perceived tilt in favor of India. Alternatively, the U.S. withdrawal from active involvement in the region, such as after the Soviet withdrawal from Afghanistan in 1988, was bound to cost Pakistan much more than its eastern neighbor. Apart from the two pillars of Pakistan-U.S. relations, namely strategy and economic development, there have been very few patterns of exchange between the two countries in other fields such as art, music, law, literature, sports, diplomacy, fashion, as well as morals and manners covering vast areas of public and private life. In this sense, the Pakistan–American relations are far less comprehensive and meaningful than the relations between the United States and various European countries across the Atlantic.[1]Accordingly, the attitudes of Pakistanis toward the United States have been influenced essentially and almost exclusively by foreign policy considerations.

From the 1980s onward, the question of whether the United States was for or against Pakistan has been generally recast in broad religious terms. People now posed the question of whether the United States was for or against Islam. This question was underlined by the public consensus that Pakistan as a premier Islamic country was inextricably linked with the destiny of the Muslim world. As an increasing number of inter-state and intra-state conflicts involved Muslims as underdogs in one or the other part of the world, the public in Pakistan grew restive and reared suspicions of the United States in its capacity as the architect of the post–Cold War world. Therefore, we need to discuss various shades of anti-Americanism in Pakistan in the context of regional and global changes.

There have been various examples of sustained patterns of collective prejudice operating in Pakistan against various individual countries as well as idea-systems identified with them, respectively. Foremost among them is anti-communism. Pakistan inherited a foreign policy perspective from British India, which was rooted in the suspicion of the Soviet

Union as a country searching for a warm water port in Southern Asia.[2] From the perceived Soviet support of successive Afghan regimes, along with their Pakhtun irredentism, up to the Soviet incursion into Afghanistan in 1979 and beyond. Pakistan remained steadfastly anti-communist and anti-Soviet Union for most of the period after independence. Moscow's occupation of the classic Islamic lands of Central Asia for over a century provided a base line for an ideational sanction against the USSR and its "atheist" philosophy of communism. As the Red Army withdrew from Afghanistan after the 1988 Geneva Accord, followed by the disintegration of the Soviet Union and the end of the Cold War, Pakistan tried to adjust itself to the new realities in the form of the emergent Central Asian Republics. However, the inter-state relations between the regional powers including Russia, China, India, Pakistan, and Iran and their conflicting or overlapping interests in Afghanistan, held back a real advance of Islamabad's relations with Moscow. The lurking anti-Russian suspicions in Pakistan will perhaps continue to keep the country away from any real breakthrough in its relations with the polar bear in the near future.

A similar historical legacy, though younger in age, operates in the field of Indo-Pakistan relations. Anti-Indianism is a legacy of the partition in 1947. There is a widespread suspicion about India not accepting partition and, therefore, the moral legitimacy of Pakistan as an independent Muslim state. Also, India is widely understood as an aggressor in Kashmir, east Pakistan, and Siachin. Common perceptions about a bellicose India next door have generally shaped Pakistani attitudes toward secularism being the latter's state "ideology." On this side of the Indo-Pakistan border, secularism is perceived to be a ploy to undermine Muslim nationalism in British India as reflected by the Two-Nation Theory. Pakistanis hold what they consider the bogus and fraudulent secularism responsible for regular discrimination against the Muslim minority in the context of contemporary Indian politics.[3]

The third example of a persistent negative feeling among Pakistanis is anti-Zionism. This was born out of the creation of Israel in 1948. Even since the first wave of emigration of Palestinians at the hands of Israel after its birth, the latter has been the target of Muslim hatred in Pakistan as elsewhere for seeking to wipe the whole Palestinian nation off the map of the world. The profile of two Palestinian Intifadas is rooted in the scenes of Israeli tanks shooting stone-throwing young Palestinians, raising their houses, building Jewish settlements on the occupied lands, and denying basic human rights to Palestinians. Not surprisingly, the state and society in Pakistan carry an anti-Zionist feeling, which is intense, permanent, and uncompromising.[4]

Pakistan's perceptions about the United States are different in both content and style. First, there is no negative historical legacy of the United States. If at all, there is a memory of a fleeting moment in history close to partition when the United States pressed imperialist powers for decolonization. Nor was the United States remembered as an occupier of Muslim lands, as opposed to the Soviet Union. Its occupation of Afghanistan, by proxy, and Iraq, more directly, in the new millennium was to come later. Similarly, there was no legacy of war with America in Pakistan, whereas the latter had been in a persistent combat position vis-à-vis India. Indeed, there had been no direct war of any Muslim country with the United States up to the 1993 Gulf War against Iraq, which was professedly fought for a Muslim (Kuwaiti) cause. It is clear from these observations that anti-Americanism has had no historical and cultural roots in Pakistan. Therefore, it never acquired the status of an ideology unlike anti-Russian, anti-Indian, and anti-Zionist perspectives.[5]

This, however, does not mean that there was no opposition to the American involvement in the political, economic, and strategic matters of Pakistan, either directly on a country-to-country basis or indirectly as part of the U.S. policy about the region as a whole. There is a long history of anti-Americanism in Pakistan, which needs to be understood in its proper context. The following sections outline three major categories of critical attitudes toward America in Pakistan:

- anti-Americanism: a friendship/betrayal model;
- anti-Americanism: a world of Islam perspective;
- anti-Americanism: an imperialist model.

As far as the critical attitudes of the elite toward the United States are concerned, these have been generally issue-specific, such as the U.S. sanctions against Pakistan's nuclear tests. For understanding this line of anti-Americanism, we need to analyze the more stable and consistent pattern of pro-Americanism among the ruling elite, which provided the context for emergence of a periodically negative attitude leading to a sense of betrayal of American friendship.

FRIENDSHIP–BETRAYAL MODEL

The major source of Pakistani perceptions about the United States, both positive and negative, lies in the way the latter addressed Islamabad's security concerns vis-à-vis India.[6] The ruling elite in the country has remained steadfastly committed to American friendship as a potential equalizer in the context of the superior military power of India vis-à-vis Pakistan. A secondary interest in Islamabad, which was indeed the first priority for Washington in the regional context, was the Soviet threat from the north. Whenever the two perspectives of Washington and Islamabad differed in terms of a joint commitment of diplomatic or strategic resources to one or the other or both, it led to exposure of Pakistan to what it considered a security threat, and hence to mistrust of Washington. This so-called official model of anti-Americanism is characterized by a sense of betrayal in the friendship with the United States.

The American tilt in favor of India in the post-1962 NEFA war situation led to the first major disillusionment with Washington in Pakistan, which had become used to enjoying American support in and outside UN in its conflicts with India. This led to what can be considered the most important policy initiative in Pakistan's history, namely turning to China, after the initial, and in the end even more consequential, initiative of turning West in the 1950s. The Pakistani establishment was shaken out of complacency because it had already started considering the American support as an immutable fact of life. A sense of betrayal of American friendship opened Pakistani diplomacy to wider options in the East. It found China a willing partner in the new relationship, in the aftermath of the latter's partial estrangement from the Soviet Union in 1959, and more recently the American tilt toward Delhi in an expedient mode of diplomacy.

The downslide in Pakistan-U.S. relations continued up to the 1965 Indo-Pakistan War, which led to the American embargo on supply of weapons to both countries. Islamabad felt deeply stung because it had virtually put all eggs in the American basket, as opposed to India, which had diversified its sources of arms supply over the years. The withdrawal of American strategic support was followed by a gradual decline of Washington's economic assistance. The sense of frustration with the United States led to Ayub Khan's description of the national destiny in terms of "friends not masters."[7] A series of events that were characterized by a sense of displeasure with Washington followed. During the 1971 Indo-Pakistan War, the promised arrival of the U.S. naval fleet "Enterprise" in the Bay of Bengal turned out to be a nonenterprise and, therefore, a bleeding wound in the U.S.-Pakistan relationship within an hour of the latter's defeat in Dhaka. Under Z.A. Bhutto, Pakistan received a stern warning from Henry Kissinger against harboring nuclear ambitions. The country remained under the U.S. embargo from 1976 to 1981. The civil and military establishment and the articulate public, in general, became fiercely critical of what they considered the American discriminatory acts against Pakistan.

The Soviet incursion into Afghanistan finally opened up a new chapter in the history of Pakistan-U.S. relations as it led to a close strategic alliance between the two countries, almost fulfilling the original purpose of Pakistan's entry into the U.S.-led military alliances, CENTO and SEATO. There was an obvious overlap in the aims and objectives of the two countries as they got deeply engaged in the Afghan conflict. For the United States, it was the presence of the Red Army in Afghanistan, which remained a critical factor in its decision to build up a resistance movement against Kabul in the first place. It did so despite its deep suspicions about Pakistan's nuclear program. In this context, the U.S. withdrawal of support for Afghan mujahideen after the signing of the 1988 Geneva Accord and departure of the Red Army from Kabul in 1989 was bound to create misgivings among Pakistanis. The presidential noncertification of Pakistan's nuclear weapons program for the next decade, as per the Pressler Amendment, kept Pakistanis tense and, therefore, committed to the idea of the United States as a nondependable ally.

Toward the end of the 1990s, Pakistan came under heavy U.S. sanctions after deciding to launch nuclear tests on May 28, 1998 as a response to the Indian nuclear tests of May 11. These were followed by the "democracy sanctions" after the 1999 military coup. Among various hiccups on the way, the nondelivery of F-16 fighter planes for which Pakistan had already paid and then the non-reimbursement of the payment for several years created deep misgivings in Islamabad. It looked as if the 1996 Brown Amendment only temporarily put a halt to the decline of Pakistan–American relations. It was only after the terrorist attacks on the World Trade Center and Pentagon that the two countries rediscovered each other, much the same way as they did in the 1950s and 1980s. The post-9/11 resumption of the U.S. interest in Pakistan as a partner in its war against terrorism has enkindled a new spirit of friendship between the two countries. In the year 2002–2003, the cycle of friendship–betrayal moves along, and efforts are afoot on the part of President Musharraf to keep Washington tied down to the region.

The periodical and recurrent gap in the Pakistan–American friendship can be defined in terms of an overlap in the objectives of the two countries: for Pakistan, strong ties with an external "equalizer" vis-à-vis its much stronger adversary next door is the first principle of foreign policy. For the United States, disappointment with India's unwillingness to join its Cold War against the Soviet Union was the prime reason to align with Pakistan in the first place. The United States never supported any of Pakistan's wars with India, be it the 1965 War or the 1971 War, or Siachin in 1984 or Kargil in 1999. But the United States joined Pakistan's war effort in support of Mujahideen fighting the Soviet forces in Afghanistan from 1981 to 1989. Not surprisingly, a sense of betrayal on the part of the ruling elite in Islamabad set in throughout the 1990s as the United States withdrew from its active presence in the region, leaving Pakistan to deal with millions of Afghan refugees on its soil.[8]

Washington and Islamabad experienced not only periodical shifts in the patterns of their strategic alliance, thus leading to anti-Americanism of the variety of friendship–betrayal syndrome in Pakistan, but also a consistent pattern of their willingness to understand each other's exclusive commitments. For example, Pakistan and the United States voted frequently on opposite sides of the UN resolutions about various contentious issues. These included Arab–Israel wars, apartheid in South Africa, specific human rights issues, NPT, and CTBT. The official and nonofficial responses to the American stance on some of these issues ranged from outright criticism of Washington to allegations of anti-Islamic discrimination. The U.S. support for Israel and the U.S. nuclear nonproliferation regime in general elicited strong anti-U.S. reactions from the elite as well as the public in Pakistan.

It is not surprising that the sense of betrayal at the hands of the United States often led to active consideration of rival–friendship patterns. Enthusiasm for friendship with China is proverbial in Pakistan. The political leadership, military elite, public intelligentsia, as well as Islamic groups have all shown great admiration for the Chinese friendship, which is described as permanent and unflinching. Similarly, Pakistan crucially and pronouncedly befriended Sukarno's Indonesia during and after the 1965 War as well as Kaddafi's Libya during and after the 1971 War. However, after the dawn of the era of Petrodollar in the post-1973 Arab–Israel war period, millions of Pakistani workers migrated to Saudi Arabia. There followed a vast networking of Islamic organizations, banking operations, media activities, and economic cooperation between the two countries. Saudi Arabia reportedly helped Pakistan through its financial crisis in the aftermath of the 1998 nuclear tests. In the hour of the perceived betrayal by the United States, Pakistan has continued to invoke its "real" and lasting friendship with both China and Saudi Arabia. However, the fact that Pakistan's foreign policy is inherently India-centered has put a constraint on the strategic impact of Pak–Saudi and Pak–China relations. Neither China nor Saudi Arabia could fulfill Pakistan's perceived security requirements and the need for diplomatic support in world forums. In the year 2002–2003, Pakistan continued to cooperate with the United States for a joint operation against terrorism. However, in the long run, the elite in Islamabad can be expected to revert to its old position of considering Washington as nondependable ally when the latter withdraws from active alignment with Pakistan in the region. Its fears about the Indian and Israeli lobbies in Washington achieving exactly that has generally kept Islamabad on its toes.

THE WORLD OF ISLAM PERSPECTIVE

If India was the crucial factor in Islamabad's quest for an external equalizer and, thus, for its periodical frustration with the United States for not matching its friendship with an equal and lasting commitment, it is the Pan-Islamist profile of the state and society that often engendered negative perceptions about Washington. The world of Islam perspective is the key to understanding the frustration of Muslims in Pakistan and elsewhere with the perceived American policies about regional conflicts. The Islamic community is a unique phenomenon in as much as it is a mini-world in the larger world. For comparison, one can argue that there is no Hindu world. The state of India comprehensively represents the world of Hinduism, with Nepal being the only other Hindu state and Bali being a remote Hindu enclave in Muslim Indonesia. There is no Buddhist world either, unless one puts together China, Campuchea, and Sri Lanka as building blocks of a faith-based community of states. Nor indeed is there a Christian world whereby countries ranging from Philippines to Kenya, Tanzania and South Africa to England, France and Germany onward to the United States, Canada, Mexico, and Brazil would make a coherent bloc of countries bound by religious ties.

The core of the world of Islam comprises 54 Muslim states. In addition, it includes significantly large historical Muslim minorities belonging to countries such as India, China, Russia, as well as the Balkan states. The third major component of this world is the expatriate Muslim community in Western countries. In the second half of the twentieth century, various regional conflicts involving Muslim communities provided what was generally defined as Islamic causes, which increasingly welded the world of Islam together. The Palestinian issue can be considered the oldest and the most consistently frustrating Islamic cause in this regard. It has cost the United States a potential loss of goodwill and political support among Muslims of Pakistan and elsewhere. A series of Islamic causes followed: Kashmir, Afghanistan, Bosnia, Kosovo, Chechynia. Muslim publics in various countries got restive about Islamic causes whenever these emerged in any part of the world of Islam. However, it would have been a U.S. foreign policy disaster, in general, if the Muslim outrage had been accommodated in the decision-making channels of Muslim states, thus pushing them against Washington in a big way. In this context, authoritarian state systems in the Muslim world are functional for the pursuit of certain policies by the United States, which are unpopular among Muslims.

In Pakistan, the 1956 Suez Crisis put the state under a severe challenge from the public outrage. People demanded condemnation of the joint British, French, and Israeli attack on Egypt, and sought to mobilize both moral and material support for the Muslim brotherly state. However, Prime Minister Sohrawardy brushed aside the idea of cooperation between Muslim countries by publicly stating that zero plus zero was equal to zero. Decades later, the Nawaz Sharif government became part of the international coalition against Iraq during the 1991 Gulf War, in the teeth of opposition from the larger public. Finally, the Musharraf government's decision to join hands with President Bush in the latter's war effort against Taliban and Osama bin Laden in 2001–2002 led to a total reversal of Islamabad's foreign policy commitments in Afghanistan even as large sections of people opposed the move vigorously. In all the three cases, that is, in 1956, 1991, and 2001–2002, the society at large reacted sharply against what it considered Western (in the last two instances American) encroachment on the sovereignty and integrity of a fellow Muslim country. In every case, the government was placed under severe pressure to stave off a moral crisis. Each time, it managed to deflect the pressure and still survive in office.[9] The clue lies in the kind of the social and political milieu of Pakistan, which has been defined in another context as an hour-glass society as opposed to the civil society.[10] The Pakistan society comprises two half spheres of activity, which are joined like an hour glass, where there is only one-way flow of authority and value from top to bottom. There are very few links available to the society at the bottom to influence and shape the policy on top. Thus, it has been possible to have a pro-American state elite and anti-American society at large at the same time.

We can argue that "official" anti-Americanism is periodical in nature and limited in scope inasmuch as the idea is to win the United States back to a fuller commitment than is forthcoming at any given time. From the early years after independence, Pakistan's ruling elite was committed to alliance with the United States and other Western countries in the context of the Cold War between the capitalist and communist blocs. The general public was far from mobilized in the sense of joining an ongoing process of political participation. From the 1970s onward, a vehement process of sharing the fate of other Muslim communities in crisis started in earnest in Pakistan. First, in the aftermath of the 1971 Indo-Pakistan War, which resulted in the emergence of East Pakistan as Bangladesh, Islamabad turned its back to South Asia. There was an acute feeling that the region belonged to India's area of influence. Under these circumstances, Pakistan turned to the Middle East in a big way.[11] This move for turning away from its eastern neighbor in the wake of a military defeat and embracing its Western neighbors with prospects of entering the larger Muslim community could not come at a more opportune moment. The post-1973 War boom in oil prices made this increasingly more meaningful in financial terms.

Therefore, we can argue that the second phase of Pakistan's history in terms of perceptions about America can be understood in the framework of the world of Islam perspective. Two new dimensions were added to the old phenomenon of the elite's pro-American policies: first, the Western perceptions about the role of Islam in the region around Pakistan were now focused on the Afghan resistance movement against the Soviet presence in Kabul. This opened up new channels of public activity, which was operationalized through the use of Islamic identity in pursuit of foreign policy objectives. Second, the focus of the new movement went beyond the anti-Indian sentiment *per se*. By the 1990s, it was the fate of Islamic community in the larger context of global politics that inspired the action and belief of the enterprising sections of the population in Pakistan and other Muslim countries.

In this process, the 1991 Gulf War seems to be the turning point in the context of Pakistani perceptions about the United States. The traditional pro–Saudi Arabian Islamic parties, such as Jamat Islami, as well as some officers in the army high command including COAS General Aslam Beg condemned the U.S.-led attack on Iraq. The transnational Islamic networks, which had operated against the Soviet presence in and around Afghanistan in the 1980s, found a new adversary in the United States in the 1990s as the latter made its presence in the Gulf noticed all around in the Muslim world militarily, diplomatically, and otherwise.[12]

The general public in Pakistan has become politically more indulgent in Islamic issues in recent years. The circuit of activity and commitment to larger Islamic causes being pursued in territories outside Pakistan—sometimes involving continental distances—has gradually expanded during the last decade. A major contribution to this phenomenon can be traced down to globalization, especially the communication and media explosion. Together, the internet and TV brought about a revolution in the perception of both the Muslim and non-Muslim worlds and their encounter in various conflict zones. Public opinion in Pakistan, holding the United States responsible for the underdog position of Muslims in different parts of the world—especially in the heart of Islam in the Middle East—found a loud and thumping voice in the 1990s. The ruling elite was no more dismissive about it as a mere reflection of a lack of information and sensibility on the part of an ignorant and gullible public. Instead, it sought to tackle it through a dual policy of change at home and continuity abroad. Thus, it opened the doors of the state to Islamic groups through elections and sought to bring them in rather than leave them out. Second, it continued to follow a policy of maintaining or reviving the old pattern of strategic alliance with the United States. It can be argued that the state has all along felt obliged to continue to focus on India as its main security concern, and, therefore, to seek to fill the perceived defence gap with that country by cultivating American friendship. On the other hand, the society at large moved on to focus on the world of Islam as its main area of commitment, and felt alienated from the United States at varying degrees according to its perceived role against one or the other Islamic cause.

ANTI-IMPERIALISM

A permanent feature of the political attitude of Pakistanis toward the United States is the current of opinion looking at the latter's role in terms of imperialism. Generally, this is the position of political activists on the wrong side of the state establishment in Pakistan. The more they felt squeezed by the federal government in Karachi and later Islamabad, the more they were alienated from Washington in its perceived role as an ally and patron of the establishment in Pakistan. The situation on the ground was crystallized by the alienated sections of the public into a perception that the ruling elite—with its core of military bureaucratic apparatuses—and the American government together represent the ultimate power in

Pakistan. The reverse position was clear too: farther from the establishment, farther from America. Thus, the antiestablishment attitude at home was largely expressed through anti-American posturing and profiling.

There were two clearly identifiable sources of antiestablishment politics and policy: leftist politics and ethnic revival. The left in Pakistan represented a ramshackle movement. It inherited from a relatively dynamic leftist movement in British India, (i) ex-members of the Communist Party of India, led by urban-based intelligentsia, and (ii) workers and professionals operating through various organizational networks, such as trade unions and peasant associations (*Kissan Sabhas*). Various leftist groups, including Pakistan Communist Party, Azad Pakistan Party, Mazdoor Kissan Party, and Pakistan Socialist Party looked at successive governments as pawns in the hands of America. They interpreted the power of the state in Pakistan in terms of the U.S. super-ordinate role in shaping the framework of politics and foreign policy in that country. The greater the perceived repression of a government, especially a military government, the more severe was the criticism of what was understood to be the U.S. policy of supporting military dictators in Pakistan. As critics of successive authoritarian governments of Pakistan—often condemned as fascist—leftists kept anti-Americanism alive in certain sections of the mobilized public at the edges of the political community.

However, in the absence of party-based national elections on the basis of adult franchise for a quarter of a century, the mass discontent outgrew the ideological framework of Marxism–Leninism espoused by the "old left." Trade unionists, public activists, and progressive students and teachers overtook the relatively sophisticated urban intellectuals talking through the idiom of "scientific socialism" and Mao's peasant revolution. Ayub was ousted from power in 1969 through a mass agitation, which clearly dubbed him and his colleagues in the army as well as others—civil bureaucracy, industrialists, and ulema—as American stooges. The "new" left in (W) Pakistan was represented by the populist leadership of Z.A. Bhutto and a large army of enterprising youth in his party, Pakistan Peoples Party, struggling to enter the state system through the ballot. The mass perception that American intervention had worked against democracy in favor of the military establishment was firmly rooted in the public psyche. Under Bhutto (1971–1977), the leading idiom of politics—if not necessarily public policy—remained "leftist" and anti-imperialist, largely couched in the emerging context of Third Worldism.[13]

Under both Zia (1977–1988) and Musharraf (1999–), the U.S. policy has been geared to the establishment of a strategic alliance with Pakistan. This was against a backdrop of a continuing Afghanistan war in the post-Soviet incursion in 1979 and the post-9/11 situation, respectively. In the public perception, the role of the United States in Pakistan is identified with protection and support for military rulers at the gross expense of democratic and liberal forces. The process of government formation after the October 2002 elections alienated large sections of the political community due to concentration of major constitutional powers in the hands of President Musharraf. However, the political class, in general, feared that Musharraf was impregnable because of the U.S. support for his role in the continuing war against terrorism. The general realization is that democracy in Pakistan was never a part of the U.S. agenda for that country. Not surprisingly, there is a feeling that Americans are responsible for creating and for increasing imbalance between the civil and military wings of the state in favor of the latter. What was initially a leftist position of anti-imperialism has gradually expanded its scope to include the liberal position of a pro-democracy movement inasmuch as the United States is understood to be an expansionist power seeking to deal with power wielders in a society, irrespective of specific patterns of authority operating there. The two positions seem to have joined hands with the emerging ideological position of "Islam in siege" in the context of the prevalent dichotomy between Islam and the West, especially as expatriate Pakistanis seek to construct a Muslim identity for themselves.[14]

At one end, the left–right dichotomy pushed activists pursuing class-based models of political change toward an anti-American agenda. At the other end, the Center–periphery dichotomy created ethnonationalist movements in various federating units—East Bengal, Sindh, NWFP, and Baluchistan—which conceived the American role in Pakistan as antagonistic to their cause.[15] Throughout the Cold War era, the perspective of ethnonationalist activists pursuing their struggle against Karachi–Islamabad was firmly couched in the larger East–West dichotomy. Not surprisingly, the Pakhtun and Baluch nationalist elite sought to cultivate links with Moscow against Washington. In this scenario, Pakistan was criticized as an agent of American imperialism out to crush movements for national self-determination. The two movements belonged to the two provinces of NWFP and Baluchistan, respectively, which were located on the borders of a traditionally pro-Soviet country—Afghanistan. The fact that the latter was situated on the borders of the USSR helped the two nationalist groups approach Moscow through Kabul.[16]

The Sindhi and Bengali movements relied on India because that was the only outside country that was geographically adjacent and politically willing to support a potentially separatist cause against Pakistan. The Sindhi nationalism never reached a level of mass mobilization, which would have seriously challenged the federation. However, Bengali nationalism was able to move forward first in electoral terms in 1970, by winning a majority in the parliament and then in terms of a militant struggle against Islamabad in 1971, with the increasingly overt help of India. Washington's perceived tilt in favor of Pakistan against the backdrop of the aborted move of the American ship Enterprise in the Bay of Bengal ignited anti-American feelings among Bengalis. We can argue that the more the state of Pakistan was identified with Washington, the more the leftist and ethnic movements cultivated anti-American feelings. Activists from the left of the political spectrum everywhere, including Punjab, which was otherwise closely identified with the establishment, joined hands with ethnic nationalists, and were often ideologically united with reference to "the national question" as well as politically. In this way, they reinvigorated each other in the pursuit of their antiestablishment, and by default, anti-American agenda.

CONCLUSION

The preceding sections have outlined three major patterns of Pakistani perceptions about the United States. Insofar as the friendship–betrayal syndrome is concerned, a persistently India-centered worldview has characterized Islamabad's attitudes toward the United States as a balancing factor vis-à-vis its stronger neighbor. However, since the United States did not share this perspective on India, there was an overlap between expectations from each other. The elite in Pakistan felt betrayed whenever the United States opted for playing a neutral role in Indo-Pakistan conflicts. At the other end, the general public is becoming increasingly anti-American in the larger framework of the world of Islam.[17] The U.S. policies are largely perceived to be against Muslims in various regional conflicts.[18] A lesser current of opinion criticizing the U.S. role in Pakistan and elsewhere is couched in an anti-imperialist mode of thinking. In Pakistan, the leftist and ethnonationalist parties and groups oppose what they consider imperialist designs of the United States and its allies, especially in the context of supporting military dictatorships in Pakistan. Together these critical approaches to the United States occupy a larger area of public space than ever before, even as the ruling elite continues to be a partner in the American-sponsored war against terrorism. As long as perceptions about the conflict between the United States and the Islamic world persist, anti-Americanism is expected to expand in the larger society, both in scope and intensity.

NOTES

1. See Denis Lacorne et al , *The Rise and Fall of Anti-Americanism: A Century of French Perception* (London: Macmillan, 1990).
2. Alastair Lamb, *Asian Frontiers* (London: Pall Mall, 1991), p. 41.
3. See S.M. Burke, *Pakistan Foreign Policy: A Historical Analysis* (London: Oxford University Press, 1973), pp. 3–11.
4. See P.R. Kumaraswamy, *Beyond the Veil: Israel–Pakistan Relations*, Memorandum no. 55 (Jaffee Center for Strategic Studies, March 2000).
5. See Mohammad Waseem, "Pakistan's perceptions of the impact of U.S. politics on its policies towards Pakistan," in *Pakistan-U.S. Relations*, edited by Noor Hussain and Leo Rose (Berkeley: University of California, 1988).
6. See, e.g., Dennis Kux, *The United States and Pakistan 1947–2000: Disenchanted Allies* (Baltimore: Johns Hopkins University Press, 2001).
7. Ayub Khan, *Friends Not Masters* (Oxford: Oxford University Press, 1967).
8. For a detailed account of the Soviet withdrawal, followed by the US withdrawal from the region. see Deigo Cordovez and Selig Harrison, *Out of Afghanistan: The Inside Story of the Soviet Withdrawal* (New York: Oxford University Press, 1995).
9. Mohammad Waseem, "The dialectic between politics and foreign policy" in *Pakistan: Nationalism Without a Nation*, edited by Christophe Jaffrelot (London: Zed Books, 2002), p. 271.
10. Richard Rose, " 'Russia' as an hour-glass society: a constitution without citizens," *East European Constitutional Review*, 1995, p. 35.
11. See Marvin Weinbaum and Gautam Sen, "Pakistan enters the Middle East," *Orbis* (fall 1978).
12. See Saroosh Irfani, "Pakistan's sectarian violence: between the 'Arabist Shift' and Indo-Persian culture," paper for conference on religion and security in South Asia, Asia-Pacific Center for Security Studies, Honolulu, Hawaii, August 20, 2002.
13. Mohammad Waseem, *Pakistan Under Martial Law 1977–1985* (Lahore: Vanguard, 1987), pp. 196–202.
14. Yunas Samad, "Imagining a British Muslim identification," in *Muslim European Youth: Reproducing Ethnicity, Religion, Culture*, edited by Steven Vertovec and Alisdair Rogers (Aldershot: Ashgate, 1998), pp. 59–61.
15. For a comparative study of ethnic conflicts, see Charles Kennedy, "Pakistan: ethnic diversity and colonial legacy," in *The Territorial Management of Ethnic Conflicts*, edited by John Coakley (London: Frank Cass, 2003), pp. 150–161.

16. See, e.g., Selig Harrison, *In the Shadow of Afghanistan: Baluch Nationalism and Soviet Temptations* (Washington, D.C.: Carnegie Endowment for International Peace, 1981).

17. See Ziauddin Sardar and Merryl Wyn Davies, *Why Do People Hate America?* (Cambridge, UK: Icon Books, 2000).

18. For the two positions for and against the U.S. policies being the root cause of anti-Americanism among Muslims, see Usaama Makdisi, "Anti-Americanism in the Arab world: an interpretation of a brief history," *The Journal of American History*, Bloomington, September 2002; and Barry Rubin, "The real roots of Arab anti-Americanism," *Foreign Affairs*, November–December 2002.

10

THREE SOURCES OF
ANTI-AMERICANISM IN IRAN

Morad Saghafi

When on November 4, 1979 a number of armed individuals (a group later called *Daneshjouyan-e Khat-e Emam* or "Students of Imam [Khomeini]'s Line") took over the U.S. Embassy in Tehran, few people knew that this was the second invasion of the U.S. Embassy since the Revolution that unseated the Pahlavi dynasty. The first occupation occurred on February 14, only three days after the Pahlavi regime was overthrown. That takeover was initiated by militant members of the Marxist–Leninist group *Fadaiyan-e Khalgh*, established a decade earlier and dedicated to guerilla attacks against the Pahlavi regime as well as U.S. interests in Iran.[1] That day, the group issued a communiqué stating that the overthrow of the regime was the first step of the revolution that had to be continued until the elimination of capitalism in Iran and that American imperialism will be the most important force opposing this event.[2] The clergy and the "Revolutionary Council" condemned the action and, following a meeting with the provisional government's foreign minister, Ebrahim Yazdi, the group accepted to leave the premises peacefully. The resolution of the crisis took only half a day.

The second takeover lasted longer: a number of Embassy staff were taken hostage for 444 days. At the beginning of the seizure, it seemed that the new hostage takers did not know exactly what they wanted. Abbas Abdi, an eminent member of the group, admitted eight years later that they had responded to Imam Khomeini's speech on November 1, when he asked "students, collegians as well as students of theological schools to expand their struggle against America to force return the Shah"[3] who had recently been admitted to a hospital in the United States for treatment against cancer. He said that they had thought the affair would last "3 to 5 days."[4] It did not, and the longer the affair lasted, the more the demands for the Shah's extradition faded out in the light of the internal political debate.

The hostage takers confessed later, "they thought the success of this experience would have marginalized the provisional government."[5] But the student movement did not consider a mere confrontation with the government challenging enough. After a while, backed by the first document found in the U.S. Embassy, reconstructed carefully and published with an eye on the condemnation of the most democratic political factions, the students requested "the ban of political parties and organizations whose actions were not aligned with the revolution's objectives and values." First the "westernized intellectuals"[6] were denounced, then it was the turn of the "army officers, the westernized managers and technicians, liberal and democratic politicians, romantic militias and communists."[7] The students even asked the religious leaders to "purify their ranks from politically wrong elements."[8]

The diplomatic relations with the United States were severed, and, in the process, the United States was branded "The Great Satan." Iran had entered a new era in the field of foreign relations. However, the U.S. embassy affair had a much deeper effect on Iran's domestic political scene.

The provisional government resigned and with it the nonradical discourse that had gained the upper hand during the eight months that separated the victory of the revolution from the occupation of the American embassy. The embassy takeover provided another golden opportunity for radical Islamist forces, who used the event to challenge secular leftists as well as rival Islamic leftist groups, which did not show the expected allegiance to and respect for Khomeini's leadership.

The domestic consequences seemed ideal: the provisional government (composed in majority of liberal Islamic and secular forces) resigned a day after the takeover; the anti-Shah and anti-monarchic ambiance was revived; and, more importantly, all radical elements were forced to fully support the Khomeini followers, who had demonstrated that they were the most revolutionary because they were the most anti-imperialist force of the country.[9]

Considering this change of equilibrium among domestic political forces in Iran, which provided Khomeini's most radical followers with a dominant position, one can say that the takeover of the U.S. Embassy was, in fact, successful. But for the sake of our study, the event underlined other more important phenomena: first that anti-Americanism, as the most important criterion for anti-imperialism, no longer was the monopoly of Leninist and leftist secular groups in Iran, but the common position of nearly all antimonarchic revolutionary groups, including religious forces. Second that relations with the United States were not only a foreign policy issue but, also perhaps much more seriously, an internal Iranian affair. In other words, within Iran's domestic political framework, America became the focus of the relationship with a foreign power—a position reserved for Great Britain for 150 years prior to the event. When, how, and why this important shift happened, are questions that this chapter discusses. For the same reason—that is, the internal dimension of Iran-U.S. relations—the answer to these questions could not be found as the sole result of a debate about diplomatic history. Nondiplomatic factors, most of which have roots in the country's internal development, should also be considered.

THE UNTRUE FRIEND

Since the mid-nineteenth century, when the intrusion of the two superpowers of the time, Russia and Great Britain, became determinant for the destiny of Iran, the country's diplomacy has evolved around two basic ideas: first, trying to use the rivalry between the two superpowers and second looking for a third force. France, Austria, Germany, and, finally, America came to play the role of this third force in Iran's contemporary history.[10] Both strategies faced severe limitations. Regarding the rivalry between the two powers, Iran appeared too weak to be able to play one against the other.

As for the involvement of this third power, it was necessary that it was necessary that it has, not just sufficient military and economic authority but also the same level of geostrategic interest that dictated Russian and British attitudes toward Iran. Notwithstanding, it was evident that the serious involvement of this third force was very much dependent on the formation of a sphere of strategic interests in Iran. In fact, the French experience during the Napoleonic wars and the German experience at the time of World Wars I and II, demonstrated that, counting on the intervention of a third force could not only be in vain but also dangerous for the country.[11] Incidentally, for four decades, the Iranians tried to create such a sphere of interest for America. The decisive moment in this long "engagement" is when Washington not only appeared to be the only government that pushed for Iran's participation at the 1919 Paris conference, but also openly opposed the Iran–English treaty of 1919, which made Iran an English protectorate.[12]

But it was during the Azerbaijan crisis following World War II that America fulfilled the Iranian dream of a third force counterbalancing the British and Russian presence in Iran.[13] The American effort to force the Soviet army to withdraw from Iran—as other allied military forces did after the end of the war—could be considered as the fruit of a century of Iranian effort to involve the United States in its destiny. The territorial integrity of Iran was no longer threatened by the rivalry or the coalition of the two great powers and Iran could think about a more active foreign policy after some 150 years of passivity.

The euphoria of such a delayed victory hid another important reality from the Iranian eyes: the fact that America could no longer be this so called "third force," as Iran had already become an essential element in the confrontation between superpowers—the world had already entered the Cold War era.

In fact, during the period between the Azerbaijan affair (1945) and the coup against Mossadegh (1953) officials of both sides lived two very different versions of the same story. Americans had seen Iran as a Third World country, which needed development aid in order to avoid the grip of communism, hence Washington's so-called Point 4 Program.[14] They saw Iran as a neighbor of their most important Cold War adversary (Soviet Union), and could not allow the growth of a communist movement in Iran. Nor could they permit the country being ruled by an unstable state.[15] Finally, they saw Iran as an oil-producing country in a position to control half of the coast of the region where 70 percent of the world oil exports were in transit at that time. Washington considered the free flow of oil as one of the pillars of the development of Europe after World War II, but also of the Middle East including Iran.[16]

On the other hand, Iranian officials saw America as their liberator from Soviet occupation, their savior, their supporter in the struggle against British domination over Iran's oil industry, and their devoted friend, eager to develop their country; in short, a friend they had desired for two centuries. Incidentally, it was this same ever-sought ally that conducted the 1953 coup. A coup not against the unpopular and reactionary Qajar dynasty—as the British fomented it three decades ago—but against a nationalist and popular prime minister who was fighting against the British for the right of the country to manage its own source of wealth. In short, America became not just an enemy but something much worse than that, a disloyal, deceitful, and untrue friend—a fact that was difficult to forgive and even more difficult to forget.

AMERICA: THE NEW AND "UNIQUE" SUPERPOWER

In analyzing the 1953 coup, Iranian Nationalist forces failed to recognize their own weaknesses in leading the oil nationalization negotiations with the British. The reality is that by counting too much on the American support, they failed not only to evaluate their real national political basis but also the world's changing realities—thus letting the negotiation to turn into an open international and national crisis. This crisis not only alarmed the Americans but also led to concerns among many conservative political and social forces regarding a possible communist takeover of Iran. Instead, and with the importance given to the role of superpowers in the destiny of Third World countries, Iran's elite put all the blame on Americans. In other words, by fomenting the 1953 coup against Mossadegh, America not only became the disloyal friend, but, in the nation's psyche, it came to occupy exclusively the place reserved for Britain and Russia since the nineteenth century. From 1953 until today, it is thought that American influence on Iran's political scene has had a decisive impact, this is why political actors who enjoyed American support think that they do not need the cooperation of other actors for their policies. As a first example of this important feature in Iranian politics, we could follow the experience of the reformist prime minister who came to office in 1961, the first American intervention in the country's domestic affairs since the 1953 coup.

The year 1953 was an important one for Iran because it was the juncture where Iran finally managed to nationalize its oil. It was also the year in which Mossadegh was removed from power. However, 1953 was certainly not a turning point in the country's short-term political life. In fact, as soon as the essential objective of the coup, namely the prevention of a communist takeover in Iran was achieved, the Americans revived their pressure on the Shah to limit his authoritarian rule and to organize real and free parliamentary elections as soon as possible. The elections to the twentieth parliament, which were supposed to fulfill the American demand, were in fact a masquerade. The Shah was forced to name Ali Amini—an American protégé—as prime minister. Amini's cabinet started its work in May 1961 with promises of political and economic reform. In the 14-month period of premiership, Amini's assurance of having U.S. backing prevented him from paying any serious attention to nationalist forces.[17] For the same reason, he did not pay enough attention to the growing discontent among teachers and to the very important problem of controlling law enforcement units which savagely cracked down on teacher and student protests.[18] He also did not pay enough attention to his most important project, that is, the land reform program.[19] Following the military crackdown on the Tehran University, Amini's government resigned and the Shah was able to negotiate a moratorium to resist the American pressures for parliamentary elections. Manoutchehr Eqbal, a pro-Shah prime minister, replaced Amini and Iran never witnessed a free election until the 1979 Revolution.

The fall of Amini's government underlined two facts in the eyes of Iran's political elite: first that their own role in Iran's domestic affairs was insignificant, and second that the United States played an essential role in the country's domestic affair. The question was no longer whether the United States played a crucial role in Iran's political life, but whether this role was to Iran's advantage or to her disadvantage. Before the 1953 coup, only Iran's pro-Soviet communists regarded the U.S. role as malefic for Iran. However, after the Amini experience, nationalists as well as rightist democratic political forces also shared the communist's point of view. The only missing opposition political element in that phase consisted of religious political groups.

THE RACE FOR ANTI-AMERICANISM

Evidently, religious authorities and a multitude of religious groups had a forceful and dominant presence as the leaders of the anti-Shah and anti-American manifestations during the turmoil that preceded the 1979 revolution. This raised important questions as to when and how religion became such a revolutionary political force in Iran?[20] And the crucial question for our discussion is why and how religious forces chose the Shah and its U.S. backers as their worst enemy in place of the atheist Iranian communists and their ally, the Soviet Union.

The Fear from Communism

It is true that the Bolshevik Revolution initially relieved Iran's political life from the menace of a powerful and threatening neighbor, but the intervention of the Bolshevik army in Gilan, the northern province of Iran during the Jangali revolt, put an end to this short period of peace.[21] However, the event that really shocked the whole political life of Iran was the 1945 Azerbaijan crisis. The Azerbaijan crisis indicated to Iran for the first time that the Bolsheviks were the true and also more active and more ideological heirs of the Russian Empire. Moreover, the crisis had also shown that this new and young imperialist force had a powerful internal ally, namely the Tudeh Party (The Communist party of Iran). The acknowledgment of the existence of internal and external forces that could drag Iran into the communist sphere of influence had a tremendous effect on the rivalry between state and religion in Iran. This effect is best seen in one of the most critical moments of Iran-U.S. relations, during the 1953 coup.[22]

It is now evident that in the course of the 1953 coup against Mossadegh, the United States not only had the backing of royalist forces and a few dissidents of the Mossadeghist movement, but also enjoyed the tacit backing of a very influential religious figure, Ayatollah Kashani.[23] Later on, radical religious movements wanting to recuperate the popularity of Mossadegh's struggle for oil nationalization praised Kashani's role during the period when he supported the prime minister and never admitted his later shift toward the monarchy. Even today, the Islamic government of Iran continues to justify their anti-Americanism partly by referring to the role that the U.S. government had played in the 1953 coup. But it is evident that at the moment of the coup, clerical leaders saw it as a defense against the potential spread of communism in the country. In an autobiography published in 1996 in Iran, Hojatol-eslam Falsafi, a very famous orator, who was related to Ayatollah Kashani, well summarizes the state of mind of religious leaders during the weeks that preceded the coup:

> In fact, religious leaders were caught between two choices: either they had to defend the greatness of Islam and the survival of Shiism, in that case they had to defend the Constitution. which recognized Shiism as the official religion of the country and this was—willingly or not—realized through the defense of constitutional monarchy. Or they had to keep quiet and free the scene for the Tudeh (communist) party to be active and potentially take power, which could have led to the eradication of Islam in the country. It was evident that religious leaders had the duty not to stay impartial and to defend the constitutional monarchy against communist activism.[24]

In the light of this event, it is essential to ask what happened between the 1953 coup and the turmoil that preceded the 1979 revolution, which gave the religious forces the opportunity to challenge the monarchical power and its American ally, without the concern that communists could benefit from the revolutionary situation and drag Iran into the sphere of Soviet influence?

The answer is that in the quarter century that separates the two events, the religious elements became the hegemonic political force of the country. This was achieved via two processes: first, by gaining the leadership of the opposition—a process helped by the Shah who eliminated all other opponents; and second, by developing a new political discourse that integrated the most important mobilizing themes of their potential rivals, specifically the nationalists (heir of Mossadegh movement), as well as leftist political forces, and thus preventing the latter two currents from gaining the upper hand in the Iranian political scene.

The 1963 Turning Point and the Search for Leadership

Khomeini's revolt in 1963 was certainly the first time that a well-known, high-ranking clerical figure intervened directly to reverse the half century long process of giving in of religious institutions to the state.[25] This attitude would probably have continued if, by the end of 1962, the Shah's authoritarian rule had not emptied the country's political scene from all political opposition that could be considered reformist.

Khomeini's entry was announced in June 1963, when he delivered a sermon in the Faizieh religious school in Qom, warning the Shah in blunt language to behave and respect clerical leaders. He was arrested on June 4. Few hours later, a crowd of protestors was formed near Tehran's Bazar and in the mid-morning, troops opened fire. The riots reached their climax on June 5 (15 Khordad) when they spread to other major cities. However, the riots were finally clamped down bearing a heavy loss of life.

When months later some of the Mossadeghist leaders were released from prison, they decided that participation in elections was unjustified, especially as election results were known in advance.[26] In their argument about refraining from elections, they also underlined the fact that after the 15 Khordad riots, prisons were filled and there was no point in producing more martyrs. They decided to adopt a policy of "patience and waiting," leaving to the religious forces the first place in opposing the Shah. Thus, with the help of the Shah, Ayatollah Khomeini and his radical followers had won the battle of leadership over nationalists and other moderate opposition leaders.

Incorporating the Leftist Discourse

The utilization of the most anti-American slogans during the pre-revolutionary turmoil in 1978 indicated clearly that the religious forces no longer expressed the fear they had in 1953. In the meantime, the religious forces were able to use leftist jargon (the promise of a class-less society and social justice for all) to mobilize people, while staying critical to the materialistic approach of communism. In fact, during these 25 years, they had become the most radical anti-monarchical political force and by incorporating in their discourse the anti-Imperialist element of the Left, they were in a good position to challenge secular leftist groups in their own backyard.

In 1943, two years after the departure of Reza Shah and the beginning of the longest period (12 years) of democracy in Iran, some religious activists were concerned about the attraction of the urban youth in Tehran and other large cities to the leftist discourse.[27] One of the first political attempts by religious activists to counterbalance the Tudeh party activities was the Nehzat-e Khodaparastan-e Socialist (Movement of socialist God-Worshippers)[28] that began its cultural and social propaganda in 1943 and became politically active six years later. During the six years of preparation for political action, they published a few booklets, explaining why Islam could give the Iranian population the means of building a more just and free society, without being obliged to let down their religion. Nakhshab, the leader of the group, who wrote all the booklets, argued that man had the moral capability to intervene into his destiny. For him, Lenin was the first person who had shown the inefficiency of materialism, because he did not wait for the materialist force of history to bring down the bourgeoisie and give the rule to the proletariat. For Nakhshab, Lenin's action for building "Socialism" voluntarily in a backward country like Russia had shown the limit of materialism and demonstrated the power of idealism. Hence, the best way of fighting for socialism was through religion and not through materialistic ideas propagated by the Tudeh party.[29]

Later, this task was assumed by Ali Shariati. He believed that another reading of Islamic history is necessary to break down the rigid conservatism of the clergy, responsible for turning Islam into a passive and soulless religion, unfit to deal with contemporary problems.[30] Therefore, he aimed at reviving Islam as the ideology of liberation of Iran as well as the ideology of freeing the Islamic world from tyranny and dependency. In doing this, Shariati made a tremendous effort to Islamize Marxism and to give a new reading of Islamic history through his new

reading of Islam. He gave a complete Islamic version of Marx's and
Engels's *Historical Materialism*, where the history of humanity starts
with early commune and finishes with the elimination of bourgeoisie,
and the establishment of a "Monolithic Classless Society."[31] He went
even further and produced a thesaurus including Islamic synonyms for
the most important notions and concepts used in the Marxist–Leninist
literature.[32] He taught his students that the real Islam had a class preference and this is the poor and disenchanted.[33] Summarizing his own
work in an open letter to his father, he said:

> what is the source of the greatest hope and energy to me is that, contrary
> to the past, it is evident that future intellectuals, leading mental figures
> and builders of our society and culture will not be the Westoxicated
> or Eastoxicated materialists, Marxists and nationalists; but they will be
> intellectuals that will choose the Islam of Ali [the first Shiite Imam] and
> the line of Hussein [the third Shiite Imam] as their school of thought for
> sociological behavior and revolutionary ideology.[34]

Shariati's revolutionary reconstruction of a new collective understanding of Islam was used by Sazeman-e Mojahedin-e Khalgh-e
Iran (People's Mojahedin Organization of Iran—MKO), a guerilla
organization that started its military operation in 1971, in an attempt
to disrupt the celebrations of the 2500-year anniversary of Iranian
monarchy. During their six years of theoretical preparation before
launching military actions, the MKO came to the conclusion that the
feebleness of Iran was not caused by the country's people, but by its
compromising leaders.[35] The MKO thought that the Iranian monarchy's dependency on the United States was, at the same time, its
source of power and its Achilles' heel. It is not a surprise then that
MKO's military operations were independently directed against the
regime and American presence in Iran. Targets of assassination included
the U.S. military adviser to the Shah, as well as the chief of Tehran
police. MKO assassinated General Price, the highest ranking American
military officer stationed in Iran, and also bombed the Coca Cola
building in Tehran. The organization was also responsible for several
explosions in Tehran on the eve of President Nixon's official visit to
Tehran in 1972.[36]

Hence, in less than two decades, while trying to achieve an hegemonic position in the struggle against the dictatorship of the Shah,
the religious political activists followed the path of radicalization and
anti-Americanism. By being a part of the more radical forces asking
for the departure of the Shah during the events that preceded the
1979 revolution, they demonstrated that they were, in fact, among

the most revolutionary political forces of the country. After the overthrow of the Shah, they had to demonstrate that they were also the most anti-American. This was done through the occupation of the U.S. embassy in Tehran. By doing so, the Islamic students put a victorious end to the rivalry between Iran's political entities, which was more than two decades old—a rivalry constructed around anti-monarchism and anti-Americanism.

FROM ANTI-ISRAELISM TO ANTI-AMERICANISM

Interestingly enough, Ayatollah Khomeini never referred to the 1953 coup and the role of the Americans in fomenting it in his pamphlets and discourses pronounced from 1962 (date of his first political intervention) till the closing months of 1979. Even when on October 27, 1964 he made one of his most furious speeches against the diplomatic immunity given to Americans working in Iran, he did not say a word about the coup.[37] He was expelled from Iran, spent 11 months in Turkey, and then went to Iraq for a long period of exile (13 years). Even there, and while the pro-Soviet and anti-Iranian Iraqi government would, probably, not prevent him from doing so, he avoided to refer to the U.S. role in 1953. While he certainly adopted an anti-American discourse, he avoided referring to an event that could give legitimacy to the nationalist movement. Instead, he enriched his anti-American discourse by using elements directly related to Islam and the Muslim people of Iran, the Middle East, and other parts of the world. The missing link was Israel.

Israel, its agents, and its conspiracies against Islamic countries had a continuous presence in Ayatollah Khomeini's discourse; but before being identified as an American agent and a source of anti-Americanism in Iran, Israel had different and very diverse roles. First, Israel was hated because of Baha'ism (a new sect developed in Iran and claiming that Bahaullah was the Prophet of God—contrary to the teachings of the Koran that Prophet Mohammad was the last prophet). Bahai's have their most important temple in Israel. For a while in Ayatollah Khomeini's discourse, one cannot distinguish between Israelism and Baha'ism.[38] Furthermore, Israel was the symbol of the Islamic community's incapability to unite against a foreign power that weakened and exploited divisions within that community. In this position, Israel was not worse than the Kashmir issue. Khomeini wanted Muslims to be united against the conspiracy of Jews and Christians, which had emerged in the creation of the state of Israel. He argued that "had only four hundred[39] million of the total seven hundred million Muslims

been united" the Jews would not have been able to establish their
state in Palestine or the Indians to dominate Kashmir. Israel was not
just the product of an American conspiracy but of the common conspiracy of both the United States and the Soviet Union, the work of
"the West" and "the East" to annihilate Islam and the Muslims.[40]

Considering the above, the question is when exactly did Khomeini's
anti-Israelism turn to anti-Americanism? It seems that this is the
precise moment when the Shah decided to offer to the American
army the support they needed to help the Israelis during the 1973
Egyptian–Syrian attack. The Khomeini declaration following that
event is undoubtedly the most radical of his declarations ever made.
After fiercely condemning the Shah's support for Israel, he urged the
Iranian masses to "oppose the interests of the United States and Israel
in Iran, and attack them even to the point of destruction."[41] From
that time on, there is no distinction for Khomeini between Israeli and
American interests.

This same declaration is also the occasion for Ayatollah Khomeini
to declare publicly, for the first time, his deep desire to see the Pahlavi
Monarchy overthrown in Iran.

> I had already warned several times about the danger of Israel and its
> elements that are led by the Shah of Iran. Muslims will not see happy
> days if they do not get rid of this corrupt element, and Iran will not be
> free as long as it is a prisoner of this family.[42]

It is true that, since his first political appearance in 1963, Khomeini
always used very direct language to talk to the Shah as if the monarch
had no knowledge about what was good and what was bad for Iran.
He gave advice to the Shah in a tone similar to the one used by a
school supervisor talking to his undisciplined and bad students. He
never asked the Shah to do anything in particular; he always warned
him to respect the constitution, to pay allegiance to Islam, to spend
his money for the poor, to be aware about the infiltration of Israeli
and American agents in Iran, and so on. But it is also true that he never
openly asked for the departure of the Shah and certainly not the
dynasty. The question then is why did he suddenly decide to change
his tone and approach? What was so special about the 1973 experience
that Khomeini decided to declare that enough is enough? The text of
his declaration contains the answer:

> Now that a large majority of the Muslim countries and several non-
> Muslim countries are in war against Israel, the Iranian state and its

undignified Shah, due to his servitude to America and to show his subordination are apparently quiet but in reality they are supporting Israel.

And the conclusion follows:

> I feel danger from this servant of America for the world of Islam, and it is now the duty of the Iranian people to prevent this dictator's crimes and it is the duty of the Iranian army and its officials not to accept this humiliation and to find a solution for the independence of their homeland.[43]

From Israel to the Shah, and from the Shah to America, this is the path that brought Ayatollah Khomeini and the mass of his followers from anti-Israelism to anti-Americanism.

CONCLUSION

Iranian anti-Americanism, compared, for example, to French anti-Americanism that includes strong cultural and anthropological aspects,[44] is almost only political. However, one should admit that it was a special political relationship.

During the course of half a century, every Iranian political force thought that by enjoying American support, it could run the country and oblige other forces to be subdued or risk being ejected or completely marginalized from the country's political scene. The victory of the Islamic Revolution showed that between 1953 and 1979, everything had been changed in this regard: now, each political force thought that all it needed to succeed was to carry the anti-American flag and be its champion. When, in 1953, Iran's ever-sought ally, namely America, turned out to be an untrue friend, its image was definitively stained for Iranians. However, America's power and authority were not affected. America became even more than before, in the Iranian vision of politics, the powerful force that could play a decisive role in Iran's internal politics. It could foment a coup d'état against a popular prime minister and bring the Shah back to his throne; it could force the same Shah to organize free elections and to step back in front of an unpopular prime minister who had the so-called American green light for organizing an agrarian reform; it could give back his confidence to his majesty and let him rule an authoritarian regime for 15 years before finally letting him down when the revolution emerged.

The American presence was supposed to free the Iranians from foreign interventions, which threatened Iran's independence. However, it turned out to be the reverse. At the dawn of the revolution, all anti-monarchic forces believed that Iran could choose freely its own destiny, only if the country could get rid of the U.S. intervention. By not realizing the Iranian dream, America became Iran's nightmare. Instead of becoming their savior, their Messiah, the United States became their troublemaker, their Satan.

While both points of view contain some truth regarding Iranian politics, it seems that they could not take account of its most decisive aspects. Like in every country, socioeconomic conditions, as well as decision of the country's leading political actors, are the essential determinants of political destiny. Of course, if most political actors continue to think that Americans (by their presence or their absence) play the decisive role in the political future of the country, then, in fact, Americans could have this messianic or satanic power. In other words, the most basic source of anti-Americanism in Iran resides exactly where its most basic source of pro-Americanism lies, namely, in the refusal of Iranians to take a serious look at their own problems and to find indigenous solutions, preferring to give the job to outside powers, and hope and pray for these to be the messianic ones.

NOTES

1. For the history of this organization see Maziar Behrooz, *Rebels Without Cause. The Failure of the Left in Iran* (London: I.B. Tauris, 1999).
2. Sazeman-e Fadayian-e Khalgh-e Iran, "Communique about the task of the provisional government," *Keyhan Newspaper*, February 14, 1979.
3. "Khaterat-e Abbas Abdi, Yeki as Daneshjouyan-e Khatt-e Emam. Barressi-ye Nahve-ye Sheklgiri-ye Harekatha-ye Daneshjouyi az aghaz" (Memories of Abbas Abdi, one of the students of Imam's line. Study about the formation of student movement from the beginning), *Keyan-e Sal (Annual Keyhan)*, New series, Year 2, vol. 2, Iran during 1365/66 (1986/87), p. 9.
4. Ibid.
5. Ibid.
6. "Etelai-ye efshagari shomare-ye 20" (The denounciation communiqué no. 20), *Asnade Lane-ye Jassoussi (Documents of the Spy Nest)* (Tehran: Markaze Nashr-e Assnad-e Lane-ye Jassoussi [Center for publishing the Document of the Spy Nest]), vol. 1–6, p. 105.
7. "Etelai-ye efshagari shomare-ye 23" (The denounciation communiqué no. 23), *Asnade Lane-ye Jassoussi (Documents of the Spy Nest), op. cit.*, p. 125.
8. Ibid., p. 126.
9. For an account of the mobilization caabilities of these leftist group and their rivalry with the Khomeini's followers, see Assef Bayat, *Street Politics*.

Poor People's Movements in Iran (New York: Columbia University Press, 1997).

10. For an academic account of the presence of Britain and Russia in Iran, see Firooz Kazemzadeh, *Russia and Britain in Persia, 1864–1914* (New Haven: Yale University Press, 1968). For the search of the third power, see R.K. Ramzani, *The Foreign Policy of Iran: A Developing Nation in World Affairs* (Charlotteville: University of Virginia Press, 1966).

11. Kaveh Bayat, "Amrika va Bitarafi-ye Iran" (America and the iranian non-alignment policy), *Goftogu Quarterly*, no. 27 (spring 1379 [2000]), 73–85.

12. Fereydoun Zandfard, *Iran va Jame'-ye Melal (Iran and the Society of Nations)* (Tehran: Shirazeh, 1377 [1998]).

13. Touraj Atabaki, *Azarbaijan Ethnicity and the Struggle for Power in Iran* (London: I.B. Tauris, 2000).

14. For the American help to Iran through the "Point 4" program, see William E. Warne, *Mission For Peace. Point 4 in Iran* (Bethesda, Maryland: Ibex Publishers, 1999). For the less state-oriented American effort to help Iran's development, see Linda Wills Qaimmaqami, "The catalyst of nationalization: Max Thornburg and the failure of private developmentalism in Iran, 1947–1957," *Diplomatic History*, vol. 19 (winter 1995), 1–31.

15. There are a significant number of books and papers that analyzes the Iranian–American relation through the logic of Cold War. See James A. Bill, *The Eagle and the Lion: The Tragedy of American Iranian Relation* (New Haven: Yale University Press, 1989). Richard W. Cottam, *Iran and the United State: A Cold War Case Study* (Pittsburgh: University of Pittsburgh Press, 1988). Habib Lajevardi, "The origins of the U.S. support for an autocratic Iran," *International Journal of Middle East Studies*, no. 15 (1983), 225–239.

16. For this point of view, which does not see the Cold War logic as the dominant logic of American–Iranian relations, see Robert MacFarland, "A peripheral view of the Cold War," *Diplomatic History*, vol. 4 (fall 1984), 335–351. Barry Rubin, *Paved with Good Intentions: The American Experience and Iran* (New York: Oxford University Press, 1980).

17. H.E. Chehabi, *Iranian Politics and Religious Modernism. The Liberation Movement of Iran under the Shah and Khomeini* (London: I.B. Tauris, 1990), pp. 140–186.

18. For a critical account of the February 1961 student protest and the savage intervention of military forces under Amini's premiership, see Kaveh Bayat, "Daneshgah-e Tehran, Avval-e Bahman-e 1340" (Tehran University, January 20, 1961), *Goftogu Quarterly*, no. 5 (fall 1373 [1994]), 45–57.

19. For an accurate and political history of the land reform, see Eric J. Hooglund, *Land and Revolution in Iran, 1960–1980* (Austin: University of Texas Press, 1982).

20. See, e.g., Hamid Dabashi, *Theology of Discontent. The Ideological Foundation of The Islamic Revolution in Iran* (New York and London: New York University Press, 1993). For a more sociological analysis, see

Said Amir Arjomand, *The Turban for the Crown. The Islamic Revolution in Iran* (New York and Oxford: Oxford University Press, 1988). For a research presenting these changes with a background of history of the shi'ism, see Yann Richard, *Si'ite Islam. Polity, Ideology and Creed* (Oxford and Cambridge: Blackwell, 1995); Shahrough Akhavi, *Religion and Politics in Contemporary Iran. Clergy–State Relations in the Pahlavi Period* (Albany: State University of New York Press, 1980).

21. Cosroe Chaqueri, *The Soviet Socialist Republic of Iran, 1920–1921. Birth of the Trauma* (Pittsburgh and London: University of Pittsburgh Press, 1994).
22. About Kashani and the way he is rehabilitated, see Yann Richard, "Ayatollah Kashani: precursor of the Islamic Republic?" in *Religion and Politics in Iran. Sh'ism from Quietism to Revolution,* edited by Nikki R. Keddie (New Haven: Yale University Press, 1983).
23. To evaluate how much these withdrawals were important for the decision of American intelligence service to program the coup, see Kermit Roosevelt, *Counter Coup. The Struggle for the Control of Iran* (New York: Mc Graw Hill, 1981 [1979]).
24. Hojatol-eslam Falsafi, *Khaterat va Mobarezat (Memories and Struggles)* (Tehran: Entesharat Markaz Assnad Enghelab Eslami, 1376 [1997]), p. 112.
25. For a documentary history of the state–clergy relationship during the Pahlavi era until 1960, see Seyyed Mohammad Hossein Manzoor ol Ajdad, *Marja'iat dar Arse-ye Jame'e va Siassat (The Sources of Imitation in the Realm of Society and Politics)* (Tehran: Shirazeh, 1380 [2001]).
26. Chehabi, *op. cit.,* pp. 180–181.
27. As an example of religious mobilization against the Tudeh Party in Shiraz, see Ali Shariatmadari, "Nokat Tarikhi, Faaliyat Hezb-e Tudeh, Melliha va Guerayesh-e Eslami" (Historical notes: Tudeh Party activities, the nationalists and the Islamist currents), *Tarikh Va Farhangue Moasser Quarterly,* no. 8 (winter 1372 [1993]), 114–127.
28. For more details, see Morad Saghafi, "Olguha-ye Noavari-ye Siassi dar Iran: Negahi be Tajrobe-ye Nehzat-e Khodaparastan-e Socialist" (Patterns of political innovation in Iran: the experience of the movement of socialist God-worshippers), *Goftogu Quarterly* (fall 1376 [1997]), 9–26.
29. Mohammad Nakhshab, *Bashar-e Maddi be Zamime-ye Chahar resale-ye Digar (The Materialist Man and Four Other Essays),* Nashr-e Karvan, Ghom, 1398 Lunar year (1982). The date of the first edition of the five essays is between 1950 to 1952.
30. Ali Shariati, *Tashayyo'e alavi va Tashayyo'e Safavi (Alavi Shi'ism and Safavid Shi'ism),* Collected Works (Tehran: Enteshar Publishing House, 1359 [1980]), vol. 10.
31. Ali Shariati, *Eslam Shenassi (Islamology),* Collected Works (Tehran: Enteshar Publishing House, 1357 [1978]), vol. 16, p. 63.
32. Ali Shariati, *Shi'e Yek Hezbe Tamam (Sh'ism, a Complete Political Party),* Collected Works (Tehran: Enteshar Publishing House, 1357 [1978]), vol. 7, pp. 95–97.

33. Ali Shariati, *Jahatguiri-ye Tabaghati-ye Eslam* (*The Class Orientation of Islam*), Collected Works (Tehran: Enteshar Publishing House, 1358 [1979]), vol. 13, p. 113.

34. Ali Shariati, *Ba Mokhtabha-ye Ashena* (*With Familiar Listeners*), Collected Works (Tehran: Hosseyniye Ershad), vol. 1, pp. 7–8.

35. For the full account, see Ervand Abrahamian, *Radical Islam: The Iranian Mojahedin* (London: I.B. Tauris, 1989).

36. Suroosh Irfani, *Revolutionary Islam in Iran. Popular Liberation or Religious Dictatorship?* (London: Zed Books Ltd, 1983), p. 95.

37. Ayatollah Ruhollah Khomeini, *Sahife-ye Nur* (*Letters from Light*), Introduction by Ayatollah Seyyed Ali Khamenei, 16 vols. (Tehran: Markaz-e Madarek-e Farhanghi-ye Enghelab-e Eslami, 1363 [1982]), vol. 1, pp. 109–113.

38. See all the Ayatullah Khomeini's discourse befor the anticapitulation in 1964. *Sahif-ye Nur, op. cit.*, pp. 8–102.

39. Ayatollah Khomeini, *Sahife-ye Nur*, vol. 1, p. 120.

40. Ibid., p. 186.

41. Ibid., p. 207.

42. Ibid., p. 208.

43. Ibid.

44. Philippe Roger, *L'Ennemi americain. Généalogie de l'antiamericanisme francais* (Paris: Le Seuil, 2002).

11

Uncle Sam to the Rescue? The Political Impact of American Involvement in ASEAN Security and Political Issues in the Wake of 9/11

Farish A. Noor

Introduction: The "Great Game" Comes to Southeast Asia

Never have the armies of the North brought peace, prosperity, or democracy to the peoples of Asia, Africa, or Latin America. In the future, as in the past five centuries, they can only bring to these peoples further servitude, the exploitation of their labour, the expropriation of their riches, and the denial of their rights. It is of the utmost importance that the progressive forces of the world understand this.

> Samir Amin,
> Arab Political Scientist,
> writing in *al-Ahram*, May 2003

Political realities are just as much the result of discursive activity as they are rooted in concrete facts and figures. This fact was demonstrated most explicitly in the discursive and ideological acrobatics performed by the leaders of Western and Southeast Asian countries in the immediate aftermath of the terrorist attacks on the United States of America on September 11, 2001. To bring home the reality of the events that took place thousands of miles away, the Kuala Lumpur Commercial Centre (KLCC) twin towers in Malaysia were evacuated the following day, after a bomb scare that came just as Malaysians were coming to terms with the loss of Malaysian workers who were lost or killed in the New York attacks. The form and content of Malaysian political discourse was subsequently altered on the basis of a simple rumor.

As the events following the aftermath of the attack were broadcast all over the world by American media channels like CNN, emotions ran high. The paranoia and xenophobia stoked by the media was soon echoed by the establishment itself. The American government responded with calls for revenge and retribution, and, in the days that followed, the president of the United States, George W. Bush, vowed that those responsible for the attacks would be made to pay and that America will lead the new global "crusade" against terrorism—an unfortunate choice of words that only added to the confusion and anxiety of the time, and which also shifted the focus of U.S. political rhetoric to a radically different register.

As a result of this discursive shift, the political game-board of Asia was reconfigured, with old allies suddenly being designated as "rogue states," while erstwhile adversaries suddenly being bestowed the title (by Washington, no less) of "moderate, progressive" Muslim states that were allied in the global "war against terror."

The discourse of the war against terror soon developed into a sophistic discursive economy of its own, replete with both positive sig- nifiers ("defenders of peace, freedom and democracy"; the "allied forces of good"; the "crusade against terror," etc.) and negative signifiers ("Muslim extremists/fanatics"; the "Axis of Evil," etc.). Mellifluously driving this rhetoric was an internal idea that was—though based mainly on unfounded and empirically un-verifiable essentialist notions— coherent and logical in its own way. Two neat chains of equivalences were drawn: on the one side stood the "forces of good" led by an increasingly unilateralist and bellicose United States and its allies, and on the other stood the "Axis of Evil" made up of those countries and movements that were said to be supportive of the use of terrorism against the West.

In time, the discourse of war against terror was globalized and hegemonized—mainly thanks to the dominance of the omnipresent American media in Asia—and the logic of the war against terror was normalized in both national and international politics in the region. The governments of ASEAN, some of which were already engaged in internal conflicts against numerous separatist movements in their own countries, were the first to put to service the discourse of war against terror to further intensify their efforts to eliminate internal dissidents and critics. The governments of Malaysia and Indonesia, in turn, found the best pretext to up the stakes in their own contestation against local Islamists from the opposition.

The war against terror has allowed some of the governments of Asia to backtrack on their earlier policies, most notably the government of the Philippines, that had earlier attempted to chart its own course by distancing itself from the long arm of Big Brother United States and forcing the United States to withdraw its troops and weapons facilities from naval and air bases on Filipino soil. A cursory overview of recent Asian history will show how the governments of Asia have tried to reposition themselves vis-à-vis the United States and their own domestic political constituencies in the wake of 9/11.

Pakistan's government under General-turned-President Parvez Musharraf was brought into the American-led coalition as its most problematic and reluctant partner with the use of a somewhat oversized carrot and an overly endowed stick. Promises of economic aid and a cancellation of outstanding loans were coupled with threats of even more comprehensive sanctions and international isolation should the Pakistani government fail to comply with the demands of Washington. In time, Islamabad agreed—but not without paying a heavy price in the form of massive demonstrations and violent protests in all the major cities of the country, courtesy of Islamist parties like the *Jama'at-e Islami* (JI) and *Jamiat'ul Ulama-e Islam* (JUI). To compound matters further, Pakistan's entry into the American-led coalition, reluctant though it was, infuriated many senior leaders of the armed forces and intelligence services who had been working with the Taliban and the numerous Jihadi and Mujahideen groupings in the country all along.

In Indonesia, groups like the *Front Pembela Islam* and *Lashkar Jihad* were immediately mobilized and took to the streets as soon as America announced its unilateral move to confront its foes abroad. But like Pakistan, Indonesia was also caught in dire straits of its own. The country's president, Megawati Sukarnoputri flew to Washington to discuss the implications of Indonesia's involvement in the international campaign against Osama bin Laden and the Taliban—though it was soon clear that the sensitive matter of Indonesia's spiraling debt problem was also put on the agenda. *Realpolitik* considerations aside, the Islamist parties and movements in Indonesia were less pragmatic in their approach to the problem. The Indonesian president was warned by the country's Islamist groups (and members of her own government like Hamzah Haz) that any attempt to appease the Americans would lead to a backlash at home with heavy political costs involved.

The Philippines was likewise forced to deal with a backlash from Islamist groups and movements in the troubled Island province of Mindanao in the south. Soon after the American response was made known to the international community, the Abu Sayyaf group renewed its attacks on Filipino government installations and outposts all over the province, and a new wave of hostage-taking was soon on the way.

Malaysia was unwittingly dragged into the global campaign that followed in the wake of the 9/11 attack. First came the news that letters containing anthrax spores that was sent to an address in the United States originated from Malaysia. It was later discovered that the letters were not, after all, contaminated and that nobody in Malaysia was involved. But the FBI's reports also pointed the finger at Malaysia when it was later revealed that Khalid al-Midhar, one of the close associates of Osama bin Laden, had met with other associates in Malaysia previously in January 2000. Later, a former member of bin Laden's Al Qaeda movement, Jamal Ahmed Al-Fadhl, also told a U.S. court that some money was deposited in Malaysia, which Malaysian authorities denied.

Developments in Malaysia—like that in Indonesia and the Philippines—soon took their course at an accelerated pace. During the U.S.-led attack on Afghanistan in October 2001, the country's biggest Islamist opposition party (the Pan-Malaysian Islamic party, PAS) declared its own jihad against the United States and its allies, Israel and Britain.[1] Loud (though nonviolent) demonstrations outside the U.S. and British embassies sent shockwaves across the country, and the foreign business community as well as Malaysia's large non-Malay, non-Muslim minority groups were taken aback by PAS's call for jihad against the infidels.

The situation was exploited to the full by the Mahathir administration, which saw it as the best justification for its own policies *vis-à-vis* the local Islamist opposition. Henceforth, the Malaysian government's crackdown on Islamist cells and networks—both real and imagined—would receive less criticism from foreign and local observers. By presenting itself as the face of "moderate" and "progressive" Islam at work, the Mahathir government had managed to outflank the Islamist opposition and reposition itself successfully.

This fact was made all the more clearer when the American trade representative, Robert B. Zoellick (who was on a visit to Malaysia and the other countries in the region) publicly stated that President Bush "was pleased with the support given by Malaysia."[2] The United States then extended its thanks to the Mahathir administration for the support it had shown despite the difficulties it had to face from the local opposition (meaning PAS). By then, it was clear that an *entente cordiale* had been struck: neither Malaysia nor the United States was prepared to let political differences get in the way of economic necessity. Trade between the two countries amounted to US$38 billion (RM144 billion) a year and America was, after all, Malaysia's biggest trading partner abroad. The American trade representative was also careful to mention all the key words that were necessary for the upward shift in bilateral relations to register: Zoellick stated that Washington viewed Malaysia as an Islamic country which could "serve the others as a role model for leadership and economic development," not only for the region but for the rest of the Muslim world as well. As an Islamic country, Malaysia was described as "modern," "progressive," "liberal," and "tolerant"—precisely the terms that were required to form a positive chain of equivalences, which the Mahathir administration was looking for.

The newly improved relationship between Kuala Lumpur and Washington was also reflected in the new understanding between the two governments. The American trade representative spoke not only about economic matters but also raised a number of concerns related to security issues. In his meeting with the Malaysian minister for foreign affairs, Syed Hamid Albar, the two men discussed the various strategies and tactics that could be used to combat the phenomenon of international "Islamic terrorism." Later, the American Pacific Fleet commander in chief, Adm. Dennis Cutler Blair (who was on a tour of ASEAN) praised the Malaysian government for its help in the global campaign against international terrorism and vowed that Malaysian and American armed forces and security services would cooperate even more in the future against the threat of terrorist networks and that militant cells posed a security threat to both countries.[3]

This new understanding would later be cemented when the leaders of Malaysia and the United States finally met for the first time (on October 20) at the APEC conference held in Shanghai a few weeks later. After the meeting between Dr. Mahathir and George W. Bush, both men agreed to seek ways and means to combat the threat of international terrorism and to increase the level of cooperation in both trade and security matters. Needless to say, these moves were strongly condemned by the members of the Islamist opposition in Malaysia, who argued that the Mahathir administration had caved in to Washington's demands and was trying to exploit the situation to the full.

The 9/11 attacks, thus, had many long-term and far-flung consequences for Muslim and non-Muslim relations. For the countries in

Asia with sizeable Muslim minorities, it opened up old wounds after decades of internal civil conflict, and served as a justification for clamping down on local Muslim resistance movements. Worse still, the fear of Islamic militancy was exploited by some as a convenient way to whip up anti-Muslim sentiment, disguised as part of the now-global "War on Terror." In Southeast Asia, the worst affected countries were the Philippines—where fears of renewed militancy on the part of Islamist movements in the south were intensified—and Indonesia, which experienced its own national tragedy with the bombing of tourist spots in Bali that only contributed to the weakening of its tattered economy.

In an effort to seize the initiative on the issue, Malaysia had played host to the leaders of Indonesia, Thailand, and the Philippines—Presidents Megawati Sukarnoputri, Thaksin Shinawatra, and Gloria Arroyo—who had visited the country to discuss matters of bilateral concern, one of which was the problem of Islamist militant networks operating in the region. Soon after, the governments of Malaysia, Indonesia, and Philippines issued a series of statements to the effect that they would, henceforth, be increasing the level of cooperation among their intelligence and security services to deal with the problem of religious militancy in Southeast Asia.

In time, however, it became clear to all that behind the scenes was the ever-present United States. With ASEAN countries caught in a desperate race to attract foreign direct investment (FDI), the governments of ASEAN were caught in a race to out-bid each other's claim to be a reliable ally to the United States, and to ensure that their countries remained in the good books of Washington and Wall Street. First to jump the gun were Singapore, Philippines, and Thailand, with each country's respective leaders categorically stating that they would offer whatever help necessary to the United States in its bid to win the war against terror.

The Singaporean government set the tone for the region's response to 9/11 by arresting a number of Singaporean Muslims who were alleged to be members of the shadowy *Jama'ah Islamiyyah* movement, which was supposed to have ties to the KMM of Malaysia and radical Muslim militants in Indonesia. The Sri-Lankan-born 'terrorism expert,' Rohan Gunaratna—author of the book on Al Qaeda[4]—was soon to be found in Singapore, based at the Institute for Defence and Strategic Studies (IDSS) of Nanyang University and feeding the Singaporean press with stories about the alleged activities of Al Qaeda in the region (though it should be noted that much of Gunaratna's "information" was fed to him by Singaporean and Filipino intelligence services as well).

Gunaratna's alarming prognosis—played to the hilt by the Singaporean government-controlled press—soon earned him the ire and scorn of the Malaysian and Indonesian governments, as well as Malaysian and Indonesian Islamist movements and parties. His allegation that Al Qaeda had transferred its operations to Southeast Asia and had established contact with the Moro Islamic Liberation Front (MILF) cast the net of association so widely that it ultimately covered not only the main Islamist party (PAS) and biggest Muslim civil society NGO (ABIM) of Malaysia, but also the ruling UMNO party under the leadership of Dr. Mahathir Mohamad.[5] In time, the Malaysian and Indonesian governments were chastising the Singaporean authorities, whom they accused of using the fear of terrorism as a means to ruin the image of their neighboring countries and to drive away much needed foreign investment and tourist dollars.

Thus, it became clear that the discourse of the war against terror was being used by the governments of ASEAN to score points against each other while also driving investment and tourism away from neighboring countries. Faced with such apparent lack of cohesion and unity of purpose, the door was opened for the reentry of the United States—and its military and intelligence operatives in particular—in the confused politics of the region. Uncle Sam was returning to ASEAN, though his presence in the not-too-distant past was far from forgotten.

LIVING UNDER UNCLE SAM'S LONG SHADOW: AMERICAN INVOLVEMENT IN ASEAN IN THE NOT-TOO-DISTANT PAST

Southeast Asia, it has to be remembered, is a highly complex and multifaceted region with a plethora of different, sometimes competing, sometimes contradictory, histories. Though historically of the same sociocultural mould (up to the twelfth century, the entire region was a patchwork of kingdoms and empires that shared a common Hindu–Buddhist heritage rooted in Sanskrit scripturalism and Brahminical culture, which originated from India), the territory of ASEAN today is made up of nation-states of different ethnic, religious, racial, and ideological hues.

The arrival of Islam from India and Singhalese Buddhism from Ceylon from the twelfth century onward effectively divided the region into two: the Malay-Muslim archipelago to the South and the Buddhist mainland to the North. From the eighteenth to nineteenth centuries onward, the entire region (save for Thailand) was carved up by Western imperial powers whose enduring legacy can still be seen in the different governmental, economic, military, and educational institutions and structures that exist till today. These institutional structures were destined to remain well into the twentieth century, when the world of Southeast Asia was once again divided according to the oppositional dialectic of the Cold War. As a result, the region today is a hotchpotch of different economic, political, and sociocultural systems, ranging from the nominal democracies and capitalist economies of Malaysia and Singapore, the centralized states of Thailand, Indonesia, and Philippines with the record of numerous military interventions in politics, and the top-heavy militarized bureaucracies of Myanmar (Burma), Laos, Cambodia, and Vietnam.

Not to be forgotten is the fact that Southeast Asia, from the post-war period onward, has been one of the most violent parts of the world and that the soil of ASEAN has been sated with the blood of millions of civilians killed in conflicts in Vietnam, Cambodia, Philippines, Indonesia, and Timor. With the end of Western European colonization in the post-war years, a power vacuum had been created in the ASEAN region, which opened the way for the arrival (and subsequent consolidation) of American hegemony.

Indonesia: Indirect U.S. Intervention by Supporting the Pro-American Military Elite

One of the first countries to openly resist the assertion of American power was Indonesia, then under the leadership of the staunch nationalist leader Sukarno. The Indonesian government under Sukarno was unwilling to accept any form of aid or military assistance from the United States for the simple reason that such a move would jeopardize Indonesia's neutral stance. In October 1950, Sukarno announced that Indonesia would no longer accept any form of aid from the United States on the grounds that such assistance often meant have to accept political conditionalities imposed by the powerful donor country as well. A few months earlier (in May 1950), the Burmese government had also announced that it would no longer accept any American military assistance.[6]

This setback did not dampen the ambitions of the Americans though: American efforts to woo Indonesia and bring it into the fold of the Western bloc intensified between 1951 and 1952, as the Korean War began to intensify. But these moves backfired for the simple reason that the communist opposition in Indonesia had grown progressively stronger and was unwilling to allow Indonesia to fall under America's shadow. The behind-the-scenes battle to win the hearts of the Indonesian leadership continued right up to the Bandung Conference that Sukarno organized in 1955.

In April 1955, Indonesia hosted the Bandung Conference that brought together the leaders of the newly independent countries of Asia and Africa. Both the United States and Soviet Russia were apprehensive about the move (while China was more inclined to support the idea since it could identify itself with the newly emerging forces in Asia). The Russians were keen to ensure that they would not be sidelined from the discussions of the conference. On the eve of the conference, the Soviet Deputy Foreign Minister Vasily Kusnetsov declared that "the Soviet Union understands fully the struggle of the nations of Africa and Asia against any form of colonial domination and economic dependence."[7]

The United States was more openly critical of the whole idea behind the conference, and many of the key strategists in Washington were certain that the Bandung Conference was nothing more than a leftist–nationalist plot to bring together the countries of Asia and Africa in an instrumental coalition against the West. The American establishment was particularly worried about how some Asian and African nations seemed eager and willing to accept Russia's (and China's) aid and military assistance packages with fewer questions asked. At that stage, however, Washington's fears of a communist takeover in Indonesia were vastly exaggerated. A few months after the conference (in August 1955) the left-leaning government of Prime Minister Ali Sastroamidjojo was toppled. Despite these developments during the 1955 elections, the Indonesian communist party (PKI) won only 16 percent of the vote (21 percent on the island of Java).

In May 1956, President Sukarno of Indonesia was invited to America by the Eisenhower administration. Sukarno's visit was hailed as a success by Eisenhower, who was particularly impressed by his willingness to be taken on a tour of Disneyland by none other than Walt Disney himself. (Sukarno was also given the opportunity to make the acquaintance of a number of Hollywood actresses during the evenings when he was free.) McMahon (1999) notes that "So impressed were US officials with the results of the Sukarno trip that in the summer of 1956 the Eisenhower administration quietly approved $US 25 million in developmental assistance for Indonesia's struggling economy."[8] This optimism was off the mark once again, as McMahon notes. If the U.S. administration really believed that by giving the president of Indonesia a private tour of Disneyland and the casting couches of Hollywood he would tilt in favor of the United States, they would be proven wrong. Soon after he returned to Indonesia, Sukarno reached a tentative agreement with Soviet Russia that would allow the transfer of $100 million worth of aid for a number of unspecified developmental projects. To make things worse, the elections that were held in Indonesia had allowed the leftist Ali Sastroamidjojo to come back to power with the backing of the PKI that was stronger than ever.

By 1958, Sukarno's attempts to build a working democracy in Indonesia had clearly failed. The regional revolts in Sumatra and Sulawesi between 1957 and 1958 had broken the back of the Ali Sastroamidjojo government and on March 13, 1958, he and his cabinet resigned. The worsening political situation in Indonesia gave Sukarno the pretext he needed for suspending the democratic process altogether and declaring martial law throughout the country.

The American government felt that this was the best time to intervene in Indonesia's domestic affairs, with the hope that by doing so they could tip the balance of power in the country and foreclose the possibility of a communist takeover once and for all. By September 1958, President Eisenhower and the American National Security Council (NSC) prepared the way for what McMahon (1999) later described as "one of the most misguided, ill-conceived and ultimately counterproductive covert operations of the entire Cold war era."[9] In an effort to strengthen the anticommunist forces within Indonesia, the Americans began to actively support the antigovernment forces that were waging a war against the central government of Sukarno. Arms and aid were soon sent to the PRRI forces that were based in Sumatra and Sulawesi. But the American efforts came to naught in the end.

The Indonesian army under the command of Gen. Abdul Haris Nasution managed to defeat the rebel forces in the interior, and, in time, were able to reveal the extent of U.S. involvement in the whole debacle. After defeating the rebels, Indonesian troops found numerous caches of U.S.-supplied weapons. They even managed to shoot down a U.S. pilot (Allen Pope) who was a CIA agent and was flying supply missions on behalf of the insurgents.[10] Sukarno cited this as proof that the United States was bent on recolonizing Indonesia by whatever means necessary, going as far as supporting antigovernment rebels who had declared war on the state. In the wake of the failed rebellions, Indonesia–American relations plummeted to an all-time low.

Indonesian–American relations would only recover after the 1965 failed coup, which brought the Pro-Western General Soeharto to power. With the rise of Soeharto and the military elite, Indonesia embarked on a ferocious purge against the leftists and communists that destroyed the PKI, forcibly annexed Irian Jaya (in 1968) and

East Timor (in 1974), and moved closer to the West in its political orientation.

The pro-American elite of Indonesia worked to improve economic, strategic, and military links with the United States, and the Americans (and British), in turn, propped up the corrupt and brutal Soeharto regime with gifts of arms, investment, and military training. From the mid-1960s to the late 1990s, Indonesia's President Soeharto rose to become the longest serving leader of ASEAN and was soon regarded as one of the most brutal dictators in the world. Soeharto's government was also dominated by pro-Western generals and military officers like Benny Moerdani, whose fear and loathing for Islamism bordered on the pathological. Needless to say, this hostility soon spilled over into open violence and confrontation between the government and the Islamists in Sumatra and Java, and only began to recede in the 1990s when it became clear that the Islamist opposition was not about to surrender.

American intervention in Indonesia, therefore, dates back to the post-war era and it should not come as a surprise if the U.S. government is still regarded with suspicion and contempt by many Islamists and pro-democracy activists in the country. But the machinations of the United States in Indonesia pale in comparison to what was done by the American government and its armed forces in Vietnam and the Philippines.

Vietnam: From Indirect American Intervention to Coups, Agent Orange and "Search and Destroy"

> The solution to Vietnam is more bombs, more shells, more napalm.
> General William Depuy,
> U.S. Commander during the Vietnam War

In the wake of the French withdrawal from Vietnam, the pro-Western emperor, Bao Dai attempted to recover his losses and rally public support behind him. In 1954, he appointed the unpopular Vietnamese Christian aristocrat Ngo Dinh Diem as his Prime Minister.[11] But what made matters worse for Diem was the fact that his government had grown even more dependent on American military and economic aid by then. (The Americans had begun to send thousands of troops to Vietnam to act as "combat advisers" to the South Vietnamese army.) In 1956, Vietnam was scheduled to hold its first free elections following the conditions laid out by the Geneva Accords. But the Western powers were certain that should a free election take place, the party of the pro-Western Emperor Bao Dai was certain to lose and communists, under the leadership of Ho Chi Minh, were sure to win. Diem, therefore, decided to cancel the elections altogether and impose direct rule. This immediately led to an escalation of violence and a new campaign by the Viet Minh. Between 1956 and 1960, the Viet Minh forces managed to kill more than 2500 government officials and launched hundreds of hit-and-run attacks on government and military installations all over the country. They were also supported by the local students, workers, peasants, and Buddhist associations, which were sick of the excesses of the Bao Dai–Ngo Dinh Diem regime. The state of crisis served as a pretext for American intervention into Vietnamese political affairs.

After coming to power in November 1960, President John F. Kennedy increased the level of U.S. commitment in the Vietnam War. He increased the level of American combat advisers in Vietnam from 600 to 16,000 within 3 years. Kennedy also authorized American troops to participate in combat operations, sanctioned the use of U.S. army helicopters, napalm, and defoliant chemicals like Agent Orange in an effort to flush the Viet Minh out of their jungle hideouts. McMahon (1999) notes that "after he grew disillusioned with Prime Minister Ngo Dinh Diem, (Kennedy) even encouraged the South Vietnamese military to assume power by extra-legal means."[12] The first coup attempt was foiled, but a second attempt on November 1, 1963 led to the killing of Ngo Dinh Diem and his brother Ngo Dinh Nhu.

Following the death of Diem, Vietnam was thrown into turmoil. Within the space of one year, nine different governments tried to take control of South Vietnam, all of them proving incapable in one way or another. Kennedy's own inept meddling in Vietnam was brought to an end by his own untimely death on November 22, 1963. But the Johnson administration that followed merely intensified the level of American involvement in Vietnam even further. President Lyndon Johnson used the 1965 Tonkin incident (where U.S. ships were bombed by North Vietnamese forces) as a pretext to escalate America's war against the communists in the North. He later increased the number of American troops in Vietnam to half a million, while authorizing a sustained bombing campaign of North Vietnam.

America's growing involvement in the Vietnam War earned it the scorn and condemnation of anticolonial and anti-imperial movements worldwide. In time, the U.S. administration was also forced to contend with growing disillusionment and criticism back home. As the war spiraled out of control, U.S. President Lyndon Johnson described the conflict as "that bitch of a war on the other side of the world."[13]

He later admitted that it was "the biggest damn mess I ever saw."[14] But, despite the doubts that were being cast on the U.S. war effort in Southeast Asia, the hawks in the Pentagon and Congress were insistent on prolonging the conflict even further. General William Depuy insisted that "the solution to Vietnam is more bombs, more shells, more napalm," while General Westmoreland argued that America should "just go on bleeding them, until Hanoi wakes up to the fact that they have bled their country to the point of national disaster for generations."[15] This trend would prevail right up to the Nixon administration, and Nixon himself would later say that he would "bomb the bastards like they had never been bombed before."[16]

Bellicose rhetoric aside, Vietnam proved to be a bigger obstacle to U.S. hegemonic ambitions in Asia than Indonesia. The Tet Offensive of 1968 caught the Americans off-guard and proved that the war could not be won by force of arms. On January 27, 1973 a formal treaty was signed between the North Vietnamese government and the forces of the South in Paris. By then, the American government realized that a communist victory was inevitable and that it would be pointless to prolong the conflict (and their involvement) any further.

In 1975, the Vietnam War finally came to its messy end. On April 21, General Nguyen Van Thieu resigned, blaming the Americans for their lack of support to his tottering regime. Thieu then flew off into exile in Hawaii as communist forces entered the Southern capital of Saigon (soon to be renamed Ho Chi Minh city). By the end of the war, more than two million Vietnamese had been killed, along with an estimated 58,000 American troops. But despite the fears of successive American administrations, the rest of Southeast Asia did not fall into the hands of the communist bloc, and most of the countries of ASEAN would remain firmly allied to America and Western interests. McMahon (1999) concludes that "in the most fundamental sense, America's failures stemmed from its gross violations of nearly all the classic rules of warfare."[17]

Of all of America's military ventures in ASEAN, Vietnam stands out as the most glaring example of the failure of U.S. intelligence to understand the nature and character of ASEAN politics and the people of the region. The Vietnam conflict also became the rallying point for anti-American pro-democracy activists in the neighboring countries of ASEAN, as it was used as a major political issue by student movements, Islamist groups, and pro-democracy NGOs in Thailand, Malaysia, and Indonesia. Compared to Vietnam, America was more successful in its attempt to construct a string of puppet regimes under its thumb in another ASEAN country, the Philippines.

The Philippines: A Long Line of Washington's
Puppets on a String

I walked into the White House and I am not ashamed to tell you that I
prayed to Almighty God for light and guidance. One night it came to
me this way . . . there was nothing left for us to do but to take (the
Philippines), and to educate the Filipinos, and uplift and civilize and
Christianize them.

American President McKinley speaking in 1899
Quoted in William Blum *Killing Hope: U.S. Military
and CIA Interventions Since World War II*
(Monroe: Common Courage Press, 1995)

The Philippines is unique in ASEAN in one vital respect: it was the
only ASEAN country that had been a colony of the United States and
was, therefore, the country where the American stamp was most visible
and deeply felt.

American involvement in the Philippines began in the late nineteenth
century when America needed a trading post in Asia to guarantee the
free movement of resources between Asia and the American West
coast. After its failed attempts to gain permanent and significant influence in Japan, Korea, and China, America began to look
to Southeast Asia for an alternative. The opportunity came with the
American–Spanish War that led to the defeat of the Spanish and the
loss of their colony, the Philippines.

America's involvement in the Philippines began soon after the
Spanish were defeated and forced to leave their colony in 1898. By
1899, American leaders like President William McKinley were openly
declaring that the United States had the right and the obligation to
intervene in Filipino affairs, and McKinley even went as far as justifying
America's imperial adventure by citing divine providence. The American
government under McKinley openly spoke of the virtues of imperialism
when addressing the Philippine question. The Philippines was bought
from Spain at the cost of US$20 million, and a force of 50,000 American
troops was dispatched to the country to "restore law and order." They
soon encountered fierce resistance from the Moros of the southern
Philippines, who did not take too kindly to the idea that they had been
"sold" by Spain and "bought" by the Americans.

The Americans attempted the strategy of indirect rule when dealing
with the Moros of Sulu and Mindanao in southern Philippines, and
this was embodied in the Bates agreement signed between the Americans
and the Sultan of Sulu in 1899. The Bates agreement was, however,
unilaterally abrogated by the Americans in 1905 when they began to

intervene directly in matters of government in the Moro sultanates. The Syrian-born Christian American agent for Moro affairs, Najeeb M. Saleeby, then proposed a new policy of tutelage and patronage that would integrate the next generation of Moro leaders. This resulted in the creation of a younger generation of Moro leaders who later became civil servants, lawyers, and merchants in the American colony.[18]

The Americans revised their own policy toward the Moros and attempted to woo some of the Moro leaders to their cause. The political reforms they introduced were intended to help assimilate the Moro communities and to give the traditional Moro leaders a place and status in the colonial administrative system they intended to set up. But attempts to introduce Western education and to disarm the Moros merely provoked them further, leading to even more conflicts. The five-day Battle of Bud Bagsak (where American troops were commanded by Gen. John J. Pershing) in 1913, led to massive Moro losses. An estimated 500–2000 Moros were killed by the end of the battle.[19] The Moros resisted American attempts to assimilate them to the end, and some of the Moro leaders even sent their petition to the American Congress in Washington. The Americans' treatment of the Moros hardly improved and when the Philippine Republic finally proclaimed its independence on July 4, 1946, the new post-colonial government invariably inherited the "Moro problem," which the Americans (and Spanish before them) had helped to create.

In 1935, the Americans created the self-governing Commonwealth of the Philippines, but it remained under indirect control of the United States and a colony of America. America propped up a number of pro-American cronies and puppet leaders as representatives to the Philippine government, and promised independence in 1945, but this was interrupted by the Japanese invasion during World War II.

On July 4, 1946, the Philippines was finally granted its independence, on the same date as the U.S. independence day. This, in itself, showed how the Philippines remained under American influence even after it gained its nominal independence. American political, military, and business interests remained in the Philippines, and Filipino independence remained cosmetic and fictional. The United States remained the de facto power behind the Philippine government and returned to its policy of selecting and promoting crony Filipino leaders, who would serve U.S. interests in the country and the region.

The first obstacle the Americans encountered was the Philippine Communist Party (PCP), which had been formed in the 1940s and had fought against the Japanese alongside the *Hukbalahap* (People's Army against Japan) that was formed in 1942. American opposition to the PCP and Huk forces was based on ideological grounds: both the PCP and Huks were left-leaning nationalists who included in their political agenda a land reform program that the Americans wanted to scuttle. In the post-war period, U.S. forces helped to reinstall traditional Filipino leaders and the feudal elite, who were used in the campaign to undermine the Huk forces.[20] The Americans were backing right-wing pro-American Filipino leaders to ensure that the new government in Manila would always follow the American line

Between 1945 and 1947, the Philippine-U.S. Trade Act and Philippine-U.S. Military Agreement were passed. The latter provided the Americans with 23 military bases in the country, and the lease was meant to last for 99 years. The pact also ensured that the Philippines could not turn to any other country for military aid and training, and the Philippine government was not allowed to buy even a single bullet from any other country without permission from Washington.[21] In 1950, the United States provided the Philippines with $US500 million worth of military assistance. The Joint U.S. Military Advisory Group (JUSMAG) helped to reorganize the Philippine intelligence services, and put their man Ramon Magsaysay as its new head. Magsaysay would later be elevated to the position of president of the Philippines, with the help of the United States and its covert intelligence units in the Philippines.

President Ramon Magsaysay was widely regarded as "America's boy" in the Philippines. In the 1950s, he was made the head of the Philippines Intelligence Services by the Americans who regarded him as a loyal and trustworthy ally on whom they could depend. The man behind the rise of Ramon Magsaysay was Lt.-Col. Edward G. Landsdale, who was the head of the CIA in the Philippines and advisor to the JUSMAG. Landsdale formed the Philippines Civil Affairs Office (CAO) that engaged in psychological warfare against the Philippine Communist Party (PCP) and other nationalist groups.

Through the CAO, the CIA intervened directly in Filipino affairs, shaping public opinion and developing the image and popularity of Magsaysay. In 1953, Magsaysay won the presidential elections with the help of the CAO and CIA, and Landsdale would later claim that it was he who "invented Magsaysay."[22] Under constant watch and supervision, Magsaysay proved to be a loyal servant to American interests: his speeches were written and vetted by Landsdale and the CAO. On one occasion, it was reported that Landsdale had even beaten Magsaysay and knocked the new president of the Philippines unconscious for not doing as he was told.[23] During Magsaysay's term of office, the United States managed to deepen and strengthen its grip on the Philippine economy and political system even further. American companies behaved as if the Philippines was a U.S. colony, and exploited the Filipinos as a captive market and source of cheap labor and resources. Magsaysay would later die in a plane crash in 1957, after which he was replaced by another American crony, Diosdado Macapagal.[24]

Diosdado Macapagal (father to the present Philippines president Gloria Arroyo Macapagal) began his career as a nationalist Filipino politician who struggled for the national liberation of his country. During the 1940s and 1950s, he campaigned for Philippine independence and attempted to mobilize popular support against the Americans who had returned to the Philippines after World War II. During the presidency of Ramon Magsaysay, Macapagal was one of the most vocal critics of the Magsaysay government, accusing the president of being a hostage to American business and military interests. By then, the American presence in the Philippines was overpowering (the CIA had helped to run and organize Magsaysay's successful 1953 election campaign) and Filipino politics was virtually run by the American-created CAO headed by the CIA operative Lt.-Col. Edward G. Landsdale.

After Magsaysay's death, the Americans began courting the support of Macapagal, who was then working with the Americans by providing them with information about the communists and other dissident groups in the country. The Americans, in turn, responded by taking Macapagal under their wing and offering him political and financial support. Through the CAO, the CIA was able to support and sustain Macapagal's election campaign in 1961. After winning the presidential elections in 1961 with U.S. support, Macapagal proved to be another loyal crony to American interests in the Philippines. The Macapagal administration was heavily influenced by Western and, especially, American interests. Macapagal signed more agreements that gave American companies the right to exploit Philippine resources and dominate the Philippine economy.

Despite his weakness and lack of popular support, Macapagal wanted to promote the Philippines as a major country within Southeast Asia. To this end, he promoted the idea of Maphilindo—the merging of Malaya, the Philippines, and Indonesia. But the idea of Maphilindo was not widely supported, and in 1963, the Federation of Malaysia was created with the incorporation of the North Kalimantan states of Sabah and Sarawak instead. Macapagal used this as a pretext to declare hostilities against Malaysia. Macapagal's leadership was weak and his U-turn during the *Konfrontasi* crisis made him look even weaker. In the same year that Sukarno was toppled, Macapagal was voted out of office and this led to the rise of America's longest-serving crony and puppet in the Philippines, Ferdinand Marcos.

Along with the other U.S.-backed leader President Suharto of Indonesia, Ferdinand Marcos ranked as one of the worst dictators in the world, as well as one of the closest allies of the United States. It was during the time of Marcos (1965–1986) that U.S.-Philippine interests coincided most closely, and when U.S. economic, military, and strategic links were strengthened. Ferdinand Marcos's period of rule witnessed the biggest volume of American aid and investment into the country ever: between 1962 and 1983, the American government gave more than $US3 billion to the Philippine government in terms of investment aid and military support. The Philippines, which was also a major ally of the West during the Cold War, also received $US4 billion in aid from international bodies like the World Bank. Apart from that, the Philippine economy was also opened up and liberalized for foreign capital penetration, thanks to the structural adjustment policies imposed by international financial advisory bodies like the International Monetary Fund (IMF). From 1965 to 1970, Marcos took the country down the road of extensive social, educational, and economic reform. Like his predecessors Magsaysay and Macapagal, Marcos was totally beholden to the Americans and the Philippine economy came under the control of American and Western multinationals.

During the Vietnam War, the Philippines under Marcos came even closer within the orbit of U.S. strategic and military interests. Marcos did not allow Philippine troops to join in the Vietnam War, but did allow Philcag Engineer units to go to Vietnam and help the American war effort there. He also allowed the United States to use the Subic Bay naval facility and Clarke Air Base as bases for U.S. naval and aerial units. It was during this time that U.S.-Philippine military cooperation was at its highest and it was also then that the Philippines became the prostitution center of ASEAN, thanks to U.S. troops who were allowed to go on "rest and recreation" leave while based there.

With extensive U.S. covert and overt support, the Marcos government helped to corporatize the Philippine army, allowing army officers to run businesses and siphon profits into their personal accounts. The American government continued to bankroll the Marcos regime and the Philippine army because of their commitment to contain the communists and NPA, and during this period (1975–1980), abuses of human rights in the Philippines reached a peak. During this time, the Philippines came closer under American control and the Philippine economy came under the indirect supervision of international agencies like the IMF. The IMF imposed structural adjustment policies (SAPs) that effectively opened up the Philippine economy to extensive foreign capital penetration, but at the expense of the local industry and business community. As the economy faltered from one crisis to another, the Marcos regime vented its wrath on its two main enemies: the communist opposition and the Moro Muslims in the southern regions of Mindanao and Sulu.

On February 25, 1986, the Marcos regime finally toppled and the Marcos family was forced to seek refuge in the United States. Corazon Aquino then became the next president of the Philippines, with the country's foreign debt estimated at around US$28 billion. On September 28, 1989 Marcos died of a heart attack in Hawaii. Imelda Marcos was later brought to trial in New York but was acquitted of all charges.

The Marcos era ended with the bankruptcy of the Philippine economy. Most of the foreign aid into the country had been appropriated and taken out of the country by the Marcoses themselves. By 1985, the Philippines had the biggest external debt burden in ASEAN and the Far East. What was more, the Philippine economy was almost totally dependent on Western investors and banks, while the local economy had been nearly wiped out, thanks to the structural adjustment policies imposed by the IMF.

Indonesia, Vietnam, and the Philippines were not the only countries in ASEAN to come under undue U.S. political, economic, and military pressure: American diplomats, intelligence personnel, and military advisors (as well as troops) had been stationed in practically every other country of ASEAN as well.

In Thailand, Malaysia, Singapore, Cambodia, Laos, and Brunei, American presence and hegemony has been introduced and maintained both directly and indirectly with the help of local elites who enlisted the help of the Americans to deal with internal dissent and opposition coming from various pro-democracy, leftist, communist, and Islamist opposition groups. In Thailand, the United States helped to maintain the army's tight grip on national politics through a complex web of patronage and support given to the Thai army and police forces who were instrumental in eliminating leftist intellectuals and communist leaders, thereby ensuring that Thailand did not fall into the hands of the Soviet bloc during the Cold War. In Singapore and Malaysia,[25] the Americans were the first to send in their intelligence personnel to help the governments of the respective countries monitor, police, and eliminate communist operatives and party workers there.

Bearing in mind the facts of contemporary post-war history, it is easy to see just how and why America's renewed presence in the ASEAN region has been a cause for alarm for many local pro-democracy, Islamist, and civil society movements, parties, and NGOs. As was the case during the heyday of U.S. unilateralism and intervention in the 1960s–1980s, America's presence in ASEAN today has led to the disruption and dislocation of local politics, distorting both internal and international politics in the region as a whole.

UNCLE'S SAM'S HEAVY AND UNEVEN IMPRINT ON THE POLITICAL TERRAIN OF ASEAN: HOW AMERICAN INTERVENTION COMPLICATED THE REGIONAL POLITICS OF SOUTHEAST ASIA

The Americans, as we have seen, were and are no strangers to Southeast Asia. From the "quiet Americans" who surreptitiously monitored, policed, and directed ASEAN's political evolution in their hotel rooms to the Marines who slaughtered Vietnamese villagers during the Vietnam War, America's presence has been felt by the ordinary people of ASEAN for decades. Even up to the 1980s and 1990s, the American presence was still a visible one, with thousands of U.S. troops cruising the red-light districts of Bangkok and Manila while on rest and recreation leave in the abovementioned countries. Needless to say, in time, the image of the ugly American, complete with his martial swagger and much-wanted dollars, became a popular image in the collective imagination of Thais, Filipinos, Vietnamese, and, to a lesser extent, Indonesians.

It is against this highly fluid, overlapping, and oft-times unstable background that the United States was poised to stage a comeback in the wake of 9/11. Needless to say, America's previous record in Southeast Asia was a major factor that informed local Southeast Asian reactions to this development. Another important factor to bear in mind is the different reaction that was bound to come from the Muslim-majority states of ASEAN.

The Muslim Reaction: Malaysia and Indonesia

Osama bin Laden is just an excuse for the United States, which has time and again shown its hostility towards Islam, to wage war against our religion.[26]

Tuan Guru Nik Aziz Nik Mat, *Murshid'ul Am* (spiritual leader) of the Pan-Malaysian Islamic Party (PAS)

The American government's declaration of a "global crusade" against "Islamic terrorism" had only succeeded in antagonizing vast sections of the global Muslim community when it was the last thing the United States needed to do. The inept handling of the complex and sensitive matter of cooperation with Muslim governments also helped to ignite local tensions that had been simmering under the surface in many of the Muslim countries.

In the ASEAN context, American unilateralism and the projection of American military power and intelligence capabilities led to growing anti-Americanism among ordinary Muslims, which cut across class, social, and geographical frontiers. The governments of Malaysia and Indonesia (the Sultanate of Brunei has been curiously silent throughout the crisis) were faced with a particularly difficult situation where they had to appease both the governments of the West and their own Muslim-majority political constituencies. The Malaysian government, in particular, was careful not to show too much support or enthusiasm for either side in the conflict.

Following America's invasion of Afghanistan in October 2001, Malaysia's prime minister, Dr. Mahathir openly stated his dissatisfaction with the American-led attack. In a press conference held in Parliament, the prime minister said that "war against these countries will not be effective in fighting terrorism."[27] Although he was also careful to state that the attack on Afghanistan should not be regarded by anyone as an attack on Islam and the Muslim world, Dr. Mahathir did question the wisdom behind the action and pointed out the negative consequences that were sure to follow.

Domestic political concerns were also not far from the mind of the Prime Minister. In a thinly veiled warning to the Malaysian Islamist parties and groups that might think of extending their support to Osama bin Laden or the Taliban, he pointed out that "we will not tolerate anyone who supports violence and will act against these irresponsible people or anyone who backs terrorism."[28]

The situation, however, was clearly out of hand by then. While the Prime Minister was trying to calm the fears of foreign investors, Western embassies, and tourists in the country, the local police and security forces were put on alert and the American embassy (which was closed as it was Columbus day in the United States) was placed under guard. On the same day (October 8), the leaders of PAS came out with their strongest statement against the Americans yet. For the *Murshid'ul Am* (spiritual leader) of PAS, Tuan Guru Nik Aziz Nik Mat, the attack on Afghanistan was clearly an attack on Islam and Muslims in general. PAS's (then) president Ustaz Fadzil Noor also stated that the attacks were not only against Afghanistan's Taliban regime but that they constituted a direct assault on Muslims the world over.

Things finally came to a climax on October 10 when PAS declared a Jihad against the United States and its coalition partners and gave the go-ahead for its members to openly join and support the Taliban. Soon after, PAS leaders like Fadzil Noor, Mohamad Sabu, and Mahfuz Omar were calling for a total boycott of all American goods and services, and even for the Malaysian government to send troops to Afghanistan to help resist the American-led attacks.[29]

In neighboring Indonesia—the biggest Muslim country in the world—the situation was made even more complex, thanks to the institutionalized divisions of racial, ethnic, and religious difference among the country's ruling elite. The Indonesian armed forces (TNI), whose presence and involvement in politics was less visible but, nevertheless, still apparent in the wake of the fall of President Soeharto in 1998, was also dominated by secular or Christian officers, who had always maintained a cautious policy of keeping the Islamists at arm's length and as far outside the political arena as possible.

Since the days of General Benny Moerdani—Soeharto's right-arm man and the most anti-Muslim general in Indonesian history—the elite component of the TNI have maintained that political Islam was a threat to the secular ideology of the state and that the Islamists were fundamentally terrorists who needed to be dealt with by force and violence.

The Indonesian Islamists managed to reposition themselves into the country's political mainstream during the economic crisis of 1997–1998, when prominent Islamist intellectuals like Amein Rais and Nurcholish Madjid were seen at the forefront of the pro-democracy *Reformasi* (reform) movement. The quiet victory of the moderate Islamists witnessed the ascendancy to power of the country's biggest Muslim party, the *Nahdatul Ulama* (NU), under the leadership of the Ulama-politician Abdurrahman Wahid (Gus Dur). It is interesting to note that even at the peak of the reform movement in Indonesia, the Western press remained silent over the Islamist background of many of the pro-democracy leaders. Amein Rais was described as a democrat and civil society activist, though it ought to be remembered that he, along with Nurcholish Madjid, Ulil Abshar Abdallah, Abdurrahman Wahid, and others were all active leaders and members of Islamic movements like the *Muhamadijjah* and *Nahdatul Ulama* of Indonesia.

The 9/11 attacks marked a radical reversal of fortunes for the Islamists in general. With a new (and weak) president as head of state—Megawati Sukarnoputri, daughter of the country's secular–nationalist founding father, President Sukarno—the army was once again in a position to play the role of power broker and kingmaker. The apparent weakness of Indonesia, coupled with renewed Islamist activism in Java and Sumatra, opened the way for the resurgence of the secular generals and their cohorts, with the backing of the Indonesian president and the powers-that-be in Washington. In time, Megawati promoted the controversial figure of General Hendrypriyono (dubbed the "Butcher of Lampung") to head the country's new integrated antiterror operations unit based in Jakarta. At the same time, Megawati also courted the help of U.S. military and intelligence services to track down the terrorists who were allegedly behind the bombings in Bali and to eliminate "terror cells" that might be operating in the country.

These moves may have endeared Megawati and her generals even more to the United States, but it also had the immediate effect of alienating her from her own Muslim-majority constituency. The move on the part of the President was immediately criticized by the country's Vice-President Hamzah Has, who was openly linked and close to the country's Islamist parties and radical Islamist movements. The more vocal and aggressive components of the Islamist fringe wasted no time before warning Megawati of the dire consequences of her diplomatic choices. Like Malaysia, though, the Indonesian government was not able (or inclined) to show excessive support to the United States for its military adventures abroad. The concerns expressed by Indonesia's political elite demonstrated their own worries about the possible reignition of radical Islamism in the country as a result of Megawati's closer ties with the United States.

The major concern expressed by the government of Muslim countries like Malaysia and Indonesia was the fact that the economic and political grievances of the Muslim world have hardly been addressed. No attempt was made—particularly by the Western/American media—to look at the root causes of Muslim anger. No attempt was made to understand how and why the attack on the United States managed to turn around such a large number of Muslim moderates and bring them on the side of Osama and the Taliban. Factual and historical analysis was put to the side and culturalist assumptions prevailed. There was talk of the bogey of the "global Islamic threat," about how Islam "condoned" such acts of violence, and the recurring image of the Muslim as the fanatical terrorist was widespread in the Western media.

Similar considerations were less evident in the non-Muslim countries of ASEAN—particularly Singapore and the Philippines—that were more preoccupied with the problem of internal Muslim dissent and increasingly vocal opposition from their Muslim minorities.

Bringing the War against Terror Home: The Reaction
of Singapore, Thailand, and the Philippines

The countries that have latched on to the discourse of the war against terror the most in ASEAN happened to be those that had the most to gain from a closer alignment with the United States and had to deal with the problem of internal dissent coming from their Muslim minority communities.

Singapore was the first to lead and the decision of the Singaporean government to support the United States in its global campaign did not come as a surprise to many ASEAN-watchers. It was well known that by the 1980s, Singapore had clearly aligned itself to the West and that unlike the other countries in the region, its economic and political lot was closely tied to Western economic, military, and economic interests. From the time of independence (in 1965), the economy of the island city-state was very much dependent on external economic variables that were beyond its control. Singapore's economy was very much tied to the import-substitution model of the colonial era and it had transformed itself into a major importer of raw materials from the neighboring states and as an exporter of manufactured goods (particularly electrical goods) destined for Western markets.

Singapore's unique ethnic profile and history also meant that its identity was shaped by considerations informed by the colonial past: the country's Chinese majority population were mainly the descendants of Chinese workers who had been brought to Southeast Asia by the British to fulfill the needs of the British colonial economy, and were thus beholden to the Western colonial authorities. With the sale of Singapore to the British by the Sultan of Johor in the nineteenth century, ethnic and political divisions appeared between the Chinese community and the original Malay–Bugis inhabitants of the island (then reduced to a minority) and these tensions have remained till today. Singapore's proximity to Malaysia and Indonesia—both of which are often described as the two Malay "giants" surrounding the tiny Chinese city-state—has also added to the anxiety of the Singaporeans and was skillfully exploited by the country's longest serving leader, Lee Kuan Yew, in order to lay the foundations for a maximalist state apparatus bent on social policing and the elimination of meaningful political contestation in the state.

Singapore's dealing with the "Muslim problem" was also colored by the idiosyncrasies of its political elite from the PAP party and its intellectual figurehead Lee Kuam Yew, who was widely regarded as one of the most conservative and reactionary leaders of the region.

Under Lee, Singapore had actively engaged and traded with South Africa, had close links with Israel and was the only Third World country that followed the United States and Britain (then under Ronald Reagan and Margaret Thatcher, respectively) out of UNESCO. Fearful that Islamic activism might open the way for stronger ties between Muslims in Singapore, Malaysia, and Indonesia, Lee Kuan Yew and the leaders of the Singaporean governmental, military, and intelligence institutions sought to find ways to diffuse the "threat" of Islamic resurgence and to isolate Singaporean Muslims from the influence of Islamic radicalism abroad.

The opportunity to do so came with the "revelation" of Al Qaeda documents in Afghanistan—whose authenticity remains disputed or at least unverified—indicating the presence of Islamic militant cells in Singapore, which were aiming to attack a number of Western targets (such as the American and British embassies) and to cause discord and strife between Malaysia and Singapore. In time, the Singaporean authorities began arresting and detaining a number of Singaporean Muslims who were accused of being members of the *Jama'ah Islamiyah* group, which was said to be working toward the reunification of Malaysia, Singapore, and Indonesia via militant means, with the objective of creating an Islamic super-state in the heart of ASEAN. These arrests, while courting international condemnation from civil society and human rights NGOs the world over, were, nonetheless, carried out and in due course, the profile of Singapore as a reliable ally in the war against terror rose accordingly.

Like Singapore, Thailand has also used the rhetoric of war against terror as a pretext for a closer realignment with the West (and the United States in particular) and renewed repression of its Muslim minority in the Southern provinces of Pattani, Yala, Satun, and Narathiwat. Though the conflict between Bangkok and the Southern Thai–Muslim provinces bordering Malaysia had reached its peak in the mid-1980s, violence and civil strife have returned to the area in the wake of 9/11.

It should not, however, be assumed that this renewed violence is mainly due to the activities of militant Islamic cells and groups operating in the provinces. Over the past few years, a number of controversial developmental projects initiated by the Thai government, as well as cross-border joint development projects between Malaysia and Thailand, have resulted in popular unrest among the local population in the areas. Compounding the problem has been the Thai police and army's reputation for siphoning off profits from such projects and profiting from the racketeering operations that have been going on there for decades. Increased economic competition for finite resources, Bangkok's strong grip on the southernmost provinces, and the appalling human rights record of local law enforcement agencies have all contributed to a general decline in law and order in the area.

But the discourse of the war against terror served its purpose as it allowed Bangkok to step up its campaign to eliminate local resistance in the area and to impose harsh standards of policing—often unregulated by a critical local media or watchdogs—in Pattani and the neighboring provinces. This has merely led to a renewed cycle of violence and the remobilization of Islamist forces, which had been dormant for some time. The Thai government that had been installed in the wake of the 1998 Asian financial crisis was widely regarded as a reformist-minded administration peopled by pro-democracy civil society actors and democrats. Following 9/11 and the adoption of the rhetoric of the war against terror by the Thai leadership, it was clear that the democratic claims and credentials of the Thai governmental elite had been compromised by their own dealings with the Muslim minority in the south of the country. It is the Philippines, however, that stands out the most as far as its own ideological U-turns and realignment of policies are concerned.

If the new political elite of Bangkok was regarded as being liberal and democratic in its profile and outlook, the political elite of Manila were thought to be even more so in the wake of the fall of Ferdinand Marcos. Yet, a cursory survey of Filipino politics from 1986 onward would suggest that the presence of the United States in the Philippines is as strong today as it ever was.

Corazon Aquino took over as president of the Philippines immediately after the fall of Marcos, but even under her government, the stamp of U.S. political, economic, and military interests was clear. Her period of government was characterized by growing instability, the inability of the Philippines government to steer the country away from dependency on U.S. direct capital investment, and growing discontent and insurgencies in the central and southern island provinces.

In 1986, Aquino proclaimed the setting up of a new national Constitution, but even that could not help to contain growing discontent among the population. One major populist move she attempted to perform was to support the anti-U.S. air and naval bases campaign, which had grown popular in the country. Under Aquino, the Americans were asked to vacate their naval and air bases in Subic Bay and Clarke Air Base, but this in turn, plunged the country into further economic crisis because, in retaliation, the United States merely moved its bases of operations to Okinawa, Korea, and Singapore, while depriving the Philippines of much needed foreign revenue income. Further instability led to an attempted *coup d'état* against the government in 1989, which in turn forced Aquino back into the hands of the Americans. Faced with rebellious military units and commanders, Aquino had no choice but to ask for American help. American military intervention came in the form of U.S. war planes and aerial maneuvers, which helped control the 1989 failed coup against her government. In the end, Aquino was forced to step down by the very same groups that supported her. In 1992 she was replaced by Fidel Ramos.

Fidel Ramos was a supporter of Ferdinand Marcos for more than two decades. Ramos's adherence to both free market ideology and U.S. military dominance was evident in his support for the Pentagon's policy of rest and recreation in the Philippines (widely understood as the U.S. military's use of Philippine women as prostitutes). He also supported and promoted further U.S. capital/business penetration into the Philippines. He formulated the "Industrial Philippines 2000 vision" project, which was aimed at making the Philippines an industrialized country by the year 2000, and to this end, he actively courted further U.S. investment. He hosted the 1996 APEC conference in Manila, where he openly supported the U.S. line of argument. Less known are the efforts he and his administration have made on behalf of the U.S. military in the Philippines.[30]

To renew its presence in the Philippines, the Pentagon turned to the policy of military access. This operated through an executive agreement implemented by the military forces of the United States and the host country. Executive agreement also governed the U.S. and Philippine military in matters concerning the bases during the Marcos regime. In the eyes of many Filipinos the present access agreement violated the post-Marcos constitution that requires Senate approval of a U.S. military presence in the Philippines. As a high-ranking military official of the Marcos dictatorship, Ramos supported the U.S. bases; as President Aquino's Minister of defense, he continued this support; as a candidate for president in 1992, he declared for access, and shortly after his election, the Pentagon got its access agreement.[31] Fidel Ramos also followed the lead of Ferdinand Marcos, in his willingness to open the Philippines to foreign capital, with minimal restraint. Like Marcos, he paid solicitous attention to the claims of the U.S. military, covered over when politically expedient by gestures of nationalist intent. Due to his openly pro-U.S. and pro-capitalist orientation, opposition against Ramos also grew and he was later voted out of office. He was then replaced by Joseph Estrada.

Joseph Ejercito Estrada (Erap) rose to power on a wave of populist support and anti-Americanism, which he tried to use to his advantage.

But, in time, he proved to be just as corrupt and ineffective as the previous leaders and was forced out of office, on corruption and embezzlement charges. During his period of office, he was actively courting U.S. support to help suppress the Moro resistance movement in the south, which only led to worsening of ties between the Christian and Muslim communities. He was later forced out of office and put on trial on corruption charges. He was replaced by Gloria Macapagal Aroyyo, daughter of the former president Diosdido Macapagal.

Like her father, Gloria Macapagal Aroyyo has proven to be a close ally and supporter of U.S. interests in the Philippines and the region. Like all her predecessors—Marcos, Aquino, Ramos, Estrada—she has not been able to deal with the chronic problem of economic underdevelopment, dependency on foreign (especially American) capital, and the growing unrest in the central and southern island provinces. By turning to the United States, Aroyyo hoped to win its support and investment in order to help build the country's economy and contain the threat of militant uprisings in the outer islands.

Even before the 9/11 bombings in New York and Washington, which the Bush administration has been using as a basis for launching its global war against terror, the Aroyyo government was busy trying to win American military and economic support. Arroyo and her defense secretary Angelo Reyes tried to negotiate with the Americans over expanding U.S. military presence in the Philippines as part of a larger security network in Asia, poised against regional security threats including anti-American "terrorist groups" and China. Philippine military leaders supported this move in order to increase the level of U.S. arms spending and aid into the country, which was at only $US2 million a year. Many senior Philippine commanders were keen to initiate and follow up on the country's arms modernization program.

Following the Abu Sayyaf kidnapping incident on Basilan island on May 27, 2001, the Philippine government and army were given the chance to renew their links with the U.S. government and armed forces. U.S. officials immediately agreed on joint counter-terror and surveillance cooperation tactics, and both sides agreed that further U.S.-Philippines cooperation in the field of arms and information gathering would be intensified. Three months later, Arroyo offered to open Subic Bay port facilities for the resupply, repair, and maintenance of U.S. warships.

After the 9/11 bombings, a 25-member U.S. Special Operations assessment team visited the Philippines for two weeks in October to review Filipino forces fighting the Abu Sayyaf. The visit led to the offer of attack helicopters, advanced communication gear, night vision equipment, surveillance capabilities, and even bloodhounds to track and destroy the Abu Sayyaf members. The Pentagon also promised a 10-fold increase in military assistance—from $1.9 to $19 million in 2002 and every year thereafter. In a subsequent Manila visit, Admiral Dennis Blair, commander in chief of the U.S. Pacific Command, also pledged to increase intelligence sharing.

Prodded by her defense and military advisers during her Washington visit, Arroyo pledged a deeper and long-term cooperation with Bush in his antiterrorist campaign. This deeper and long-term cooperation, which practically goes beyond fighting the Abu Sayyaf, led to further deals that extended military rights that the American forces used to enjoy under the U.S.-Philippine bases pact. A joint statement said that the two presidents discussed an integrated plan including a joint-training package, equipment needed for increased troop mobility, a maintenance program to enhance overall military capabilities, specific targeted law enforcement and counter-terrorism cooperation, and a new bilateral defense consultative mechanism. The Bush government then increased defense and economic aid commitments to $US40 million.

Between 1999 and 2003, the government of Aroyyo has overturned many of the post-Marcos constitutional blocks and legal restrictions that would allow the Americans to come back and establish their power in the country. The most recent infringement of the post-Marcos constitutional set up was the war games between U.S. and Philippine forces code-named Kalayaan-Aguila 2002 or Mindanao Balikatan 02-1, held in Basilan and Zamboanga and led by the American Special Operations Forces (SOFs). Kalayaan-Aguila 2002 marks the largest U.S. military intervention engaged in actual combat against real human targets on Philippine soil since the Philippine–American War (1899–1901). It deployed the largest number of U.S. troops for combat in the Basilan–Zamboanga area since the Moro Wars (1901–1911).[32]

Arroyo, who was actively courting the political support of the United States for the 2004 presidential elections, completely disregarded the post-Marcos Constitution, which prohibits foreign military troops on Philippine soil, unless covered by a treaty to be concurred in by the Senate. All the existing security agreements of the Philippines and the United States—Mutual Defense Treaty, Military Assistance Agreement, Visiting Forces Agreement—do not have provisions for the deployment of foreign military forces, advisers, foreign military trainers, or coordinators in actual combat operations. Philippine undersecretary for foreign affairs Lauro Baja admitted that this form of operation in an actual combat zone is not even covered by any

Memorandum of Understanding between the two countries. But by then, the Philippines' realignment back into the fold of U.S. hegemony was almost complete, as was made apparent by the president herself during her recent visit to the United States when she stated that:

> While Asia must take greater responsibility for its own political and eco-nomic security, it must also recognise that strong relations with the United States of America will contribute greatly to regional peace and prosperity, stability and security, especially from terrorism.[33]

It is clear that the Philippines has always been a client state of the United States and that American political, economic, and military interests extend deep into the country's domestic politics and political/ governmental institutions. Furthermore, half a century of American colonization, coupled with half a century of indirect U.S. intervention into Philippines politics, means that, in terms of both its domestic and foreign policies, the Philippines is no more than a proxy state acting under the direction of the United States.

How the War against Terror has Divided the Governments of ASEAN and Allowed the United States to Assume Center Stage Once More

ASEAN, today, is at a crossroads of its history. Since its formation in 1967, the regional grouping has been trying to carve a place for itself as a major actor in global politics and its membership has now been expanded to include Brunei, Myanmar, Laos, Cambodia, and Vietnam. Yet, despite the pomposity and grandeur of ASEAN meetings and conferences, the regional grouping has little to show in terms of concrete political success.

ASEAN's attempts to put forward and implement the Zone of Peace, Freedom and Neutrality (ZOPFAN) was soon exposed for the cosmetic phenomenon that it really was. Despite claims to neutrality during the Cold War, it was clear that ASEAN was quietly neutral "on the side of the West." Committed as they are to free market principles and being among the first countries to embrace the globalization process, the nation-states of ASEAN have been important trading allies and strategic partners to their Western counterparts—though the relationship between the two sides was never one based on equality of stature and respect. The governments of ASEAN turned to the

West, and most notably to the United States, to save them from the grip of Soviet expansion and America remains the number one trading partner of every ASEAN state, including the Muslim-majority states of Malaysia, Indonesia, and Brunei.

This unequal relationship, brokered between Washington's elite and its nominated counterparts in ASEAN, has also been based on very real differentials of political, economic, and military power which the leaders of ASEAN are more than aware of. As a result of this enduring legacy of dependency that has been underwritten by American intervention (or threats of intervention), sponsorship, and patronage, the governments of ASEAN have also been at the mercy of the whims of America's political elite and economic managers.

This was most clearly evident in the wake of 9/11 when each and every leader of ASEAN echoed America's concern over the danger of "global Islamic terrorism" and the "threat" that it posed for global economic and political relations. Despite the cautious words of warning issued by the political leadership of Malaysia and Indonesia about America's subsequent military exercises in Afghanistan and Iraq, both countries have played along with the American line and Malaysia has even gone as far as laying the foundations for a regional ASEAN Anti-Terror Center that is meant to coordinate the intelligence activities of the security services of the ASEAN states, with the Americans (via the CIA and FBI) giving close support. Malaysia has also shifted the focus of the Five-Nation Defence Group (comprising of Malaysia, Singapore, Britain, Australia, and New Zealand) toward the issue of "terrorism" and religious extremism in its bid to ensure that its military and strategic links with the West are not broken.[34]

As we have seen, the divisive nature of intra-ASEAN rivalry and competition has also meant that some ASEAN governments have been able to exploit Washington's ambitious agenda to the pull, paying lip-service (if not more) to American designs on the region as a whole. Already the governments of Singapore, Thailand, and the Philippines have gone out of their way to ingratiate themselves to the Bush administration and both Lee Kuan Yew and Gloria Arroyo have openly called for a more visible and lasting U.S. military presence in the region.

The Americans, in turn, have reciprocated these demands with their own renewed commitment to ASEAN's future, no doubt with the intention of ensuring that ASEAN's future development will be in line with U.S. political, economic, and strategic-military interests. During her recent trip to Washington (May 2003), Philippine president Gloria Arroyo was given the assurance that America will protect the interests of the Philippines, which the U.S. president described as America's "oldest ally" in the region. The Philippines was also described by the U.S. president as a "major non-NATO ally" and a key country in the global war against terror.[35] While the American government was busy improving its ties with the Philippines and Singapore, the military campaign conducted by the Indonesian armed forces against Islamist "rebels" in the north Sumatran province of Aceh, received scant attention. Despite numerous reports of atrocities being carried out by Indonesian troops against the civilian population in Aceh (including the burning down of hundreds of schools, colleges, and religious seminaries), it was clear that Washington was more concerned about the ongoing war against terror in Southeast Asia at the time.[36]

This trend, if continued unchecked, can only help to deteriorate the already poor and weakening state of human rights and democracy in ASEAN as a whole and to foreground long-existing tensions and rivalries between states and religious and ethnic communities in the region. In countries like Malaysia and Indonesia with Muslim majority communities, the dubious presence of the United States is bound to lead to even more vocal (and possibly violent) anti-American sentiments spilling out onto the streets. While in those countries with Muslim minority communities, like Singapore, Philippines, and Thailand, the unwelcome intrusion of American military and intelligence personnel to deal with the so-called Muslim problem will also lead to greater alienation and feelings of discrimination among the Muslims, who increasingly feel that they have been typecast as the "fifth column" within. The net effect of U.S. intervention in the region would be the emergence of a politics of divide-and-rule, with Washington in the pivotal position to play the role of patron–protector to regimes of its choice—regardless of the human rights records of the governments in question.

Under such circumstances, what hope is there for an ASEAN bloc with a meaningful independent foreign and domestic policy to call its own? Those ASEAN leaders, like Dr. Mahathir of Malaysia, who have spoken up against the misguided policies of the United States in Afghanistan and Iraq have been summarily put down and chastised by America's ambassadors with the warning that such talk could jeopardize the economic and political stability and future of their own countries.[37] The "Great Game" has returned to Asia with a vengeance, and American global hegemony is set to rise once more as it rewrites its history and pursues its "manifest destiny" as part of a global crusade against terror.

NOTES

1. On the same day (October 8) that the United States invaded Afghanistan, the leaders of PAS came out with their strongest statement against the Americans yet. For the *Murshid'ul Am* (spiritual leader) of PAS, Tuan Guru Nik Aziz Nik Mat, the attack on Afghanistan was clearly an attack on Islam and Muslims in general. Speaking out in defence of the Taliban government, he claimed that: "The US hates the *Taliban* because the latter is firmly committed to upholding Islamic values. Osama bin Laden is just an excuse for the US, which has time and again shown its hostility towards Islam, to wage war against the religion," Mohd Irfan Isa, *Osama an Excuse to Wage War against Islam: Nik Aziz* (Malaysiakini.com, October 10, 2001). PAS's (then) president Ustaz Fadzil Noor also stated that the attacks were not only against Afghanistan's Taliban regime but that they constituted a direct assault on Muslims the world over. Speaking to local and foreign journalists in a press conference of his own, Fadzil Noor said that "America has attacked a small and defenceless country like Afghanistan without showing the world strong reason or proof, (and) they are war criminals," *US Embassy under Guard, PAS Labels Americans "War Criminals"* (Malaysiakini.com, October 8, 2001). He then added: "If the Americans are really waging a war against terrorism, why don't they attack Israel, who are terrorists against the Palestinians?" (ibid.) The President of the Islamist party ended the interview with a clarion call to arms when he stated that: "all Muslims must oppose these criminals—this time, there is no denying a call for *Jihad*." (Ibid.)

2. See Tong Yee Siong, *US Thanks Mahathir for Support, Understands Malaysia's Dilemma* (Malaysiakini.com, October 15, 2001). At a special press conference held in Kuala Lumpur, the U.S. Trade Representative Zoellick stated that the United States "respects Malaysia for all the internal challenges and tensions it has to deal with, which makes its support more meaningful." He also denied that the Mahathir government's objection to the U.S. air strike on Afghanistan could jeopardize the countries' bilateral trade: "Our trade ties are based on close economic relationship. The support we received in many areas will only strengthen the nature of our relationship." He added that "I don't see any negative variety [of views] in there. The difference of views is understandable."

3. See "Admiral Blair: contain terrorism for political stability," *New Sunday Times*, November 25, 2001.

4. See Rohan Gunaratna, *Inside al-Qaeda: Global Network of Terror* (London: Hurst and Co., 2002).

5. See Farish A. Noor, *Fighting Demons of Their Own Making*, in Malaysiakini.com, July 6, 2002.

6. Robert J. McMahon, *The Limits of Empire: The United States and Southeast Asia Since World War II* (New York Columbia University Press, 1999).

7. Ibid., 1999, p. 73.

8. Robert J. McMahon, *The Limits of Empire: The United States and Southeast Asia Since World War II* (New York: Columbia University Press, 1999), p. 85.

9. Ibid., p. 88.

10. Ibid., p. 89.

11. Ngo Dinh Diem was, however, totally out of touch with the Vietnamese people like Bao Dai. He ruled like a feudal warlord and was dependent on his own network of Catholic advisers, Chinese business cronies, and family members. Diem also preferred to speak in French, had spent years abroad, and was known to be supported by the Americans who saw him as their last chance to block a communist takeover of the country.

12. Ibid., p. 107.

13. Ibid., p. 115.

14. Ibid., p. 115.

15. Ibid., pp. 130–131.

16. McMahon (1999) notes that "in a no-holds-barred effort to block a North Vietnamese victory, Nixon would unleash the most intensive bombing campaign of the war . . . Removing previous restraints, the President ordered the sustained bombing of Hanoi and Haiphong, the mining of Haiphong harbour and a naval blockade of the entire North Vietnamese coast" (p. 167).

17. Ibid., p. 130. McMahon notes that "the grossly inflated body counts pro-duced by US and South Vietnamese forces as the principal index for military progress never even approximated the real figures. Nor could any mere statistical measure capture the indomitable will and determination of the other side, that was conditioned by historical experience and cultural values that few Americans knew and even fewer still appreciated" (p. 131). Vietnam would remain under Communist rule for the next two-and-a-half decades, though, by 1978, it would find itself at war again, this time against its communist ex-allies, Cambodia and China.

18. For a more detailed account of the development of American policy toward the Moros, see Thomas C. McKenna, "Appreciating Islam in the Muslim Philippines," in *Islam in the Age of Nation-States*, edited by Hefner and Horvatich (New Haven: Yale University Press, 1997), pp. 48–67.

19. Ibid., p. 51.

20. Blum, 1995, p. 40. By the end of 1945, the Americans were training a local force of 50,000 Filipino troops that were later used to contain the Huk uprising. When the Huk leaders attempted to reintegrate themselves into mainstream Filipino society, their moves were blocked by the Americans and pro-American Filipino leaders. Luis Taruc, the leader of the Huks, was prevented from taking his seat in the Philippines Congress even though he had won the elections fairly.

21. William Blum, *Killing Hope: U.S. Military and CIA Interven-tions Since World War II* (Monroe, Maine: Common Courage Press, 1995), p. 41.

22. Ibid., p. 44.

23. Ibid., p. 43.

24. See Edward G. Landsdale. *In the Midst of Wars* (New York, 1972); Blum, *Killing Hope*.

25. American military and intelligence personnel were stationed in Malaysia after World War II, tagging along with the British. At the time was a detachment of security and intelligence personnel from the American Office of Strategic Services (OSS), which arrived to survey the political terrain in the region. The American agents were based at the offices of the OCBC bank in Kuala Lumpur, close to the Chinatown district of the capital where they could observe the activities of the Chinese communist and leftist movements there. Among the American OSS agents based at the OCBC building were Brig.-Gen. R.C. Fape, L.J.W. Smith, and Captain Post. It was at the OCBC office that the OSS agents attempted to lure members of the MCP-backed MPAJU, and one of the MPAJU leaders, Koon Swan, even tried to gain the support of the Americans in the MCP's struggle against the British. None of the MCP's efforts were to prove successful, and, in the end, it was the OSS (with the help of the Malayan intelligence expert C.C. Too) who managed to win over the communist leaders (like Chan Tai Chee) to their side. Though small in number, the American presence in Malaysia was destined to be a long-lasting one. As they had shown in the Philippines, the Americans were keen to impress upon the people of Southeast Asia that they were the new power to be reckoned with.

26. See Mohd Irfan Isa, *Osama—an Excuse to Wage War against Islam: Nik Aziz* (Malaysiakini.com, October 10, 2001).

27. See *We Do Not Support War Against any Muslim Nation: PM* (Malaysiakini.com, October 8, 2001).

28. Ibid.

29. See Tong Yee Siong, *Mahfuz Wants Gov't to Provide Military Aid to Taliban* (Malaysiakini.com, October 11, 2001).

30. Since the Philippine Senate defeated the bases treaty in September 1991, the Pentagon has been trying to reestablish its military presence in the Philippines in order to be able to use that country again as a springboard for U.S. power projection. President Ramos and his administration have been the Pentagon's main allies in this effort.

31. In November 1992, at the initiative of high U.S. military officials in the Pacific, their Philippine counterparts agreed to give the U.S. military access to Philippine ports, air fields, and military installations for purposes of ship visits, air transit, and small unit military exercises (as was reported in the press at the time). In November 1994. the Pentagon, with Ramos's support, proposed to broaden the limited access agreement of 1992 with an Acquisition and Cross-Servicing Agreement (ACSA) giving the U.S. military rights in the Philippines, and the use of Philippine territory as a launching pad for possible U.S. intervention.

32. Under the name of the annual Balikatan (Shoulder-to-Shoulder) Military Exercise, 1200 Philippine troops and 660 U.S. troops engaged in a

six months to one year joint military operations against the Abu Sayyaf. Previous Philippine-U.S.military exercises in various parts of Luzon and Mindoro have avoided areas of rebel or dissident operations, obviously, to prevent a deeper involvement by U.S. forces in internal conflicts. Even at the height of U.S. military activity on the U.S. bases in the 1960s and 1970s, U.S. military forces kept a low profile in the counter-insurgency campaign in the surrounding Central Luzon provinces. American troops deployed in the Philippines thus far, between 2001 and 2003, include: in late 2001—Initial military presence: 250 American troops based all over the country to help with counter-insurgency work, training, and intelligence gathering; most operatives based in Basilan and southern island provinces; in late-2001–early-2002—additional 660 American troops, including 160 Special Operations Forces (SOFs), Navy SEALS units, and Green Beret commandos. Used as U.S. contingent in U.S.-Philippines Balikatan joint exercise with Abu Sayyaf as live human targets. Mostly based in Southern Mindanao; and American forces that have been picked for their expertise in counter-terrorism. They are licensed to conduct covert and overt operations given the fact that some of them are operatives of the Central Intelligence Agency (CIA) and other U.S. spy networks wearing soldier's uniform.

33. Quoted in BBC, *US Pledges Troops for Philippines*, May 19, 2003 (BBC world service—BBC.co.uk).

34. See *Five-Power Defence Group Shifts it Focus to Terrorism* (Malaysiakini.com, June 2, 2003).

35. See BBC, *US Pledges Troops for Philippines*, May 19, 2003 (BBC world service—BBC.co.uk).

36. See BBC, *Schools Torched in Aceh Conflict*, May 20, 2003 (BBC world service—BBC.co.uk).

37. See *Malaysia–US Ties Heading Towards New Low, Warns US Envoy* (Malaysiakini.com, May 29, 2003).

REPORTS

Growing American-Philippine Military and Diplomatic Co-operation and its Impact on Malaysia/ASEAN. Background report for ABIM Bureau of International Affairs (ABIM/BIA/Rep.no.02/0203/ Philippines-US).